# Música Norteña

D0861117

IN THE SERIES *Studies in Latin American and Caribbean Music,*
EDITED BY PETER MANUEL

# Música Norteña

*Mexican Migrants Creating a Nation between Nations*

CATHY RAGLAND

TEMPLE UNIVERSITY PRESS
Philadelphia

TEMPLE UNIVERSITY PRESS
1601 North Broad Street
Philadelphia PA 19122
www.temple.edu/tempress

Copyright © 2009 by Temple University
All rights reserved
Published 2009
Printed in the United States of America

⊛ The paper used in this publication meets the requirements of the American National
Standard for Information Sciences—Permanence of Paper for Printed Library Materials,
ANSI Z39.48-1992

*All attempts were made to locate the owners of the photographs published in this book.*
*If you believe you may be one of them, please contact Temple University Press, and the*
*publisher will include appropriate acknowledgment in subsequent editions of the book.*

Library of Congress Cataloging-in-Publication Data

Ragland, Cathy.
   Música norteña : Mexican migrants creating a nation between nations / Cathy Ragland.
      p.   cm.
   Includes bibliographical references, discography, and index.
   ISBN 978-1-59213-746-6 (hardcover : alk. paper)
   ISBN 978-1-59213-747-3 (pbk. : alk. paper)
   1. Conjunto music—History and criticism.   2. Folk music—Mexican-American
Border Region—History and criticism.   3. Music—Social aspects—Mexican-American
Border Region—History.   I. Title.

ML3570.9.R35  2009
781.62'68720721—dc22                                          2008039545

2  4  6  8  9  7  5  3  1

R0431100308

# Contents

# Preface

I conducted the primary research for this book in different stages and in different locales throughout the United States and Mexico between 1998 and 2005. I have also drawn on research that I conducted as a music journalist in Austin, Texas, in 1995 and 1996 and as a folklorist working in Texas and Washington throughout the 1990s. My ability to obtain access to artists, communities, and the industry often depended on my role as journalist, folklorist, or academic researcher. Each role allowed me a particular level of access and affected the kind of information I was able to obtain and the ways in which informants responded to me and my questions.

As a journalist, I often found it much easier to gain access to well-known norteña artists such as Los Tigres del Norte, Ramón Ayala, Luis y Julián, and Los Terribles del Norte. Generally, I had a better chance of convincing managers or record labels to connect me with these artists when they knew an article would be published in a major newspaper. However, when I contacted these sources as an academic researcher, the response was less enthusiastic, and gaining access took much longer, if I managed it at all. I had to be much more persistent and devise new ways to connect with musicians, other than through managers and record labels.

I also sensed that part of the problem had to do with gender. To begin with, few researchers (particularly non-Mexicans) are interested in contemporary *música norteña* (or simply norteña), but fewer still are women. Most of the women who were interested in meeting Ayala were fans or groupies.

As a researcher, I had to prove myself by summarizing what I knew about the history of norteña music and giving a rundown of the other well-known artists I had interviewed in the past. Furthermore, in order to make sure I would be taken seriously, I talked about the published articles I had written about the music industry, recordings, and particular artists. In many cases, it was only after such detailed discussions that I gained access and could arrange my interviews.

Sometimes I had to devise more aggressive and "creative" tactics to gain access to these artists. For example, when Ramón Ayala's manager did not respond to my requests for an interview, I decided to try to locate Ayala myself at a concert in San Antonio, Texas. Two hours before his performance, I searched for Ayala's tour bus behind the building. Norteña musicians in this area typically travel in large buses with their names and logos emblazoned along the sides and, because the buses are heavily guarded, musicians often prefer them to dressing rooms and tend to stay in them until just before the show. There I spoke with the driver, who led me to the road manager, who—in turn—led me to Ayala's manager. After a long explanation of my project and a strategic mention that I had interviewed other well-known norteña artists both for this work and previously as a journalist for the San Antonio Express-News, I was told to return in an hour to be introduced directly to Ayala. When I returned, I had to tell my whole story again to a different road manager, but eventually I was introduced to Ayala, who gave me both his home and cell phone numbers to arrange an interview.

If I had spoken to Ayala as a journalist, we would probably have gone immediately into the bus and conducted a fifteen- to twenty-minute interview. That had been my experience in the past, but for a mere researcher and scholar, the situation was a bit more complicated. However, when I told Ayala about my interest in the history of norteña music as a border genre and his role in its modernization and development, he invited me to his home in Harlingen, Texas (within a couple of miles of the border), where we spoke for over two hours. I found that when I was able to talk to artists of Ayala's stature, they were eager to participate in a project documenting the history of norteña music, even if their managers and other handlers did not see the significance of this work. Ayala noted that, at least in Texas, norteña music is rarely researched seriously in the way that tejano music has been. Other artists, like Julián Garza, of Luis y Julián, said that they would like to see more "scholarly" research done on norteña and noted its neglect in comparison to tejano music.

Aside from my work as a journalist, I conducted research as a folklorist in Austin, Texas, and in Seattle, Washington, among Mexican immigrant communities, locating artists who performed both tejano and norteña music for various programs and projects. In Washington, I conducted a two-year research project within the Chicano and Mexican communities in Seattle and the Yakima Valley, where I learned more about the role of norteña music in Mexican immigrant communities away from the border region. These projects allowed me to learn about the social, cultural, and political divisions that existed between the more assimilated Chicanos (who tended to speak only English or were bilingual, were U.S.-born, and had little connection to Mexico) and the less assimilated Mexican immigrants (who spoke only Spanish or were somewhat bilingual, were Mexican-born, and still maintained economic and social ties to Mexico). I discovered conflicts between these communities, which centered on music preferences and class-based distinctions.

I also noted that many of the long-time Chicano residents and extended families in Washington had actually migrated there from Texas, particularly the Rio Grande Valley region, prior to the 1960s. Texas-Mexicans ceased migrating for work by the mid-1960s, and since then the overwhelming majority of migration to this area has come from Mexico, particularly the states of Jalisco, Colima, Michoacán, Guanajuato, and (more recently) Oaxaca. By the time of my research, the rapidly growing Mexican immigrant population had greatly eclipsed the Chicano presence, and there was concern that the Texas-Mexican, or tejano, music preferred by the local Chicanos was rapidly losing airtime on local Spanish-language radio stations. Mexican genres, such as norteña, *banda*, *ranchera*, and *tropical* (see the Glossary), were considerably more popular and more accessible in local shops and at festivals and dance clubs, but the Chicano population insisted on equal representation for tejano music, though it was difficult to obtain due to limited distribution and live performances of this music were rare.

In the summer of 1998, accepting a fellowship from the Rockefeller Foundation, I left Washington to conduct research in northern Mexico, particularly in the states of Nuevo León and Tamaulipas, to compile data to construct a history of norteña music in the region. I met with a number of *cronistas* (amateur historians) from towns and municipalities. Typically, the cronistas were dedicated fans of norteña music who owned vast collections of records and documents dating back to the early twentieth century. Because very little scholarly work has been done on norteña music, these individuals took it upon themselves to build extensive personal archives of interviews, recordings, newspaper articles, and their own handwritten accounts of the music's evolution and its important historical figures. Though I realized that I had to be selective about the information that these cronistas were eager to share with me, I found their archives, their stories, and our discussions about the music's role in the local society to be wonderfully useful and revealing.

Discussing the music's origin, the cronistas revealed a strong sense of pride in and deep connection to the history of norteña music, a genre that is now claimed by many Mexican immigrants living throughout the United States (and particularly in California). The cronistas and other researchers, musicians, and fans in Monterrey and border towns constantly describe this area as the "birthplace" and home of norteña music. I soon learned that norteña's history is part of everyone's history here, but a particularly personal one for those who have deep family ties in Mexico's far North.

My next opportunity to conduct research occurred in New York City, where I worked for the Center for Traditional Music and Dance as a folklorist and project director. My research experience with newly arrived Mexican immigrants in New York differed greatly from my experience in Texas and Washington State. When I arrived in the fall of 1999, I learned that the Mexican community in New York had little social or political presence within the city and state power structures. The majority of the Mexicans I encountered and worked with spoke only Spanish, some of the newest arrivals spoke only Nahuatl or other indigenous languages of rural Mexico, and few had lived in the city more than ten years. Additionally, most have come from southern states such as Puebla, Guerrero, and Oaxaca.

For this community, I was one of the first non-Mexicans interested in learning about its music, culture, family life, and history. Moreover, through my work at the Center, I helped present some of the first local, community-based artists in city-wide concerts focusing on traditional and popular music of Mexico. While local mariachi musicians were already performing in restaurants and events sponsored by the Mexican Consulate, norteña groups were never invited as "official" representatives of Mexican music and culture. For the local Mexican elite, the music's themes of illegal border crossing, drug trafficking, and criticism of U.S. and Mexican political corruption made it inappropriate as a cultural representation of a united and "civilized" Mexican immigrant community.

Finding and working with four norteña groups in the city as part of a five-year-long initiative at the Center, I brought together musicians, artists, community leaders, and activists to establish a cultural organization to present Mexican music and dance in some of the city's public settings, such as the American Museum of Natural History, Lincoln Center, and Central Park. An after-school mariachi program that offers free classes to children ages eight to seventeen in East Harlem also resulted from the initiative. Of the groups I located, one in particular, Suspenso del Norte, was of particular interest to me because it was a family group, made up of the three Javier brothers—Santiago, Pablo, and Fernando—and Santiago's son, Dionicio. Like many other norteña groups performing in the city and surrounding boroughs, Suspenso played almost exclusively for private parties, rarely in clubs or at festivals. Most of the songs played by Suspenso and other groups are *mojado* themed (about the undocumented immigrant experience), such as "El Mojado Acaudalado" (The Wealthy Wetback), and narcocorridos, such as "Jefe de Jefes" (Boss of the Bosses) and "Mis Tres Animales" (My Three Animals). When I asked in an interview how the members of Suspenso felt about playing narcocorridos even though they do not support that lifestyle, the accordionist, Santiago Javier, explained, "All of these songs have more than one meaning, you know; they are not just about drug trafficking.

These guys risk their lives and send money back home to their families and villages, like we do. I don't agree with how they make their money, but sometimes you don't have a choice" (personal communication).[1] The group also plays a number of classic border corridos celebrating legendary bandit heroes, and though they are from Puebla, the Javier brothers speak reverently of Monterrey and the border region as norteña's birthplace.

In the summer of 2003, I traveled to the brothers' hometown of Santa Inés, Puebla, to visit their father, Roberto Javier, who had taught his sons how to play the accordion and *bajo sexto* (a hybrid bass-rhythm guitar with ten or twelve strings) and many classic norteña songs. There I learned about the deep connection norteña music had to working-class (in this case rural) communities in southern Mexico. Roberto told me about the first time he heard Los Alegres de Terán. It was on a jukebox in a restaurant/bar in Mexico City, where he was working as a cook during the early 1960s. "I had traveled to the city to make some money because there was nothing here," he recalled. "Even then, it was the music of migrants . . . of workers like me, and I thought it was the best thing I'd ever heard" (personal communication).

Though we were hundreds of miles from the northern border, norteña music appeared to be alive and well among laborers struggling to make ends meet throughout this region. Most of the senior Javier's neighbors also had sons and daughters living in New York whose undocumented status prevented them from returning home for a visit for many years. During my stay, Roberto stood outside his house (which still had no electricity) and pointed to several neighboring houses that had family members in New York. He also pointed to a partially constructed house next to his that his son Santiago was building and hoped to live in one day. The next day Roberto gave me an old button accordion to take back to New York for his son Pablo. Roberto was not playing it anymore, he said, and he had heard that Pablo's son Oscar was interested in learning. Roberto had never met Oscar, who had been born in the United States ten years earlier. Since Roberto could not be there to teach Oscar, he hoped his accordion might do some of the work for his grandson. "This will get him started until we meet one day in the future," Roberto said with a positive note in his voice. "God willing, I hope that day will come." Three years have passed since I drove that accordion across the border from Puebla to New York. Oscar now plays with his father's group, and when Pablo lost his job for a time, the two played the New York subways to help make ends meet. Today, Pablo is working again, but the subway money turned out to be pretty good so they occasionally work as a duo for a few hours on the weekends.

In New York, several months after my visit to his hometown, Pablo said to me, "Every Mexican wants to return home. We all have that dream: Mexico lives

---

[1] All interview translations are my own unless otherwise noted.

in our hearts. We might stay thirty years or more, and we may even become legalized and get our U.S. citizenships, but if you ask, most of us want to be buried in Mexico. That's what the song says, you know" (personal communication). With that, he recited the refrain from the song "El Mojado Acaudalado" written by Teodoro Bello for Los Tigres del Norte:

> Me está esperando, México lindo
> por eso mismo me voy a ir.
> Soy el mojado acaudalado,
> pero en mi tierra quiero morir.
>
> [You're waiting for me, my beautiful Mexico
> for this reason, I'm going back.
> I'm the wealthy wetback,
> but I want to die in my country.][2]

---

[2] From the CD *Jefe de Jefes*, recorded by Los Tigres del Norte (Fonovisa FDCD-80711, 1997). All translations of song lyrics in this book are my own unless otherwise noted.

# Acknowledgments

T his book draws on many years spent as a researcher and writer in various locations and in different capacities. Therefore, it is not possible to thank all of the people who have given their time and support to the research and writing of this book. I would, however, like to acknowledge some individuals and institutions whose support made this work possible.

I would first like to thank Dr. Peter Manuel, for his patience, insightful criticism, and support during the early stages of this work. He kept me focused on the crucial arguments and encouraged me to balance my own ideas and fieldwork findings with an effective theoretical perspective. Other early readers of this work also offered invaluable suggestions and support: Dr. Ellie Hisama, Dr. Barbara Hampton, Dr. Juan Flores, Dr. Michael Stone, Dr. Allan Atlas, and Dr. T. M. Scruggs.

I am forever indebted to those foundations and institutions that provided financial support for the research of this book. I want to acknowledge the initial support I received in 1998 from the Guadalupe Cultural Arts Center in San Antonio, which awarded me a Ford Foundation Research Fellowship through its Gateways Program. This fellowship allowed me to travel to northeastern Mexico for an extended period to conduct initial research on the history of norteña music. I cherish the invaluable contacts, scholarly exchange, and new friendships that led me to develop new avenues of research and ideology in this study. I am also very grateful to the Social

Science Research Council for awarding me a generous Arts Program Fellowship in 2002. It allowed me to return to northeastern Mexico and the Mexico-Texas border region and to conduct new research among immigrant communities in Chicago and California. I appreciate the organization's support of new work in the social sciences and, in particular, its dedication to projects that consider the impact of international migration on cultural life and the arts. I also want to acknowledge the Center for Latin American, Caribbean, and Latino Studies at the City University of New York (CUNY) Graduate Center for the award of a 2002 summer travel grant that allowed for follow-up research in Nuevo León and Puebla.

While research funding was imperative for this project, the enormous task of organizing and cataloguing an overwhelming amount of research data and turning it into a book would have been impossible without additional financial support. I am extremely grateful for the generous support I received during the writing phase of this work from the Graduate Center at CUNY: the Baisley Powell Elebash Dissertation Fellowship, the Andrew Silk Dissertation Grant, and the CUNY Writing across the Curriculum Fellowship Program. I want to acknowledge the Centro Regional de Investigaciones Multidisciplinarias at the Universidad Nacional Autónoma de México (UNAM) campus in Cuernavaca, Morelos, for awarding me a Rockefeller Residency Fellowship that allowed for additional research and writing for this project. I also want to express my gratitude for assistance from the Gustave Reese Publication Endowment Fund of the American Musicological Society.

I want to thank Ethel Raim, the artistic director at the Center for Traditional Music and Dance, who hired me to direct a community cultural initiative project for three years with a predominantly new Mexican immigrant community in New York. This work allowed me the unique opportunity to develop and foster connections with local norteña musicians and community members. Thanks also go to Ellen Simon and María Quiroga at the Union Settlement Association in East Harlem, which has contracted me every year since I arrived in New York in 1999 to produce its annual *Día de los Muertos* (Day of the Dead) program in East Harlem. Finally, I want to acknowledge Northwest Folklife in Seattle and Texas Folklife Resources and Pat Jasper, former director of Texas Folklife Resources, in Austin for providing invaluable opportunities to conduct research and develop valuable contacts in Mexican immigrant communities throughout Texas and Washington State.

My deepest thanks go to the many musicians, promoters, radio personalities, and record companies who make this music happen on a daily basis on both sides of the border. I am especially grateful to those who took time out of their busy schedules to talk with me and take me under their wing. In particular, I want to acknowledge Pepe Garza and Luisa Fernanda Patrón of Grupo Tayer, who welcomed me to their home in Monterrey, Nuevo León, for several months and put me in contact with so many musicians, promoters, and scholars of norteña music throughout the region. I am also grateful for the many casual conversations about norteña music that I had with Pablo, Santiago, and Fernando Javier of Suspenso del Norte in New York. These musicians, along with their father, Roberto, whom I visited in Puebla, helped me develop a deeper understanding of the music's impact on working-class people in Mexico and on undocumented immigrants in the United States.

I also extend my warmest thanks to the musicians who opened their homes and lives to me and spent hours talking to me and taking me to performances at private events in remote villages, where I was treated like royalty and graciously introduced to friends, fans, musicians, and other individuals who proved to be crucial to my work. I owe thanks to Julián Garza, Gilberto García Sr., the late Lalo "El Piporro" González, Ramiro Cavazos, Ramón Ayala, Bobby Salinas, Poncho Villagomez, Juan Salazar, Miguel Luna, the late Narciso Martínez, and many others.

Meeting and talking with other Mexican music historians and fellow researchers while in the field was a uniquely rewarding part of this work. I am eternally grateful for the opportunity I had to exchange ideas and research notes with Juan Alanís Támez, Guillermo Berrones, Raúl García Flores, Armando Ortiz, Héctor Galán, Carlos Gómez Flores, Celso Garza Guajardo, and others. I would also like to mention the Mexican music promoters Oscar Flores and Joel Cano, the Mexican-border deejay Rogelio García, the Texas record-label owners Freddie Martínez Jr. of Freddie Records, and Rick and Roland García of Hacienda Records, who provided me with a great deal of invaluable information about the history and inside politics of the norteña industry on both sides of the border. I am indebted for the support and friendship of fellow music journalists and norteña and tejano music lovers and researchers Vilma Maldonado and Rafael Molina.

For helping me solidify my framework and formulate my ideas in a coherent manner, I want to thank my dear friend Karen Fleshman, whose knowledge of Mexican immigration history and U.S.-Mexico border relations proved invaluable in the research and writing of this dissertation. Thanks also go to Karen for sharing many hours over many years talking about norteña music and its relationship to undocumented immigrants and for acting as a soundboard for the development of some of this work's core ideas. I am grateful to Cornelius Dufallo and Tony Corsano for the countless hours they spent assisting me with the musical transcriptions and to EDIT911.com for editorial assistance with the manuscript.

I extend my most heartfelt appreciation and gratitude to my mother, Millie, and her husband, Jim, for their consistent love and support and for providing me a safe haven in San Antonio, Texas, from which I set out across the border on numerous occasions, leaving them to wonder where I was headed and how I would get there. I am also deeply grateful to my sister, Danette Maddox, who has always given an encouraging word and a boost of confidence when I needed it the most. I want to thank my partner and friend, Badal K. Roy, for always being there, particularly during the "rough patches," and for providing well-placed words of humor and sarcasm when I was taking things much too seriously. I am also greatly indebted to my very good friend Jorge Martínez, who not only designed an amazing book cover but also gave me an almost daily dose of positive energy and encouragement that kept me focused and determined during the final stages of editing and formatting the book.

There are surely other names that I am leaving out, but among the many who deserve recognition are Carmen García, Johnny A. Rodríguez, Eva Ybarra, John Marcell, and Diana García, for their undying support and lifelong friendship. I conclude by dedicating this work to my longtime friend Ram Ayala, proprietor of the San Antonio institution Tacoland, whose life was cut short by a random act of violence. Ayala was one of San Antonio's greatest supporters of music and creativity. He is sorely missed and will never be forgotten.

# Introduction

During the summer of 1996, Roberto M., a Tejano (Texas-Mexican) friend who was an arts presenter in San Antonio, asked me to take him to a dance featuring *norteña* (northern Mexican) music. Having grown up in the city, he told me about the many *tardeadas* (afternoon dances, usually held on Sundays), weddings, and community festivals, where he often danced to local Texas-Mexican conjunto groups. But he had never been to a norteña dance and had paid relatively little attention to the music. Tejano conjunto and norteña groups feature the same instrumentation: a three-row button accordion; a bajo sexto, which has twelve strings with six double courses; an electric bass; and drums. Despite the similarity in instruments, the communities who listen to these genres in South Texas are very distinct. Roberto, a fourth-generation Texas-Mexican who had worked for over twelve years promoting "Mexican American" culture and arts in the city, told me he felt somewhat guilty that he knew very little about the Mexican immigrant population, which seemed more connected with its Mexican roots than he was and spoke better Spanish than he did. "What do I really know about Mexico?" I remember him saying to me as we drove to the outskirts of the city. "My family, my heritage is from there, but I'm a Texan."

I took Roberto to Mi Ranchito (My Little Ranch), a run-down club with a small dance floor on the outskirts of the city. It was across from a flea market that I frequented because it had more Mexican goods than most. Shoppers could find cheap cassettes and CDs of Mexican music (almost all pirated), great homemade tamales and tacos, a variety of leather goods, and live chickens and goats; moreover, there was always a norteña group playing for shoppers, dancers, and beer drinkers. I knew that after the flea market closed on Saturdays and Sundays the party moved across the street to Mi Ranchito, which featured norteña bands that drove in from just across the border. When we walked into the club, Roberto immediately noticed how distorted the sound system was. "It's so loud, and the bass is overpowering everything," he said. "The sound is so messy." The dance floor was crowded, and there was no air-conditioning, which seemed to bother no one but us.

The band played one song after another without stopping, and the bajo sexto player talked rapidly over the brief accordion introductions to read dedications and acknowledge as many people at the dance as possible. Roberto noted that it seemed unusual to him that the bajo sexto player appeared to be the bandleader and lead singer. In tejano conjunto, the accordionist is always the bandleader and is expected to take many solos and show off his virtuosic playing skill. Many popular tejano conjunto groups are known by their accordionists' names, such as Santiago Jiménez Jr. y Su Conjunto, Flaco Jiménez y Su Conjunto, Esteban Jordán y Su Conjunto, Mingo Saldívar y Sus Tremendos Cuatro Espadas (Four Tremendous Swords), and Eva Ybarra y Su Conjunto. I explained that in norteña, the focus is on the lyrics, on the story being told, and the accordion is merely an accompanying instrument, given an occasional solo only between stanzas.

As we danced, Roberto, who is one of the best conjunto dancers I know, had trouble with the rhythm. "It's too fast," he said, "too jumpy. I can't glide across the floor and do all of the turns I'm used to doing." As we left the club, Roberto said that, though he was not sure that he really liked norteña all that much, he wondered why these two musical genres, which share the same origin in the Texas-Mexican border region, now exhibit such different stylistic features and have come to represent different Mexican American communities.

Some years later, while researching norteña music and interviewing musicians in northeastern Mexico, I often brought up the issue of the stylistic and identity-based distinctions made between tejano and norteña music. In an interview I conducted with Miguel Luna of the pioneering norteña group El Palomo y el Gorrión (The Dove and the Sparrow), which he had formed with his brother when they were teenagers in the 1950s, the accordionist and songwriter readily pointed out stylistic distinctions and poignantly ascribed them to economic disadvantages and class-based divisions. For Luna, tejano music is associated with advances in technology and virtuosity, while norteña is more closely connected to the sentiments of its listeners and is clearly more working-class:

> Tejano music is more refined, more delicate, more difficult to play, but rhythmically it is steadier. I attribute this to the fact that in the United States, the musicians have more devices and better sound and this gives them the advantage of being more prepared and perfecting their sound.

There [in the United States] is where they first used drums and electric bass, in a complete group. Norteña music is rougher, but with more feeling, and it is simpler. The people feel it more. In northern Mexico, and among the immigrants in the United States, are the people who work "sunup to sundown" and practice [music] only during the evenings, but with feeling and nostalgia. (personal communication)

Over the years since my last conversation with Luna, norteña and tejano music (also *música tejana*) have absorbed influences from each other as well as from North American[1] and Latino popular music genres. Nevertheless, the two genres have remained relatively separated by geographical, experiential, economic, and class-based divisions within the ethnic Mexican communities in the United States. Among the North American population at large, there is a tendency to conceive of the Spanish- and Mexican-origin population, particularly in the Southwest (which once belonged to Spain), as a homogeneous group (Gutiérrez 1987, 81). Similarly, the U.S. Latino and North American mainstream music industry tends to lump tejano and norteña (and their listening audiences) together.

## Differentiating Cultures and Their Music

Despite outsiders' perceptions of homogeneity, however, historical, racial, and economic boundaries have contributed to the fragmentation of Mexican American identity in the United States. Increased migration and new patterns of travel have produced multiple collective identities based on regional associations, rural versus urban origins, indigenous identity, immigration status, and economic integration. For example, a *Tejano* is a person of Mexican heritage, typically born and living in Texas. The term was initially used in the early 1800s to distinguish between the Anglo-American settlers in the state and the Mexican Americans. On the other hand, many people of Mexican heritage living in the United States use *Chicano*. The term became popular in the late 1960s among Mexican Americans involved in the civil rights movement who sought to create an autonomous cultural reality in the United States. Today, the term is used primarily in the Southwest as a general description for Mexican Americans. Tejanos and Chicanos—who benefited from the civil rights and Chicano movements—gained political

---

[1] I use the term *North American* here and throughout this book to refer to inhabitants of the United States only. I have purposely avoided use of the term *American* to refer to people and places in the United States, because this use of the term has been debated in recent years and many people believe that it disregards other nations throughout the Americas. Throughout the Spanish-speaking world, use of the term *estadounidense* (literally, "United Statesian") is growing. Some consider the term more appropriate than the common term *norteamericano* (North American). While *North American* can and does include inhabitants of Canada and northern Mexico, I have chosen it over *American* for lack of a more appropriate term at this time.

and economic power, implemented equal education reforms, and elevated the region's Spanish and Mexican social and cultural visibility. However, these benefits did not extend across the continental United States, where new Mexican immigrants were traveling and working.

Tejano music has remained predominantly regional and has embraced elements of North American popular music genres, particularly Texas swing and country and western, and its listening public is made up of individuals claiming a combination of Spanish, Tejano, and Mexican American roots and having a relatively distant relationship with Mexico. Norteña music—which synthesizes a Mexican border ballad tradition with updated lyrics that merge themes of border crossing, experiences of migration, sociopolitical commentary, and the real and imagined exploits of modern-day bandit heroes, drug smugglers, and undocumented travelers—evolved and became popular among Mexican immigrants living and working in locales throughout the United States, as well as among their families and community members back in Mexico. The norteña music industry and the subgenres that have emerged in its wake (e.g., *onda grupera,* banda/*technobanda, sonidero, música duranguense*) have been shaped (and reshaped) by fluid notions of ethnic and regional identity, national affiliation, home space, and sociopolitical associations in both countries. Throughout the Mexican diaspora, this loose-knit community has been continually impacted by growing numbers of undocumented migrants, its lower-class status, increased limitations on work and economic improvement, and racial tension. Norteña music embodies these tensions and other factors that marginalize this community, offering both an escape and the opportunity to be heard.

A long history of border-crossing themes is one of the primary elements that distinguish norteña from both tejano and other popular Latino genres. In this case *Latino* refers to Latin American popular music genres that have become popular initially (or only) in the U.S. market (see Pacini Hernández 2001). And while the narrative ballad (corrido)—one of the primary song forms of the norteña genre—has been studied by linguists, sociologists, folklorists, and historians on its own, it has received little attention in the context of popular music and cultural studies. Though norteña is popular in Mexico, primarily among rural and working-class audiences, it is often excluded from being seriously considered "Mexican" popular music, largely because the bulk of its audience and recording activity is located in the United States and the northernmost region of Mexico, which has a historically estranged relationship with the government and cultural center of Mexico (Ramírez-Pimienta 2004).

Since the early 1990s, diasporas and the dynamic communities that are created by travel and migration have been the subjects of research, both in general theoretical writings (e.g., Appadurai 1990; Clifford 1994; and Kaplan 1996) and in specific case studies. This research has explored the profound impact migrating and displaced communities have had on the music, culture, economics, and politics that have shaped the world and, in particular, North American society.

These communities have effected a blurring of the boundaries that once defined "home" and "abroad" and a merging of cultures and identities, causing a reconsideration of many traditional ideas about society. Still, the word *community* suggests a place of belonging. It is based, as the sociologist Amitai Etzioni writes, on the notion that "free individuals require a community, which backs them up against encroachment by the state and sustains morality by drawing on the gentle prodding of kin, friends, neighbors, and other members, rather than building on government controls or fear of authorities" (1993, 15). The border folklorist and novelist Américo Paredes asserts that the redefinition of the Rio Grande from river to "dividing line" disrupted the traditional sense of community in the border region, thus making former relatives and neighbors suddenly "foreigners in a foreign land" (1958, 15). However, corrido composers and musicians responded with songs documenting this disruption, invasion of territory, and loss of traditional border life, thus instilling a sense of solidarity through shared experience. The maintenance of the corrido in modern norteña today reminds the Mexican listener of this "tradition of community" that so defined border life (and inspired uprisings that led to the Mexican Revolution) and helps to extend that experience across the Mexican diaspora.

## Historical Patterns of Migration

The migration of Mexican laborers into the United States dates back to the mid-1800s, after the signing of the Treaty of Hidalgo and the conclusion of the U.S.-Mexico War. From 1942 to 1964, the Bracero Program, which was first negotiated by the United States and Mexico as an emergency measure during World War II, encouraged large migrations of Mexicans to the United States to work on building railroads throughout the Southwest. Under the program's terms, American agricultural enterprises could also legally bring in Mexican contract laborers for seasonal work. However, in the off-season many did not return home but settled on the border instead, adding to the swelling population of the region and often locating where people from their home state were already established. Many of these migrants came from areas other than the northeastern Mexican border states (Galarza 1978, 197, 107–115). After 1964, there was a significant increase in undocumented workers coming into the United States.

Since the mid-1960s, increased militarization of the border as a result of border crossing has paralleled a steady rise in immigration, resulting in heated controversy among politicians and impacting social and economic interests within the United States at large. Norteña has emerged as a veritable soundtrack of the circular, back-and-forth migratory experiences of the Mexican migrant and immigrant laborer community. It is, perhaps, the single most popular music style throughout Mexico, flourishing in its regional heartland (northeastern Mexico) and as the favored genre of migrant laborers. As a hybrid music form that combines European dance rhythms, primarily the polka and waltz, with the corrido, norteña has a history located in the geographical space of the U.S.-Mexico border region. However, its modern-day audience is spread over multiple sites throughout the United States and Mexico.

Research into and documentation of a Mexican popular music phenomenon that is expressly tied to globalization, migration, displacement, and economic necessity speak to a plethora of multidisciplinary issues in ethnomusicology and the social sciences. The migration of Mexican working-class laborers since the turn of the twentieth century, growing to mass proportions since the 1960s, has perpetuated the development of a Mexican American culture (traditionally defined by a "distinct" border community and, later, by the Chicano experience) into a postmodern community that lives and works in multiple sites and within expanding borders. Música norteña not only represents a means by which this community can have a voice and speak out about its experiences; it is also a uniquely rich poetic oral tradition, an eloquent record of the past that spills over into the present. It is not only a history of the Mexican migrant experience in the United States but one that is intimately shared and understood by families, friends, and neighbors in Mexico as well. Taken collectively, the songs describe the making of a nation between nations. Everything about norteña reflects not only how life is lived within this community but also how it is both remembered and imagined. Tracked alongside changes in immigration legislation, the ebbs and flows of U.S. and Mexican political change and economic struggles, complex ethnic and cultural allegiances, increases in violence and criminal activity, and critical public opinion from both sides of the border, the modern evolution of norteña embodies it all, offering a fascinating opportunity for exploration and study.

# 1

# Mexicanidad and Música Norteña in the "Two Mexicos"

## The Corrido and Norteña Music

### The Corrido

Scholars in Chicano studies, Spanish literature, linguistics, and folklore in the United States and Mexico have produced ample research and writing on the corrido, but there is very little on norteña music, the popular music vehicle for the contemporary corrido. The traditional Mexican corrido is a topical narrative ballad sung, without a refrain, to a basic melody in waltz time (3/4); many contemporary corridos are played in a fast polka rhythm (2/4) more appropriate for a two-step type dance popular in northern Mexico and Texas. The corrido consists of eight-syllable lines organized in stanzas of four (quatrains) and maintains an *abcd* rhyme pattern, though this can vary at times. As a popular narrative song form, the corrido was the primary vehicle for the exploits of prerevolutionary and revolutionary bandit heroes from the mid-1800s to the early 1930s, and song topics range from stories about revolutionary heroes to U.S.-Mexico border conflict to illegal border crossing and drug smuggling. Since the early nineteenth century, the corrido has been associated with peasant and working-class communities of Mexico.

In an early study of the corrido, Armand Duvalier (1937) argues that the corrido descends from the Spanish *romance* (a classic poetic song form dating back to the 1500s, featuring octosyllabic lines alternating in pairs with rhymed assonance in the even lines). Vicente T. Mendoza (1954) agreed, attributing the corrido's features to the *decimal,* a Spanish poetic form consisting of one or more stanzas, each with ten octosyllabic lines. The origin of the corrido has since been a source of contention for scholars, particularly for the border scholar, folklorist, and Chicano Studies pioneer Américo Paredes (1958, 149–150), who challenged Mendoza and Duvalier by giving evidence of the rise of the romance corrido in New Spain during the mid-1700s and marking the appearance of the "true" corrido in the border region during the mid-1800s. Mendoza (1954, 1964) traces the corrido's profound connection to Mexican history and culture as it evolves from this period through to the height of its development in the 1930s (see the example of a typical corrido, Chapter 2, page 36). However, all three scholars agree that the corrido ceased to be a true "epic" genre after the 1930s, since the songs could not be traced to specific persons, places, or events (Nicolopulos 1997). Paredes points out, moreover, that by this time the corrido had shed its "proletarian" audience and references as a result of commercialization of songs through the recording industry (on both sides of the border) and influence from the Mexican film industry (Paredes 1993, 136–138).

The majority of corrido recordings during the 1940s and 1950s were on independent labels located on both sides of the border, such as Ideal and Falcon in southern Texas and Orfeo in Monterrey, Nuevo León, Mexico. María Herrera-Sobek (1993) arranges many of these songs according to Paredes's research and collected recordings, ordering them chronologically and by popular themes. She identifies six primary themes of songs collected from 1848 to 1964, when the Bracero Program ended:

1. Cowboys and Outlaws
2. Working and Traveling on the Railroad
3. Revolution and Hard Times
4. Migrants and Renegades
5. Repatriation and Deportation
6. The Bracero Program

Herrera-Sobek (1993) identifies seven themes after 1964:

1. Songs of Protest
2. Border-Crossing Strategies
3. Racial Tensions
4. Poverty, Petroleum, and Amnesty
5. Love
6. Acculturation and Assimilation
7. Death

While there is no specific mention of mojado- or *narcotraficante*-themed songs, these protagonists (particularly the mojado) dominate nearly every genre except the first three (Cowboys and Outlaws, Working and Traveling on the Railroad, and Revolution and Hard Times), all of which were of the pre-1930s epic-heroic variety classified by Paredes. In fact, many of the songs listed under the remaining themes prior to 1964 are actually from before the 1930s, except for those associated with the Bracero Program, supporting Paredes's and Limón's assertions that the corrido went into decline (and decadence) after the 1930s. As Guillermo Hernández (1999) and James Nicolopulos (1997) have noted, however, a resurgence of corrido activity occurred in the late 1960s, with new compositions focusing on contemporary themes more closely linked to economic, social, and political developments among the Mexican immigrant laborer community in the United States.

The 1940s witnessed stylistic and compositional transformations of the corrido by composers and recording artists such as Los Alegres de Terán, Los Donneños, El Piporro, and Los Gorriones de Topo Chico, who responded to interest from Mexico City–based major labels; from both nationalistic and commercial motives, the labels sought out regional norteña artists with a potential for popularity throughout the country. These artists popularized the norteña ensemble along with newly composed *canción-corridos* that eliminated some of the traditional corrido characteristics, such as the opening address; the statement of location, year, and time, and the final farewell at the end of the song. While many of these recording artists were composing corridos with refrains and modifying corrido song form characteristics, they also introduced the norteña ensemble—featuring accordion, bajo sexto, and *tololoche* (traditionally handmade contrabass)—that would serve as the primary musical vehicle for the modern corrido, as well as rancheras (also known as *canciones rancheras* or *canciones típicas*; they are pastoral or "country" songs) and later the *canción romántica* and the Mexican *cumbia* (also called *tropical* or *colombiana* and based on the Afro-Colombian popular song and dance genre). Like the corrido, the ranchera is associated with rural life and culture and, since the 1920s, with working-class Mexicans on both sides of the border (Peña 1999a, 50–51). It is typically played in 2/4 time (derived from the polka) with the stress on the off-beats (two and four, in terms of eighth notes) for dancing. However, Paredes (1993, 139), along with later scholars such as José Limón (1992, 40–42) and María Herrera-Sobek (1993, 225–228), notes that contemporary norteña groups are still performing and commercially recording many pre-1930s epic corridos, thus preserving and perpetuating the song form.

While the canción-corrido maintained the corrido's strophic form and rhyme scheme, it added other popular song features such as refrains and instrumental interludes after stanzas. Early corridos had lasted twenty minutes or more, depending on the singer's elaborations on the storyline, but songs were shortened to the three minutes required by 45 rpm vinyl recordings. However, though the canción-corrido dominated recorded output after the 1940s, later corrido scholars, such as John Holmes McDowell (1972, 1981) and Herrera-Sobek (1990,

1993), focused on corridos written and composed in the traditional style that Duvalier (1937) and Mendoza (1964) had outlined. Some scholars, such as Limón (1992, 40–42), believed that continued research into "authentic" heroic and conflict corrido texts would remind the Mexican American community of the traditional heroic-epic songwriting and would serve as a historical and ideological expression of resistance, political and cultural autonomy, and the fight against commercialization.

Paredes dismissed these shorter canción-corridos as "movie corridos" (1958, 139–140) or "popular pseudo-corridos" (1958, 140; 1993, 138). Nevertheless, the late 1940s through the early 1950s proved to be an important period in the creation of a modern norteña music genre that would be instrumental in defining the intense demographic and cultural changes occurring in the region. Many popular artists, for example Los Alegres and Los Donneños, had experienced traveling and crossing the border as migrant workers, and their lyrics spoke of nostalgia, class and racial conflict, and the breakup of family life and love relationships. They recorded classic corridos from before the 1930s, composed their own border-crossing and conflict corridos in the traditional form, some of which are included in Herrera-Sobek's research (1979, 1993), and they wrote popular canción-corridos that drew on new and very personal feelings and experiences of the migrating community that had gone largely dismissed or unnoticed by scholars. Los Alegres and other norteña artists also competed with Texas-based groups such as those of Santiago Jiménez Sr., Narciso Martínez, and Lydia Mendoza, who were recording on regional labels and marketed to working-class Mexican American and new immigrant communities. Even after Mexico City–based labels moved away from recording and promoting regional popular music artists in the 1950s, Los Alegres and other border-based groups continued to record on independently owned Mexican and Mexican American labels located on both sides of the border. With a large part of the community traveling illegally during this time, partly because of the Bracero Program's end in 1964 and more ambiguous and complex immigration laws, the corrido resurfaced, incorporating features of the traditional corrido and the canción-corrido.

Two new corrido protagonists emerged: the narcotraficante and the mojado. Numerous corridos recorded in the 1960s and 1970s and still popular today feature either the narcotraficante or the mojado as a hero of the underclass. Hernández (1999) champions the narcotraficante and views him as a throwback to the heroic figures of resistance in both border conflict and revolutionary corrido narratives. While the fantastical narcotraficante in narcocorridos emerges as a powerful figure who overcomes North American domination, I contend that the mojado, as an outlaw, is also portrayed as heroic. He confronts authority, racism, displacement, and economic misfortune, emerging triumphant as a result of his bravery and self-sacrifice, two traits that were central to both heroic and conflict corridos in the border region.

In the majority of drug-trafficking and border-crossing corridos before the 1960s, the protagonist dies, goes to jail, or loses his family and money; these songs tend to deliver admonitions against such illegal activity (Nicolopulos 1997). However, a few scholars, such as Guillermo Hernández, James Nicolopulos, and Mark Cameron Edberg, have recognized the narcotraficante's role as a modern-day social bandit who rises from his poor and marginalized community to be a successful businessman of the drug trade by subverting authority, flirting with death, and knocking down social and political barriers. Mexican scholars, such as Luis Astorga (1996a, 1996b) and Juan Carlos Ramírez-Pimienta (2004, 1998), have likened corrupt Mexican politicians to narcotraficantes, both having the power and wealth to control and destroy the lives of individuals, one group legally and the other illegally. In these binational representations, the narcotraficante in today's corridos has superhuman qualities that allow him to subvert authority on both sides of the border; an admirable feat in the eyes of Mexican migrants, many of whom live in the United States illegally. The greater part of scholarly writing (e.g., Herrera-Sobek, Guillermo Hernández, Ramírez-Pimienta) and journalistic work (e.g., Quiñones, Wald) on corridos in recent years has focused on the narcocorrido as a means by which the underclass can vicariously transcend borders and subvert authority, both North American and Mexican.

Few of these scholars have discussed the mojado, who appears in many more modern corridos than the narcotraficante (and in some cases is also involved in drug smuggling) and might be viewed as the narcotraficante's alter ego. In Edberg's study (2004), the narcotraficante emerges as a vibrant persona who maintains distinct Mexican, or more specifically northern Mexican, cultural roots that are also transnational. Edberg asserts that the narcotraficante draws cultural meaning from the conditions of poverty created by U.S. domination and global capital, a long history of race and class-based border conflict, the Mexican tradition of individual power and agency (the strongest representation of this is among the Norteño people), and the "real" and "imagined" images of the lawless border region's brave and macho bandit hero, such as Pancho Villa and Heraclio Bernal (2004, 122–123). In the case of Villa, well-known throughout Mexico, his heroic status was also attributed to his fame as a border raider who went up against General John Pershing's forces and, by extension, North American encroachment (Paredes 1976, 39). However, the mojado, as the sociologist Glenn A. Martínez (1998) suggests, has also garnered meaning from similar circumstances by evading border control agents and resisting assimilation in the United States by maintaining long-distance connections to his region of origin, avoiding capture by authorities, and maintaining a strong work ethic and family ties. It is not surprising that a popular music genre and defiantly independent industry would be formed around a narrative ballad tradition that was initially shaped by powerful images of a community's fight to establish an identity and place in a conflicted border environment.

## Norteña Music

While no scholarly publications exist about norteña music beyond those discussing its association with the corrido, it is sometimes mentioned in relation to the development of the regionally specific Texas-Mexican conjunto, a southern Texas variant of norteña with the same instrumentation that, beginning around the late 1940s, became specifically associated with Texas-Mexicans and later with more assimilated Chicanos throughout the Southwest. The folklorist and ethnomusicologist Manuel Peña's seminal research on conjunto music, which he describes as the working-class music of Mexican Americans of the Southwest, suggests that conjunto is a powerful expression of the modern working-class Tejano or Chicano experience, which contributed to its emergence as a highly stylized North American regional music phenomenon (1985). As this popular music became more assimilated, bilingual, and upwardly mobile, other more "Americanized" genres emerged from conjunto's core. *Orquesta tejana* evolved in the 1940s and 1950s in response to an expanding middle class of Texas-Mexicans. This genre merged North American popular styles such as rock and roll, Mexican folk song forms like rancheras and corridos, as well as popular Latin rhythms such as cumbia and salsa and elements of conjunto. This style is the predecessor to contemporary *música tejana,* or tejano, which evolved in the 1980s and 1990s (Peña 1999b).

Tejano spread throughout the Southwest and, owing to a prolific and active independent recording industry, gained some national recognition in the United States, alongside other popular pan-Latino styles, such as salsa and cumbia. While Peña's work broadened the interest in and subsequent reach of Mexican American and Chicano studies and contributed to North American popular music literature, it did so by moving the focus on Texas-Mexican border music and the Tejano community away from the border region and its nearby Mexican roots. Similarly, the local and global impact of norteña—which has a much larger audience; is more directly associated with nonassimilated, Spanish-speaking Mexican immigrants; and has a wider reach on both sides of the border than conjunto—has been largely ignored and there is little room for norteña in the North American popular music industry's marketing strategy for Hispanic and Latin American music. When some of norteña's most popular names, such as Ramón Ayala y Los Bravos del Norte, Los Tigres del Norte, and Los Tucanes del Norte, come up in the North American popular music market, they are often erroneously associated with the conjunto or tejano genres.

This confusion is understandable because tejano and conjunto are often presented to the public at large as the first truly "Chicano" or Mexican American music. Peña, for example, makes scant reference to norteña and its artists, simply referring to the genre as an "offshoot of música tejana" (1999a, 15). Tejano music is celebrated as the voice of a bilingual, middle-class Mexican American community whose members can trace their roots back to the early Spanish settlers in southern Texas or to families that immigrated from cities and towns in Mexican border states and crossed over just after the Mexican Revolution and before the Bracero Program was instituted. In contrast, norteña, with its focus on the narrative corrido or ranchera repertoire of songs, whose themes document the hardships of crossing the border, is associated with the displaced and marginalized.

Tejano and conjunto music are geared to a dancing public, and the lyrics deal with issues of love and celebrate Tejano/Chicano pride. The "folkloric" Texas-Mexican conjunto and the more modern *música tejana* hold a deeply powerful and symbolic role in the creation and strengthening of a distinct Texas-Mexican culture and identity, as Peña's writings clearly indicate (1985, 1999a, 1999b). While Mexican history and culture are invoked in these Texas-based traditions and are part of the reason conjunto still exists, they are imagined or "recreated" nostalgically. However, norteña, which has spawned a much larger transnational recording and touring industry, is the music of immigrants who are carving out a distinct Mexican diaspora community that celebrates Mexican culture, history, community relations, hard work, and resistance to assimilation.

## Writings on the Corrido and Norteña Music

In recent years, the popular press on both sides of the border has weighed in, particularly on the subject of narcocorridos. The popular music journalist Sam Quiñones, a freelance writer based in Mexico since 1995 whose articles have appeared in such newspapers as the *Los Angeles Times,* the *Houston Chronicle,* and the *San Francisco Examiner,* has written frequently about the popularity of narcocorridos among Mexican laborers in rural villages and municipalities throughout Mexico. He also published a book, *True Tales from Another Mexico: The Lynch Mob, the Popsicle Kings, Chalino, and the Bronx* (2001), filled with stories about immigrant communities scraping out a living in a variety of creative and unthinkable ways—one of the few popular publications that takes a realistic look at the thoroughly modern and uniquely transnational Mexican diaspora. One of the most fascinating moments in Quiñones's book is the tragic real-life account of the narcocorrido composer—mojado, drug kingpin, and former prisoner—Chalino Sánchez, who almost single-handedly breathed new life into the norteña industry and the narcocorrido by writing songs that were more "realistic" and violent than those of Los Tigres and other norteña groups who came before him. Influenced by gangsta rap in Los Angeles, Sánchez brought a younger audience to the genre and, by living the life of many of his protagonists, he proved to be the ultimate "badass" by getting himself murdered in Sinaloa.

Elijah Wald is also a journalist turned book author, whose writings about narcocorridos and the genre's most popular group, Los Tigres del Norte, began to appear in the mainstream press just after the release of the group's influential recording *Jefe de Jefes* (Boss of Bosses) in 1997. In an article for the *Boston Globe,*

Wald (1998) notes that mainstream North America has been out of touch with Mexican immigrant culture and its popular music, in particular the narco-corrido. He writes that Los Tigres are clever innovators of the narcocorrido tradition: They celebrate the ability of the marginalized Mexican immigrant laborer to subvert authority while calling the U.S. government to task for its role in rampant drug trafficking across the border. Wald's 2001 book, *Narcocorrido: A Journey into the Music of Drugs, Guns, and Guerrillas*, is a travelogue that chronicles his journey through Mexico in search of legendary composers of popular narcocorridos such as Andrés Contreras, Teodoro Bello, Enrique Franco, Julián Garza, and Gabriel Villanueva. Wald's approach resembles that of a cultural tourist who is fascinated by the "exotic" lawlessness of these modern-day social bandits. However, since he focuses his attention on musicians and composers as folk artists making a living as best they can, he tries to eschew any serious debates about celebrating this lifestyle or exoticizing "the other."

While many Mexican scholars and journalists treat norteña and its most popular artists, Los Tigres del Norte, as a symptom of neoliberal policies of the Mexican government or of migrants' increased exposure to North American pop culture and decadence, some still insist that the genre is uniquely Mexican and worthy of proper study. The poet and musicologist Mario Arturo Ramos published *Cien corridos: Alma de la canción mexicana* (2002), an anthology of one hundred corridos dating from 1810 to the present, which was well received by the academic community and in the popular press. The book was distributed to elementary and high schools across Mexico for nearly two years. When the legislators of several Mexican states discovered that the book contained four narcocorridos (some of which were actually mojado-themed corridos), they removed it from schools and libraries, and the government ordered the book's publisher, Editorial Océano, to cease production and distribution (García Hernández 2005).

Meanwhile, the popular book by the Spanish novelist Arturo Pérez-Reverte, *La reina del sur* (The queen of the South), which is based on one of the first narcocorridos (made famous in the 1970s by Los Tigres del Norte), continues to be available in Mexican bookstores and libraries throughout the country. It would seem that from an "official" standpoint, the narcocorrido as pulp fiction is acceptable and celebrated, but as a contemporary manifestation of the proletariat corrido tradition, it is unworthy of serious scholarly study. Finally, while the debate continues about the narcocorrido and mojado-themed songs, little can be found on the extraordinary impact of norteña music as the genre popular with immigrant laborers on both sides of the border. One book, Toño Carrizosa's *La onda grupera: Historia del movimiento grupero* (1997), makes a valiant attempt to examine the cumbia-laden popular music industry that exploded in the early 1980s in Monterrey and swept through the U.S.-based Mexican immigrant population through the early 1990s. While norteña music and the narcocorrido seemed to be on a hiatus during this period, cumbia (also, *onda grupera*) groups from Monterrey, dressed in glitzy western garb, like Los Bukis, Bronco, and

Selena (from Texas) brought this popular genre to the attention of major international labels' Latin divisions, such as Discos Sony, WEA Latin, and Capitol EMI Latin. However, this trend was short-lived, and with the resurgence (again) of the narcocorrido—thanks in part to Chalino Sánchez and primarily California-based new groups like Los Tucanes de Tijuana (The Toucans of Tijuana)—norteña was back on top, with independent labels like Fonovisa (San José, California), Disa (Monterrey), and DLV (Monterrey) competing with these same major label players. For some scholars (Edberg and Ramírez-Pimienta in particular), norteña has been transformed and commodified by both the music industry and the drug trafficking industry as a highly marketable product with broad appeal, particularly among the marginalized, impoverished, and undocumented, bringing into question whether the narcocorrido is a true narrative of resistance.

## Music, Migration, and Mexicanidad

The impact of migration, particularly in the United States, has forced scholars to consider music, both traditional and popular, not as belonging to one place or another but as being associated with both here and there or, as the title of Los Tigres del Norte's song "Ni Aquí ni Allá" suggests, as belonging neither here nor there.[1] Music is no longer static and associated with a specific geographical site. The movement of people, along with new developments in technology, has spurred interest in issues of authenticity, tradition, and expanded networks for the performance and consumption of music. And while the music of migrating communities is being "reinvented" or "redefined" in new locales, it still allows community members to remain connected to a sense of history, culture, and identity (Hobsbawm 1983, 1–3). The long history and political and racial dynamics of the migration of Mexican laborers into the United States have profoundly influenced its society and culture. With over ten million Mexican Americans living legally in this country, it is no wonder that Mexican traditional and popular music and culture have significantly influenced North American society and culture (Arizpe 2004, 20–22). This culture is so visible in some regions such as the Southwest that mariachi music is taught in local schools and universities; new migration trends in the Midwest, Pacific Northwest, and Northeast are bringing mariachi schools and programs to these regions as well.

Researchers examining Mexican migration trends have noted the transnational and transcultural nature of migration over the past twenty-five years (e.g., Arizpe 2004; Massey, Durand, and Malone 2002; Smith 2000). Early migration, particularly from northern Mexican states to predominantly southwestern

---

[1] This title, like those of many songs and albums by Los Tigres del Norte and other popular norteña artists, uses the English-language form of capitalization. (According to Spanish-language rules for capitalization, only the first word and proper nouns are capitalized in titles.) As the norteña music industry became increasingly focused on the immigrant population in the United States, these titles, like the music itself, embodied the merging of Mexican and North American cultures. I have adopted this format throughout the book.

U.S. states, expanded an already Hispanicized and Mexicanized region. Many immigrants settled in this region, finding the linguistic, cultural, and social adjustments not so extreme, though they still experienced racism and discrimination. However, after 1973 and peaking in the mid-1990s, high unemployment rates and income inequality became the norm. Mexican immigrants could not find jobs in this region as easily as they had in the past, and they began fanning out across the United States (Durand, Massey, and Parrado 1999, 520). Before the Immigration Reform and Control Act (IRCA) was instituted in 1986, those who did travel for work outside the Southwest often stayed temporarily, returning to Mexico (many to border towns to work temporarily in *maquila* factories). The IRCA changed that pattern. The law offered amnesty to long-term undocumented workers at a time when Mexico was experiencing unusually severe inflation and unemployment, and many chose to remain in the United States. While the IRCA required undocumented immigrants to remain in the United States while their amnesty petitions were reviewed, the law's tighter control of the border, which included an increase in border patrol agents, encouraged new undocumented workers to remain in the United States rather than risk crossing back (1999, 521–524). Today, Mexicans make up almost 60 percent of the nation's undocumented population of over eleven million, and 80 to 85 percent of the migration from Mexico in recent years is undocumented (Passel 2005). The U.S. government has continued to fight migration at the border (and out of view of the North American public at large), but Mexican migration and its ensuing cultural impact have increased, becoming more visible in urban centers and rural towns throughout the United States.

Norteña music, with the corrido ballad song form at its core, is the popular music genre that initially traveled with migrant workers and, after the Bracero Program ended, with the undocumented traveler in particular. Though it is not unusual to encounter the occasional regional Mexican *son* ensemble (string band) among immigrant communities, norteña is the modern popular music genre that became specifically associated with this community, the experience of migration, and the search for work. Thanks to pioneering artists like Los Alegres de Terán, El Piporro, Ramón Ayala y Los Bravos del Norte, and Los Tigres del Norte, the norteña ensemble sound was modernized and eventually tailored to the experiences and aesthetic tastes of this community. Similarly, the corrido was transformed from a heroic epic ballad to a topical narrative popular song form that expressed the ordeal of travel, displacement, cultural and racial conflict, and societal change. In large part as a result of the massive migration of this population, years of complex and ambiguous U.S. immigration policy, a volatile and increasingly criminalized border region, and escalating undocumented migration, norteña's audience grew. Movement is at the core of norteña's development. It was the migration of people that brought the corrido song tradition and the accordion and bajo sexto together. Travel to urban and rural locales farther north into the United States broadened this music's popularity, and the high mobility of its audience and performers meant that the industry evolved on both sides of the border, first in Texas, then Monterrey, and later in California.

The advent of cassette technology in the 1970s and 1980s brought another kind of mobility to the music, and, in cassette format, norteña began to travel back to Mexico, where it became associated with working-class populations throughout the country. Cassettes enabled individuals within this transnational migrant network to share the music with each other and with families and friends in Mexico. That cassettes were inexpensive to manufacture and duplicate not only made the music more accessible and readily available but also opened the industry to pirating, thus subverting the economic interests of major label control of popular music, as did the popularization and dissemination of Indian popular music in the 1970s and 1980s that Peter Manuel (1993) describes. Today, the music remains mobile, accessible, and exploitable thanks to technological advancements (e.g., CD and DVD duplication and the Internet) that have extended its popularity. Continued migration beyond the Southwest has secured markets for norteña throughout the Mexican diaspora (as well as among border-crossing migrants from Central America, Colombia, Ecuador, and Peru), situating the music as an important cultural agent in the creation of a "new Mexican global nation" (Arizpe 2004, 22).

The continued popularity of norteña music, a genre that is not viewed as purely "Mexican" by the mainstream Mexican music industry and that cannot cross over into the North American mainstream market, represents a new Mexican identity—or *mexicanidad*—shaped by the collective experience of travel and the constant flow of information, ideas, and culture. While mariachi ensembles—which feature songs from the Revolution, regional folk songs, and romantic ballads—are often promoted in the United States as the music of the Mexican "nation" by Mexican consular offices and cultural institutions, norteña has emerged as the voice of the present-day Mexican migrant experience. Because this experience has become so deeply rooted in the Mexican consciousness and in working-class society on both sides of the border, norteña has morphed from a regional genre of peasant laborers to a mass-produced popular music genre that speaks to the political, social, and cultural inequalities experienced by Mexican immigrant workers in the United States and their families and communities in Mexico.

Though song lyrics certainly document the hardship and alienation of this experience, they also remind immigrants of the importance of loyalty to one's family and country. In this case, mexicanidad is asserted through embracing a heritage that is indigenous as well as Mexican. Mexico's government and political elite have generally viewed border-crossing migrants and indigenous Mexicans as outcasts. Celebrating indigenous culture and identity was at the core of the emerging Mexican nationalistic movement of the 1930s and 1940s. Among Mexican immigrants today mexicanidad is represented through solidarity and connecting with communities across the diaspora and is based on pride of origin,

---

### Soy Potosino

| | |
|---|---|
| Soy de tierras potosinas | I am from Potosino country* |
| y mi orgullo es ser de allá | and I am proud to be from there |
| Mis venas traen sangre azteca | I have Aztec blood in my veins |
| de mi tierra les quiero contar | I want to tell you about my country |
| Cien por ciento mexicano | One hundred percent Mexican |
| Mi sangre de indio no voy a negar | I will not deny my Indian blood |
| | |
| Soy de donde se da la tuna | I am from where you find the *tuna*\* |
| donde el águila bajó | where the eagle lands |
| Cuando mató a la serpiente | when he kills the serpent |
| y en la bandera quedó | and is pictured on our flag |
| Lo dicen los potosinos los compas | As good friends of Potosinos say |
| que bajan de otra región | who come from other regions |
| | |
| Tuve que dejar mi patria | I had to give up my country |
| con los gringos yo emigré | I had to emigrate to live with the gringos |
| Aunque estoy en tierra gringa | Even though I'm in gringo land |
| mis raíces yo no olvidaré | I will never forget my roots |
| Así hay como tanto hispano | Like so many Hispanic people |
| que llega a esta tierra | who come to this country |
| ya me acostumbré | now I am accustomed |

---

FIGURE 1.1 "Soy Potosino." Written by José G. Martínez in 2002. Recorded by Los Terribles del Norte in 2003. *Potosino country = San Luis Potosí; *tuna* = cactus pear. (From the CD *La tercera es la vendida . . . eso!* [Freddie Records JMCD-1858]. Lyrics courtesy of Freddie Records/MARFRE Music.)

both regional and national. Norteña's focus on the shared experiences of Mexican migrants in the United States combined with nostalgic references to the past embodies this postmodern sense of mexicanidad. In the popular corrido excerpted in Figure 1.1, "Soy Potosino" by the Texas-based norteña group Los Terribles del Norte, the border-crossing migrant clings, simultaneously, to his regional, indigenous, and Mexican national identity while affirming that he is "accustomed" (but not assimilated) to life in the United States. For its author and for many of his fellow migrant travelers, this song constructs an imagined community and nationality through both symbolic and experiential references to mexicanidad while it implies strong resistance to North American social domination and acculturation.

The sociologist Robert Smith argues that tighter immigration laws and the inability to travel freely have prompted communities from which large groups of Mexican immigrants hail to maintain long-distance connections via grassroots organizations and through continuous involvement not only in family businesses and household decisions but also in local politics and community service (2003, 299–305). While immigrants are returning home less often, whether because of financial independence, growing family ties in the United States, or their undocumented status, they are participating in a more fluid and autonomous notion of a Mexican diasporic nation. Although it might seem that such limitations on physical travel would discourage commitment to Mexico, new technologies, an expanded number of Spanish-speaking Mexican enclaves throughout the United States, and the large percentage of undocumented travelers unable (or unwilling) to assimilate into Chicano or North American populations have reinforced these long-distance ties to Mexico. Traditionally, migration studies supported the notion that Mexican migrant populations maintained a "unidirectional shift," meaning that in spite of the fact that they often moved between communities on both sides of the border, they eventually focused their involvement in one. However, Roger Rouse (1991, 13–15) argues that advancements in communication technology and travel have allowed for a continued interest in remaining culturally, socially, and economically involved in more than one community or locale at the same time. Ironically, in my own observation, even though many undocumented immigrants cannot travel, many maintain businesses, relationships, and even residences in both locales (many living with the hope of returning one day). The Mexican government not only recognizes but also encourages a sense of dual nationality, in part because the country depends on remittances from this population. A recent example of this was legislation passed in March 2005, which gave immigrants the right to vote in Mexican elections from the United States (even if they have obtained U.S. citizenship). By reaching out to a population it had ignored for so many years, the Mexican government has signaled its recognition of the Mexican diaspora and the power this community holds financially, politically, and culturally. Mexican immigrants, in turn, have responded with a fervent revitalization of mexicanidad.

More than any other traditional, regional, or popular Mexican music genre, norteña embodies an immigrant notion of mexicanidad and, by extension, the new Mexican global nation. The genre's origins in the historically autonomous northernmost region of Mexico, its stylistic and popular evolution among migrating Mexicans who brought to it musical ideas and technological innovation from both sides of the border, and its initial commercial growth and marketing focus in the United States have positioned it as the voice of a nation of Mexican immigrants who are living in one locale and imagining themselves in another. In the corridos and rancheras of norteña music, the immigrant lives as an outcast (or outlaw if he or she is illegal) and can find a sense of belonging that is based on a shared understanding of history, migration, and values. Though this definition of norteña aligns it with the growth and dispersion of the immigrant community in the United States, norteña is also very widely disseminated and popular in Mexico. A long and highly politicized history of migration to the United States has profoundly and significantly affected Mexico, economically, socially, politically, and culturally (Smith 2003; Arizpe 2004). With one in every ten Mexicans migrating to the United States and with remittances and investments from immigrants totaling as much as $23.98 billion (Malkin 2008), Mexico has begun to embrace its diasporic population, recognizing the hybrid culture and nomadic lifestyle of that population, even though remittances have dropped in recent months because of the U.S. housing slump and economic crisis (Malkin 2008).

## Defining a "Mexican" Diaspora

According to Américo Paredes, "Every Mexican knows that there are in fact two Mexicos, just as he knows that there being two is not a purely metaphysical concept, although it has transcendental implications." There is the "real" Mexico, as he describes it, the territory physically occupied by a nation, and then there is the other Mexico, the one known to Mexicans as "México de afuera" (Mexico of the outside), made up of Mexicans living throughout the United States (Paredes 1993, 3). North American society's uneasiness with the social and cultural impact of "two Mexicos" is evidenced by moments in North American history when Mexicans have not been made to feel welcome, such as California's ill-conceived Proposition 187 in the mid-1990s and the U.S. government's aggressive stance on immigration, most recently after the "reforms" of 1996, which restricted or prohibited state and federal public services (such as health care) for certain immigrants, placed greater restrictions on immigration, and sought to strengthen policing of the border. Paredes's work focuses on the second of the two Mexicos, "México de afuera," which he asserts is made up of all persons of Mexican descent living in the United States (1993, 3). However, one cannot assume that all Mexicans in "México de afuera" are the same. In fact, to understand the role of norteña music as a means of understanding a complex and vast Mexican diaspora, one must distinguish the Tejano from the Chicano and the Mexican American from the Mexican national. There are also regional distinctions, within both the United States and Mexico, and divisions within the population that are based on such criteria as level of education, work experience (in a rural or urban context), and length of time away from the "first" Mexico. The popularity of norteña music has ebbed and flowed on the basis of the social and cultural dynamics of local and transnational distinctions that exist within Mexican communities. This study's documentation, research, and analysis of norteña music in both Mexicos examines these distinctions and the role they have played in the "coming together" and the transnational flow of the two Mexicos.

The once "regional" characteristics of norteña music and culture have been historicized, sensationalized, localized, and transformed by an expanding population of border-crossing Mexicans, particularly those labeled "illegal" (or mojado) who travel from all regions of the country. The most appealing character of norteña is the postmodern working-class "outlaw," who consistently eludes authority (both Mexican and North American) and bears no clear discernible attachment to either of the two Mexicos. This has long been the case with the Norteño people, who have been virtually self-ruling for decades and maintained an ambivalent (and somewhat distant) relationship with Mexico's administrative and nationalistic core amid what the historian David G. Gutiérrez describes as "the continuing social, cultural, and economic integration of the United States–Mexico border region" (1999, 509). Like the Norteño himself, traveling Mexican laborers from all regions of the country have grown accustomed to living and working in communities on both sides of the border. Perhaps it is more appropriate to look at norteña music and the working-class Mexican immigrant as together constituting both a blurring of boundaries that once defined "home" and "abroad" and a merging of cultures and identities.

The academic research and writings of James Clifford, Arjun Appadurai, Caren Kaplan, George Lipsitz, Homi Bhabha, and others have shown that migrant and "displaced" communities have had a profound impact on the culture, economics, and politics that have shaped the world and, in particular, North American society. Lipsitz has observed that Latin American immigrants (not unlike other diasporic communities) are perhaps more modernized and more accustomed than their countrymen who stayed behind (as well as many North Americans themselves) to the globalization of the United States. Because they were "created by the machinations of world capitalism over the centuries" and are thus "accustomed to code switching, syncretism, and hybridity," these communities may be better prepared for the more complex and sinuous notions of place, identity, and nationalism that are shaping the world today (1994, 31). This idea pertains especially to members of the Mexican immigrant population, who—from the social, cultural, and economic border-based conflicts between Norteño Mexicans and Anglo-American newcomers of the mid-nineteenth century to the current oppressive immigration laws and discrimination—have emerged resilient and ever more determined to seek a better life and economic freedom in the United States. Their experience in negotiating diverse social, political, and cultural landscapes has better equipped these immigrants to form transnational communal allegiances than to remain dependent on any one nation.

In the case of Mexico, this notion is best understood when considering the northernmost region and the borderlands, where a regional identity was formed partly in response to encroaching capitalism by an aggressive "foreign entity" and the oppressive authoritarianism of a distant nation. For more than a century, both real and imagined ideas and experiences of the U.S.-Mexico border have shaped a Mexican American history and imagination. These experiences created the foundation for defining a separate society and ideology, particularly in the Southwest. The historian Mario T. García (1996, 90) describes both the symbolic and the concrete effects the border has had on travelers and notes that each generation's interpretation of the border has profoundly shaped its political and cultural developments for years. The border figures prominently in the collective memory of what constitutes a "homeland" for many Mexicans and Mexican Americans, perhaps more so than Mexico itself. Conflicts within both Mexican and North American societies have contributed to the characteristics of a Mexican diaspora that can only be fully imagined by those who have crossed the border, regardless of which side they happen to be living on. Norteña music exists simultaneously as "border" music and as the music of immigrant Mexican laborers. It is a mechanism by which regional interpretations of the Mexican diaspora have been artistically and collectively expressed, particularly as divisions within the ethnic Mexican population itself have widened and become increasingly complex.

The reality of traveling for work has a long history in northern Mexico— from the Tlaxcalteca Indians who were brought to the area by Spanish colonizers from the Tlaxcala region of central Mexico in the seventeenth century to work in local mines to the Mexican cowboys who joined North American cattle drives in the 1800s to the Mexican laborers who now cross the U.S.-Mexico border for work on a daily basis. For these travelers, the experience of displacement and migration has merged with a global flow of ideologies, technology, and imagination that, through the years, has had a crucial role in shaping the shifting ideas of what constitutes Mexico and the United States. For the Mexican immigrant, norteña music, like the diaspora whose experiences it expresses, began in the border region, extended into the United States, and then extended into Mexico's interior. Because of its association with northern Mexico and border culture, norteña music and its social history have now become "slippery," to use Appadurai's term (1990, 44), as the genre's stylistic features and meaning have been affected by the fluidity of travel, the politicization of the border, and the localization of communities on both sides.

## Race, Class, and Identity in the Mexican Diaspora

Issues of race, class, and identity have been tied to the development of popular music in the United States. Though popular music genres such as country, jazz, rhythm and blues, rock, hip hop, and rap evolved from a merging of African and European musical elements, they are also the result of marginalization and oppression. Prior to the civil rights movement, musicians and audiences were segregated, but as musical ideas and influences continued to flow back and forth, these once distanced and isolated communities came closer. While the coming together of cross-cultural musical ideas transcends the experience of discrimination and marginalization to some extent, our society is still grappling with racial, economic, and social inequalities in its musical and artistic life.

In the United States, race has been viewed in black and white terms; the issue has become much more complex as immigration continues from so many locales and racial mixing grows more common. The Mexican American or Chicano in this country has long been a racialized and marginalized minority. While many Mexican Americans came into this country through immigration, a large population in the Southwest suddenly found themselves in the United States after the Mexican American War ended in 1848 and the Treaty of Hidalgo ceded to the United States more than 525,000 square miles of former Mexican territory (Arizona, California, western Colorado, Nevada, New Mexico, Texas, and Utah). The agreement also established the U.S.-Mexican border at the Rio Grande and Gila rivers. Many Mexican residents in this new U.S. region were viewed as second-class citizens in the racial and class-based hierarchy imposed by Anglo-Americans. They were, as David G. Gutiérrez notes, "doubly marginalized as orphans of the Mexican nation and as outcasts within the newly expanded United States" (1999, 485).

Over the years, racial divisions between Mexicans and Anglo-Americans in the Southwest became more rigid and institutionalized, making it more difficult for Mexicans to integrate into North American society. Gutiérrez depicts a segregation and impoverishment that extended by the turn of the twentieth century throughout the Southwest in "run-down barrios and rural colonias," which he says also provided a safe haven for preserving traditional customs, language, and religious practices (1999, 488). The Mexican Revolution and the subsequent economic upheaval from 1910 to 1920 prompted the first large wave of Mexican migration into the United States, largely through illegal channels. During this time, rapid development in the Southwest produced jobs in mines, railroad construction, and farm labor (Gutiérrez 1999, 120–123).

Living in isolated communities and working in backbreaking jobs as migrant laborers, Mexicans experienced discrimination throughout the Southwest. In Texas, the Anglo-American population maintained a social policy of segregation and discrimination along with a cultural memory of the Alamo. Furthermore, native Spanish-speaking populations in this area (many of whom were descended from Spanish, rather than Mexican, settlers) campaigned to be accepted as "American" and lobbied to distance themselves from what they considered to be "lower-class" immigrants (Gutiérrez 1999, 129). Such attitudes set the stage for long-enduring class- and race-based divisions in Texas and the lower Rio Grande Valley, an agriculturally fertile area that borders Mexico. In this region and among the Mexican migrant workers who were forced to leave their villages and families for work "en el otro lado" (on the other side) the traditional border corrido and the accordion/bajo sexto–based norteña ensemble first came together. Manuel Peña describes this working-class norteña ensemble as a "proletarian expression" that would achieve cultural autonomy within the white hegemonic society that dominated the region's politics, society, and economy (1985, 145). As Paredes (1958, 1993) also suggests, the norteña ensemble, like the corrido, was a means by which this community could maintain control of its own forms of cultural and religious expression and thus exert power and resist total domination by the local society.

Peña's exhaustive work examined the evolution of the Texas-Mexican conjunto (as the norteña ensemble came to be known by Mexican-Americans in Texas) as the voice of a post–World War II emerging Mexican American (as well as Tejano and Chicano) middle class, which sought to assimilate but not to acculturate into North American society. The African American community's struggle for civil liberties in the 1950s and 1960s inspired many second- and third-generation Mexican Americans (many of whom now called themselves Chicanos and Chicanas) to embark on their own campaign for improvements in socioeconomic and educational conditions and to assert their rights as citizens of the United States (Gonzales 1999, 191). Peña (1985) notes that in this period Texas-Mexican conjunto declined as a popular music genre of the Mexican working class, being eclipsed by the more "sophisticated" orquesta tejana genre that replaced the accordion with brass instruments (and later keyboards) and the bajo sexto with electric guitar and bass.

Because, according to Peña, Texas-Mexican conjunto was a "counter-ideological response by Tejano (Texas-Mexican) workers to subordination under North American political, economic and cultural hegemony" (1985, 110), it lost relevance as Chicanos and Tejanos achieved a higher social and economic status within North American society. By the mid-1960s, Texas-Mexican conjunto's evolution as a popular music genre ceased; it became "folk music" and was celebrated as a "symbol" of the Texas-Mexican's (and Chicano's) working-class past and struggle for recognition within the dominant Anglo-American culture. Outside interest in the music (for instance, by the Smithsonian Institution and independent audiophile record labels, such as Arhoolie Records and Rounder Records) and the commercialization of orquesta tejana (later known as *música tejana,* or simply tejano) have contributed to the perpetuation of the music as "folkloric" and increasingly "regional."

What Peña leaves out of this discussion, however, is the continued "Mexicanization" of the border region and the impact the surge of Mexican migration into the United States had on Mexican immigrant popular music, particularly after the end of the Bracero Program in the mid-1960s. While Tejanos and Chicanos were establishing a place for themselves within North American culture and society, increasing numbers of new Mexican immigrants were coming into the United States each year, many of them illegally, and finding work beyond the Southwest (e.g., in Chicago, Michigan, Oregon, Washington State). These migrants represented a new labor class, discriminated against by both North American employers and bilingual, upwardly mobile Chicano/Tejano residents. While the Chicano movement brought about numerous educational, socioeconomic, and cultural reforms (e.g., bilingual and bicultural education, recognition that the United States is a multicultural society, Chicano and Latino university programs, farm labor reforms, recognition of Chicano arts and artists), many of these benefits did not affect the lives of new Mexican immigrants and eventually contributed to further divisions within the ethnic Mexican community at large, divisions based on education level, language skills, immigration status, and class distinctions. It is clear that while the advancements brought about by the movement established a vibrant Mexican presence and cultural heritage that has maintained a high profile in North American society since the 1970s, the increasing numbers of undocumented immigrants have generated a negative reaction (Gonzales 1999, 223). And as the general population grew apprehensive about these numbers, it began to blame Mexican immigrants for everything from job shortages to increases in drug-related crime. In many regions of the Southwest, attitudes toward Mexican immigrants grew hostile. Fearing a return to the discriminative and oppressive atmosphere experienced by their parents and grandparents, many Chicanos and Tejanos sought to distance themselves from this new "Mexican" population, only further marginalizing the latter as impoverished laborers and "second-class" residents.

During this period norteña emerged as the popular music associated with this growing and doubly marginalized community. While Texas-Mexican conjunto became detached from the migrating Mexican and the increasingly "Mexicanized" border community, norteña emerged as a distinct genre with its own style. Though conjunto and norteña featured the same working-class instrumental core (accordion and bajo sexto) and had assimilated from rock and roll such modern instruments as the electric bass, drum set, and occasionally the saxophone, they grew apart stylistically. While conjunto became a dance hall phenomenon that increasingly showcased the accordion (now a symbol of Tejano and Chicano identity) and relied more on English-language lyrics, norteña groups, who typically sang in Spanish, focused more on the corrido and traditional rhythms such as the European-derived polka and waltz and the regional Mexican *huapango,* a dance rhythm with rapidly alternating patterns. For many migrating Mexicans, the corrido evoked the Revolution (a time when peasants and bandit heroes changed the course of Mexican history); the fetishized and eternally macho Norteño cowboy; and the humiliating and, now increasingly dangerous, border-crossing experience.

Unlike the Texas-Mexican conjunto, norteña represented neither a working-class past nor a constructed Mexican heritage; rather, it represented the present-day experiences of a Mexican laborer community that confronted racism and disenfranchisement in the struggle to better the lives of its families and communities. These immigrants—in part because of the overwhelming percentage of undocumented workers among them and because they formed distinct communities and Mexican enclaves throughout the United States—have tended to sustain stronger ties to their communities of origin; they have not assimilated and have lower naturalization rates than any other immigrant community in the United States and have maintained a profound sense of Mexican identity. Norteña music has perpetuated this immigrant notion of mexicanidad through songs that invoke solidarity and collective identity by means of musical documentations of "real life" immigrant experiences and both documented and fictive exploits of the modern-day border cowboy, the narcotraficante.

As a popular music form rooted in a race- and class-based community in North American society, norteña has grown into a transnational popular music phenomenon that has also penetrated the U.S. Latino popular music industry, albeit via strikingly independent and individualistic means. Norteña's popularity and dissemination throughout an expanding Mexican diaspora has been fueled by the ability of the immigrants in this community to imagine themselves as Mexican no matter where they have settled. In this imagining, history and experience take precedence over place (Appadurai 1996; Bhabha 1994). The popularization and perpetuation of norteña music, along with a clearly defined notion of a global Mexican nation, have helped the Mexican immigrant (particularly the undocumented) to rise above the class-based discrimination, oppression, and displacement imposed by a North American government that continues to criminalize its border zone and blame immigration problems on the migrating Mexican.

# 2

# Regional Identity, Class, and the Emergence of "Border Music"

The Norteño people, like the norteña music that originated in this region, are self-sufficient and resilient. In the Mexican imagination, the Norteño resembles the North American cowboy. Depicted in most Mexican films as male—macho in attitude and physical presence—the often pistol-packing Norteño represents a colorful image of Mexico's wild and untamed frontier. The country's northernmost region remained largely rural, poor, and sparsely populated during the first part of the last century; in the 1930s and 1940s, the population grew when numerous government-sponsored agrarian and irrigation projects began, but when these programs dissolved in the 1950s, many migrants and rural residents moved to border cities like Ciudad Juárez and Tijuana, whose populations quadrupled by the late 1960s. From there, many people crossed over into the United States, where jobs were more abundant and wages were often higher. Most people did so illegally because of stringent and vaguely worded U.S. government stipulations for legal entry (Gonzales 1999, 176–178).

The area bordering the United States exists in the consciousness of both Mexicans and North Americans as a no-man's-land of sorts, where illegal crossings produce both outlaws and traitors. The novelist Gloria Anzaldúa has described the border as "una herida abierta" (an open wound) and as "the lifeblood of two worlds merging to form a third country" (1987, 3). This region, the Rio Grande Valley of southern Texas and northeastern Mexico (see the map, Figure 2.1), gave birth to early forms of música norteña and its

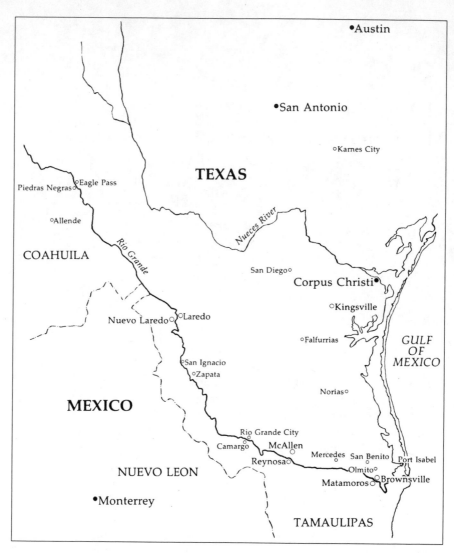

**FIGURE 2.1** Lower Rio Grande Valley of Texas bordering three Mexican states: Tamaulipas, Nuevo León, and Coahuila. The map also features border towns well-known for early recording activity and radio broadcasts of norteña music such as McAllen, Reynosa, Matamoros, and Brownsville. The large industrial city of Monterrey, Nuevo León, would become the major hub for recording commercial norteña by the early 1960s.

(Reprinted from Américo Paredes, *A Texas-Mexican Cancionero* [Urbana: University of Illinois Press, 1976], xii, with permission of the author's estate.)

pioneering artists: Narciso Martínez, Los Montañeses del Álamo, Antonio Tanguma, Los Alegres de Terán, Los Gorriones de Topo Chico, El Piporro, Luis y Julián, Carlos y José, Cornelio Reyna y los Relámpagos del Norte, Ramón Ayala, Los Cadetes de Linares, and many others. Early folk music ensembles in this region featured elements of Spanish, Mexican, Czech, Polish, German, and later North American musical influences (Moreno Rivas 1979, 57–58). The first record labels and studios for Mexican music were launched on the Texas side, in the lower Rio Grande Valley, in response to the growing popularity of this new genre and the many migrant-laborer artists who were available. However, Monterrey, Nuevo León—the state's large industrial capital and cultural center—soon responded with its own recording studios and labels as well as one of the first and most powerful radio stations in Mexico.

Though many of norteña's fans live in the United States and are mostly undocumented, norteña has evolved into a multimillion dollar industry with artists touring extensively on both sides of the border. Other genres—such as banda (or the more modernized version, *technobanda*), cumbia (also known as *tropical*), mariachi, *sonidero,* and *rock en español* (rock music sung in Spanish)— are either popular youth genres imported from Mexico or an updated tradition now associated with a specific region, like the *technobanda* phenomenon of southern California.

Mariachi holds the unique status of the "national music of Mexico" and is an urbanized genre that originated with the regional *son jalisciense* string ensemble tradition of western Mexico, particularly the states of Jalisco and Colima. After the Mexican Revolution of 1910, the mariachi became a symbol of nationalism primarily for its use by Mexican presidents for official and political functions. Popularized in 1930s Mexican films as the quintessential Mexican folk-derived musical ensemble, it grew more significant in its global representation of a united Mexican heritage and culture and as a symbol of modernity. It owes its importance and longevity to several factors: First, during the peak of Mexican rural to urban migration in the 1930s and 1940s, the mariachi ensemble took in other regional son influences, such as son *jarocho* and son *huasteco* (requiring more violins and replacing the harp with the *guitarrón* (a large deep-bodied, six-string acoustic bass), identifiable by nostalgic migrants. In addition, the mariachi also embraced the modern influences of the time, including in its repertoire the bolero, newly imported from Cuba via the Yucatán, and incorporating the trumpet, a nod to the worldwide acceptance of the North American big band jazz craze.

Mariachi is also the style best known to non-Mexicans and is celebrated as the ultimate expression of Mexican identity among Mexican American and Chicano communities throughout the United States. Since the early 1960s, mariachi education programs and U.S.-based groups have sprung up among communities, initially in the Southwest and now throughout the country. Today, while some mariachi groups, such as the Los Angeles–based Sol de México and Los Camperos, have enjoyed minor recognition as recording artists, the tradition remains a dormant artifact of class-based colonial Mexico with relatively little new music composed and performed. The majority of Mexican pop music is dictated by a larger "Latino" or "International" commercial market that views mariachi as too "folkloric" and, perhaps, too "Mexican." Norteña, however, is primarily driven by the tastes, activities, and attitudes of the working-class, immigrant community. New songs, new composers, and new groups are the driving force behind this genre, which the dominant Latino industry sees as too "working-class" and too "Mexican." Nevertheless, norteña has maintained its commercial success primarily among Mexican (and increasingly Central American) workers in the United States since the 1960s and has grown into the focus of a significant independent recording industry that is closely tied to a large and complex touring network covering major cities and rural communities across the United States and, more recently, central and southern Mexico. It is not considered to be folkloric, nostalgic, or educational, like mariachi, nor is it part of the pan-Latino popular music market. Norteña music's popularity lies somewhere between the folkloric and the commercial, between regional and transnational, and between Mexico and the United States. In essence, neither here nor there.

## Northern Mexico and the Norteño People

To better understand norteña music's unique transformation, one must consider Norteños themselves. They are the people of Mexico's far North who have a distinct and exceptionally autonomous identity within Mexican history and society. Northern Mexico's geographic isolation and turbulent past, one that is closely tied to the U.S.-Mexico border and migration, have led to its estranged relationship with Mexico's core. Many scholars and writers (Américo Paredes, Mario T. García, Guillermo Gómez-Peña, Néstor Rodríguez, and others) identify the far North as a separate country, describing it as neither of the United States nor of Mexico, while the historian David G. Gutiérrez distinguishes this region as the "third social space that is located in the interstices between the dominant national and cultural systems of both the United States and Mexico" (1999, 488).

The Norteño people have a long history of being fiercely independent and autonomous. For centuries, both indigenous and mestizo communities navigated the rugged mountain ranges and vast deserts of this region in near isolation. Until the mid-nineteenth century, they built families and communities with little interference, or support, from the national government. Northern Mexico is made up of the states that border the United States—Tamaulipas, Nuevo León, Coahuila, Chihuahua, Sonora, and Baja California—and parts of the northern regions of states located just to the south of these bordering states, such as Durango, Zacatecas, Sinaloa, and San Luis Potosí. Because of its harsh terrain and desert-like climate, early Spanish explorers paid little attention to this region. The earliest Spanish settlements were in what is now Nuevo León and parts of southern San Luis Potosí during the late sixteenth and early seventeenth centuries. This area was given the official name Nuevo Reino de León (New Kingdom of León), and some of the first cities in the region were established here, among them Monterrey in 1596, Cerralvo in 1582, Bustamante in 1686, and Cadereyta in 1637 (Osante 1997, 17–24). However, Spanish colonists aggressively moved northward in the early eighteenth century when precious metals were found in the region. During the colonial period, mining activity inspired the settlement and growth of some of the region's most vital cities: Monterrey in Nuevo León, Saltillo and Torreón in Coahuila, Durango City in Durango, Real de Catorce in San Luis Potosí, Hermosillo in Sonora, Chihuahua City and Parral in Chihuahua, and Culiacán in Sinaloa.

The Spanish also built missions in northern Mexico and Texas in order to convert Native Americans to Christianity and to guard against French encroachment from Louisiana. Early missions included Nueva Extremadura (Nuevo León, 1596), San Bernardo (Coahuila, 1703), Nuestra Señora de Guadalupe de los Nacadoches (Texas, 1716), and San Antonio de Valero (Texas, 1718) (Osante 1997, 18). The south-central Texas and northern Mexico region was colonized in 1746 as Nuevo Santander (see the map, Figure 2.2), and it was one of the last northern provinces of New Spain (Mexico). It extended from the San Antonio River in Texas to the Gulf of Mexico, south to the Pánuco River near Tampico, Veracruz, and west to the states of Tamaulipas and Coahuila. This area had become a haven for rebellious Native Americans who fled Spanish settlements in Nuevo León. The indigenous inhabitants, who belonged to several different tribes and ethnic groups that were identified by language and/or political structure, such as the Karankawas, Pasitas, Janambres, Comepescados (Fish Eaters), and others, were eventually extinguished.

Northern Mexico has long distinguished itself as self-governing and self-sufficient. It is no surprise that the Mexican Revolution (1910–1917), which overthrew the oppressive Porfirian regime, was born here. The thirty-year reign of President Porfirio Díaz (1876–1880 and 1884–1911) brought political stability and industrialization to the country, but such progress came at the price of impoverishing the peasant and laborer classes. It also brought about thousands of deaths among the Yaqui Indians in Sonora and various indigenous communities south of Mexico City. Though this was the period when most of Mexico's great railroads were built, Díaz allowed them to be exploited by North American and European entrepreneurs for the exportation of mineral and oil resources (Herrera-Sobek 1993, 49). Díaz also made extradition deals with North American authorities—the Texas Rangers in particular—that angered northern Mexican farmers and ranchers who were slowly losing their property (Paredes 1958, 135–136). Díaz was merciless in his campaigns to quash any peasant uprisings, particularly in northern Mexico and close to the border.

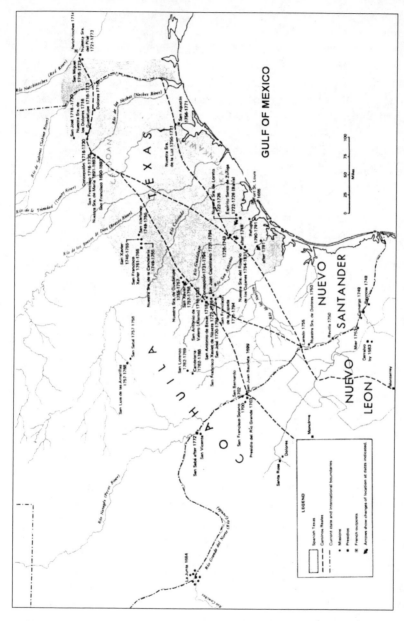

**FIGURE 2.2** Map of Spanish territories showing missions, presidios (penitentiaries), and roads that established the northern reach of New Spain during the seventeenth and eighteenth centuries. (Adapted from Herbert E. Bolton, *Texas in the Middle Eighteenth Century* [Berkeley and Los Angeles: University of California Press, 1915].)

The Texas-Mexican border folklorist and musicologist Américo Paredes notes that Díaz was concerned with the border early on in his presidency and dispatched tyrannical *rurales* (created in the image of the Texas Rangers) to keep peasants and laborers incapacitated (1958, 135). In 1906, he ordered the massacre of striking miners in the town of Cananea in the northern state of Sonora. Many historians believe that this event sparked the Revolution, and it was later followed by a steady stream of additional uprisings, particularly in the northern states of Coahuila and Chihuahua (McLynn 2001, 21). These uprisings inspired revolts in indigenous communities in southern Mexico as well, many of which were led by Emiliano Zapata, the peasant who had recruited thousands of laborers and landless peasants to attack haciendas and reclaim their lost land (McLynn 2001, 50–51). The ensuing Mexican Revolution would eventually reshape every social, economic, and political aspect of Mexican life and would open the door to the development of a new national identity. It would also balance nationalism with anti-U.S. sentiment.

## The Mexican Revolution and the Bandit Hero

In northern Mexico, the impetus of the revolution, combined with the Robin Hood–like banditry of working-class heroes such as Pancho Villa, Heraclio Bernal, Toribio Ortega, Juan Nepomuceno Cortina, and Pascual Orozco, breathed new life into the narrative ballad of the corrido, which was popular throughout Mexico. In northeastern Mexico—particularly the area bordering Texas and the Rio Grande Valley—the corrido was further transformed as it articulated the collective experiences, beliefs, and attitudes of the border community. A strophic poetic and musical form, the border corrido was traditionally sung by a male duo and accompanied by the *guitarra sexta* (six-string guitar). The border *corridista* (composer/ singer of corridos) never sings in the first person, but is "an impersonal authoritative voice," an informed, community-based observer of events and the actions and reactions of local heroes (McDowell 1981, 46). In the late nineteenth and early twentieth centuries, the border corrido was a musical newspaper of sorts, since most people in this region were illiterate. As the popular norteña ensemble tradition, featuring the *acordeón* (accordion) and bajo sexto at its core, became established in this region during the 1930s, the corrido was further transformed as its topical narrative merged with the canción ranchera styles.

Early border corridos were written about popular Norteño revolutionary figures like Villa, who led one of the most important military campaigns of the Mexican Revolution. Villa became a powerful icon among the Norteño people, primarily through the documentation of his exploits with his band of fighters, División del Norte, who often acted independently, even against the wishes of revolutionary leaders. The appeal of Villa and other outlaw heroes in Mexico is based on their fiercely independent personalities; they were almost always of humble origins, consistently rebelled against the tyrannical authority of the

Mexican government, and were equally suspicious of increasing U.S. encroachment in the region. As María Herrera-Sobek (1993, 11–12) and others have noted, Villa fits Eric J. Hobsbawm's definition of the "social bandit" hero who champions the interest of the "folk" in his disregard for authority and his Robin Hood–like exploits. However, critics of Hobsbawm's "social bandit" model claim that one must focus not on the bandit's "deeds" but rather on how the bandit is perceived over time by the local community through stories and songs (Chandler 1978, 240–241). In the early border corrido tradition, many heroes were themselves peasants who connected with the community because they emerged from society's margins to fight against American encroachment and to maintain their border culture and society. This is best exemplified in one of the most popular corridos, "Gregorio Cortez," in which fellow workers and peasants assist Cortez as he flees from the Texas Rangers. For the Norteño, Villa was not only a heroic figure, but a fellow underclass peasant who represented the fight for equality, justice, and respect.

Born in San Juan del Río, Durango, in 1877 or 1878, Pancho (also known as Francisco) Villa (his birth name is actually Doroteo Arango) was a laborer, cattle rustler, bank robber, murderer, womanizer, and champion of the poor. The charismatic Villa recruited thousands of Norteño peasants into his army. In 1910 he came down from the mountains where he was hiding out as a bandit and joined forces with Francisco I. Madero. Madero was the son of a wealthy landowner from Coahuila who led the revolt against the then-president Porfirio Díaz. Many elite families in the North knew that aligning themselves with local revolutionaries was far safer than siding with a distant Mexican military regime (McLynn 2001, 14–15). Before his involvement with Madero, Villa had skillfully avoided oppressive mining bosses and government authorities. His transition from bandit to revolutionary once he had joined forces with Madero was an unprecedented historical moment (McLynn, 18). Villa's exploits were both chronicled and romanticized in the border corrido, which, in turn, inspired numerous fictional and nonfictional books and films about his life.

Villa became the most celebrated hero in the history of the corrido, prompting Paredes to document three distinct Villa personae in the corrido tradition: the legendary social bandit, the historical revolutionary military leader, and the border raider (1976, 38–39). It is in this third aspect, as defender of border communities against U.S. encroachment, that Villa emerged as a powerful mythic hero to all Mexicans (Paredes 1976, 39). Ever since the international boundary was established in this region, ballads and songs have depicted the intercultural conflict between the Anglo-American and Mexican societies. During the early stages of the Revolution, Villa had the foresight to envision the border as an emerging melting pot of social, economic, and political interests. He brought North American freedom fighters and Mexican laborers together in his campaign for political reform and social justice. However, when the U.S. government turned against him and supported the rival Revolutionary leader Venustiano Carranza, Villa retaliated by invading several border towns and, eventually, defeating U.S. troops in Columbus, New Mexico, an action that is still considered to be the only successful foreign military invasion of the United States (McLynn 2001, 322). While many North Americans regard Villa as an outlaw and bandit, Mexicans, particularly Norteños, view him as an important avenger of Anglo-American expansionism and a consummate defender of the Mexican working class (Paredes 1976, 39). Most Mexicans today, like Norteños since before the Revolution, celebrate outlaw bandit figures like Villa for their selfless acts of resistance against two powerful forces: Mexican nationalism and North American imperialism (Paredes 1976, 61–63).

In northern Mexico, the earliest examples of such proletarian heroes were renegade revolutionaries like Pancho Villa, Emiliano Zapata, and Jesús Leal. Early corridos about Villa generally describe particular battles, his fighting spirit, or his undying dedication to the revolution. Corridos written about Villa after the 1930s tend to be phrased in much broader terms, describing his valor, leadership, and defiance. "El corrido de Durango," one of many corridos still sung about Villa, was probably written in the 1930s, several years after his death in 1923. It was composed by Miguel Ángel Gallardo, who was conscripted into the División del Norte at the age of fourteen and participated in many battles under Villa's command. (In addition to composing numerous corridos, Gallardo was a well-known cinematic actor.) This corrido features a variant on the typical formal opening address to the listener or audience, describing where Villa is from (Durango) and what he was before the Revolution (bandit). As in other corridos, the verses shown in Figure 2.3 celebrate Villa's heroic character, bravery, and skills in battle and lament his passing because he was one of a kind. In the final stanza, the corridista bids farewell to his audience. That popular norteña groups continued to record this corrido throughout the twentieth century demonstrates the enduring popularity and relevance of this seemingly immortal border figure. Even today most Mexicans remember Villa with great pride for having led the most important military campaigns of the Revolution, in which his troops were victorious throughout the country. Villa is a particularly heroic figure for Norteños (and border-crossers) who continue to struggle with North American economic and political oppression, racism, and authoritative power.

## The Border Corrido

Vicente T. Mendoza wrote in his groundbreaking study, *El romance español y el corrido mexicano* (1939), that there is a direct link between the Mexican corrido and the Spanish romance. In later writings, Mendoza (1954), clearly caught up in the early-twentieth-century wave of Mexican nationalism, suggests that the Mexican corrido solidified as a unique narrative ballad form, noting its use in

## El Corrido de Durango

| | |
|---|---|
| En Durango comenzó | In Durango he started |
| su carrera de bandido | his career as a bandit |
| en cada golpe que daba | and after every assault |
| se hacía el desaparecido. | he seemed to disappear. |
| | |
| Al llegar a La Laguna | On arriving at the Laguna, |
| tomó la estación de Horizontes | he captured the depot in Horizontes. |
| desde entonces lo seguían | They've been following him since then |
| por los pueblos y los montes. | through towns and mountains. |
| | |
| Pero un día allá en el noroeste, | But one day in the Northwest, |
| entre Tirso y La Boquilla, | between Tirso and La Boquilla, |
| se encontraban acampadas | Pancho Villa and his forces |
| las fuerzas de Pancho Villa. | were camped out. |
| | |
| Gritaba Francisco Villa: | Francisco Villa shouted out: |
| "Yo el miedo no lo conozco. | "I don't know the meaning of fear, |
| ¡Que viva Pancho I. Madero! | long live Pancho I. Madero, |
| ¡Que muera Pascual Orozco!" | and death to Pascual Orozco!" |
| | |
| Gritaba Francisco Villa | Francisco Villa shouted out |
| en su caballo tordillo: | as he was riding on his dapple-gray horse: |
| "En las bolsas traigo pesos | "I carry pesos in my pockets |
| y en la cintura casquillos!" | and bullets in my belt!" |
| | |
| ¿Dónde estás, Francisco Villa? | Where are you now, Francisco Villa? |
| General tan afamado, | A most famous general, |
| que los hiciste correr | who made them all |
| a todos como venados. | run like deer. |
| | |
| Ya con ésta ahí me despido, | Now I must say goodbye, |
| a la sombra de un durazno | from the shade of a peach tree, |
| aquí termino cantando | I have finished singing |
| el corrido de Durango. | The corrido of Durango. |

FIGURE 2.3 "El Corrido de Durango." Written by Miguel Ángel Gallardo (date unknown). Recorded by Los Dorados de Durango in 1916.

(From the four-CD boxed set *The Mexican Revolution: Corridos about the Heroes and Events, 1910–1920 and Beyond!* various artists [Arhoolie CD-7041-44, 1996]. English translation of lyrics from CD liner notes courtesy of Arhoolie Records.)

documenting heroic exploits and events of the Mexican Revolution. Another researcher of border corridos, Francisco Ramos Aguirre (1994), found evidence that the corrido derived from an octosyllabic poetic form called *ensaladilla* (medley or hodgepodge), which was introduced in the region by Spanish soldiers colonizing Nuevo Santander during the mid-1700s. Ramos Aguirre noted that many of the songs he and other local scholars collected from this period, which typically immortalized individuals who died in skirmishes with the local indigenous population, contained features similar to those of the corrido, such as the date the song was composed, and details of the hero's deeds and how he met his fate (1994, 12–13). These homages to deceased soldiers were likely delivered to their families in Spain as documentation of their heroic service to the colonizing efforts. Paredes's research on corridos and folk songs in the Lower Rio Grande border region (once part of the province of Nuevo Santander) suggests that the corrido tradition developed expressly in response to the changing worldview of Mexicans, as a means of documenting the historical events that were rapidly altering the social fabric of their community and their way of life (1958).

Paredes's documentation of the border corrido, however, reveals a characteristic tradition that was created out of the conflicts that, he asserts, "arose from the bipolar ordering of the society that took hold in the Rio Grande Valley" (1978, 69). Corridos during the early part of the twentieth century, such as "El Corrido de Gregorio Cortez" and "El Corrido de Juan Cortina," spoke not only of bandits or smugglers but of men who fought for their rights and those of their families. For Mexicans living in the agriculturally rich Lower Rio Grande region of Texas, which borders Mexico, corridos spoke primarily of the plight of a Mexican and Mexican American community who for at least one hundred years was caught in the middle of civil wars on both sides of the border in the midst of racial, political, and social friction and inconsistency (Paredes 1958, 1976).

In the border region, at least, the corrido evolved during the first thirty years of the twentieth century as a vehicle for preserving the history and identity of the people of northeastern Mexico and the border region. Paredes (1958, 1963) believes that the genre is based on Spanish forms other than the romance, such as the highly poetic *décima* and the rhyming *copla*, a popular song form with four, octosyllabic verses in which the last words of the second and fourth lines rhyme (Hagan, Dickey, and Peña 1979, 7). Corridos from this period generally featured ten- or eight-syllable lines with four-line verses and were sung primarily to a waltz rhythm of 3/4 (typical of most lyrical songs in the region); they followed the structure of the *copla*'s octosyllabic quatrains with a rhyme scheme of *abcb*. Corridos are generally in major keys and remain within the vocal range of an octave. This relatively short range is a distinctive feature of the corrido, as Paredes indicates: "[It] allows the corrido to be sung at the top of the singer's voice, an essential part of the corrido style" (Paredes 1976, xxi).

The typical corrido is said to have six primary components, outlined by Armando Duvalier (1937, 1):

1. The composer/singer's opening address to the audience
2. Place, time, and name of the primary character
3. Background of the main character and his situation
4. The message
5. Farewell from the main character
6. Farewell from composer/singer

However, through the years, many contemporary composers and singers have taken the liberty of eliminating the opening address and the farewell (*despedida*). The singer may start the corrido with the action of the narration to pique the listener's interest (Hagan, Dickey, and Peña 1979, 50–51). The Spanish literature scholar and corrido researcher Guillermo Hernández asserts that true corridos must feature at least three of the aforementioned components, typically "(2) place and name of the main character, (4) message, and (5 or 6) the farewell. They must also maintain an arrangement of four or six lines per stanza" (1999, 70). For Hernández, a primary characteristic of the traditional border corrido is that its protagonists are normal, everyday individuals whose convictions have motivated them to participate in actions that have a profound impact on the local community. However, while an ordinary person, the protagonist "serves as a model of conduct under extraordinary circumstances" (1999, 73). The corridista scrutinizes and analyzes the hero's action for the benefit of the community-based listener. The protagonists, and the situations in which they find themselves, render the corrido "adaptable," which "helps explain why the history of the genre has shown the capacity to portray protagonists with such a wide variety of occupations, regional characteristics, political affiliations, and social identities" (Hernández 1999, 75).

According to Paredes, the border corridos about the prerevolutionary bandit heroes (e.g., Gregorio Cortez) are better described as "proletarian" rather than "epic" because they celebrate individuals who emerge from the margins of society to fight for social justice and the basic rights of their fellow man (1958, 137). Other than revolutionary heroes and outlaws (often one and the same), corridos also told stories of Norteño gunfighters (*pistoleros*), travel for work (initially on cattle drives and then migrating for work to northern Mexico and across the border), tragedies, humorous events, and agrarian reform. Paredes (1958) and Mendoza (1954) agree that after the 1930s no truly "heroic" corridos were produced and that those that are sung now have been preserved by corrido scholars and in the oral history and folklore of the border region. Popular music commercialization and marketing have affected the newer corridos about border crossing, tequila and drug smuggling, and Anglo-Mexican conflicts, and Paredes laments the demise of the traditional corridos. However, in taking up this argument, Limón posits that the traditional "heroic" and "proletarian" corridos have not been completely forgotten, particularly by Mexican immigrants, and are still sung (alongside the newer and more "decadent" corridos) to "remind their listeners of the prior period of open, epic confrontation, and thus go on playing an active role as an ideological focal point and expression of resistance" (1992, 41). The heroic and proletarian qualities of these traditional corridos, in Limón's interpretation of their impact on the listening public, still inform contemporary songs that celebrate modern-day quasi-heroic figures from the humble mojado to the lawless narcotraficante.

In later years, particularly after the Bracero Program ended in 1964, many corridos focused on migrant labor, drug smuggling and trafficking, workers' rights, and more recently an ambiguous Mexican identity in the expanding diaspora of Mexican laborers on both sides of the border. Heroic outlaws and smugglers remain popular in modern norteña corridos, primarily as a defiant alter ego of the now predominant mojado. Some recent corridos also deal with lifestyle issues affecting the Mexican immigrant, illegal or not, such as changing relationships between men and women and conflicting feelings about establishing a new life in the States and rearing children who know little of their Mexican heritage or the Spanish language.

The core instrumentation of norteña music, the accordion and bajo sexto, has not changed since the 1940s, and many of its artists still perform polkas, traditional rancheras, corridos, and contemporary cumbias. The corrido, in particular, has been both preserved and transformed, in large part, by the intensity of demographic and cultural change among this autonomous and marginalized community of farmers and laborers over the past quarter century. From the narrative accounts of cattle drives by Mexican cowboys employed by Anglo-American ranchers and the accounts of "border conflict" described by Paredes (1958, 1963) to more recent themes concerning immigrant rights, economic hardship, and discrimination, the corrido has become a repository of countless stories of travel and displacement. These songs document issues of personal and collective identity and affiliation in the U.S.–Mexico borderlands (where such issues are especially volatile) and continue to be spread by Mexican laborers to communities throughout the United States and back again to Mexico.

"Los Tequileros" (The Tequila Smugglers) (see Figure 2.4) is one of the earliest smuggling songs. Containing most of the components outlined by Duvalier (1937, 1), it tells the tragic fate of three tequila runners from the state of Guerrero. They are killed by that famously violent special police force, the Texas Rangers, who patrolled the border trying to end lawlessness and disorder along the Rio Grande (Paredes 1958, 24). The Texas Rangers (rinches) appear in numerous corridos written in the late nineteenth and early twentieth centuries. They symbolize the growing oppression and racial tension at the core of the many conflicts between Mexican and North American communities in the border region. During Prohibition in the United States, tequila was the liquor most

## Los Tequileros

### (2) Place/time of event

El día dos de febrero,
¡qué día tan señalado!
Mataron tres tequileros,
los rinches del otro lado.

On the second day of February
What a memorable day!
The Texas Rangers from the other side
killed three tequila smugglers.

### (3) Background of the main character(s) and his (their) situation

Llegaron al Río Grande.
Se pusieron a pensar.
"Será bueno ver a Leandro
porque somos dos no más."

They reached the Rio Grande
and they stopped to think.
"We had better go to see Leandro
because there are only two of us."

Le echan el envite a Leandro,
Leandro les dice que no:
"Fíjese que estoy enfermo,
así no quisiera yo."

They invited Leandro to go with them,
and Leandro said no:
"You know I am sick,
I don't want to go."

Al fin de tanto invitarle,
Leandro los acompañó,
en las lomas de Almiramba,
fue el primero que murió.

They kept asking him to go,
until Leandro went with them,
in the hills of Almiramba,
he was the first one to die.

La carga que ellos llevaban
era tequila anisado,
el rumbo que ellos llevaban
era San Diego afamado.

The contraband they were taking
was refined tequila,
the direction they were taking
was toward the famed San Diego.

Salieron desde Guerrero
con rumbo para el oriente,
allí les tenían sitiado
dos carros con mucha gente.

They left Guerrero
in an easterly direction.
There they had waiting for them
two cars with many people.

Cuando cruzaron el río
se fueron por un cañón,
se pusieron a hacer lumbre
sin ninguna precaución.

When they crossed the river
they traveled along a canyon.
Then they stopped to make a fire
without any regard for danger.

El capitán de los rinches
platicaba con esmero:
"Es bueno agregar ventaja
porque estos son de Guerrero."

The captain of the Rangers
was speaking in measured tones:
"It is wise to stack the odds
because these men are from Guerrero."

*(continued on next page)*

FIGURE 2.4 "Los Tequileros." Written by Tomás Ortiz del Valle in the 1920s or 1930s.
This song has been recorded by many norteña artists, including Los Alegres de Terán.
(Lyrics courtesy of Editor Tica Publishing.)

## Los Tequileros (continued)

Les hicieron un descargue
a mediación del camino,
cayó Gerónimo muerto,
Silvano muy mal herido.

They fired a volley at them
in the middle of the road.
Gerónimo fell dead,
and Silvano was hurt badly.

Tumban el caballo a Leandro,
y a él lo hirieron de un brazo,
ya no les podía hacer fuego,
tenía varios balazos.

They shot Leandro off his horse,
wounding him in the arm.
He could no longer fire back.
He had several bullet wounds.

El capitán de los rinches
a Silvano se acercó,
y en unos cuantos segundos
Silvano García murió.

The captain of the Rangers
came close to Silvano,
and in a few seconds
Silvano García died.

### (4) The message

Los rinches serán muy hombres,
no se les puede negar,
nos cazan como venados
para podernos matar.

The Rangers are very brave,
there is no doubt.
They hunt us like deer
so they can kill us.

Si los rinches fueran hombres
y sus caras presentaran
entonce' a los tequileros
otro gallo nos cantara.

If the Rangers were really brave
and met us face to face,
then we would be singing a different
song about the tequila smugglers.

### (5) Farewell to the main characters

Pues ellos los tres murieron,
los versos aquí se acaban,
se les concedió a los rinches
las muertas que ellos deseaban.

So, all three of them died,
and these stanzas are at an end.
The Rangers were able to accomplish
the killings they wanted.

El que compuso estos versos
no se hallaba allí presente,
estos versos son compuestos
por lo que decía la gente.

He who composed these stanzas
was not present when it happened.
These verses have been composed
from the accounts of other people.

### (6) Farewell from the composer

Aquí va la despedida,
en medio de tres floreros,
y aquí se acaba el corrido,
versos de los tequileros.

Now I say farewell,
in between three flower vases.
This is the end of this corrido,
the verses of the tequila smugglers.

FIGURE 2.4   Continued

commonly smuggled across the U.S.-Mexico border. *Tequileros* generally operated in groups of three or four and devised creative ways to bring the liquor into the United States, such as in spare car tires or in homemade boats or rafts that they pushed across the river at night (Paredes 1958, 42–43). The stanzas in Figure 2.4 that satisfy Duvalier's corrido components are labeled.

## Border Conflict

Northern Mexico has been a highly politicized and volatile region, in part because of its proximity to the U.S. border. As a result, Norteño identity has been shaped by North American cultural and political affiliations. In northern Mexico and the border region, Mexican nationalism and North American imperialism converged and, by the beginning of the twentieth century, had the effect of further isolating the local population from the rest of Mexico. After gaining independence from Spain in 1821, Mexico struggled to build a unified national identity for a country that was culturally and regionally fragmented (Gutiérrez 1999, 484). Nearly a century later, that struggle intensified. After the Mexican Revolution (1910–1917), the Mexican government organized new efforts to expand its reach throughout the country. However, the country's indigenous South and far North maintained territorial autonomy, distinct cultural communities, and allegiances to their own local heroes.

As the first to cross the U.S.-Mexico border for work in the late nineteenth century, Norteños had performed a rebellious act of survival and self-preservation. During and after the Revolution, thousands of Mexican nationals (mostly from northern states), crossed the border and became part of a large laborer community that the U.S. government set out to "Americanize" and discipline (Gutiérrez 1999, 491–492). In response, the Mexican government began an ephemeral campaign to seduce communities to privilege a Mexican national identity over their own regional and cross-cultural affiliations. The border historian Andrés Reséndez (1999, 671) points out that government officials issued printed propaganda and other artifacts, such as flags and coins, and distributed them in the region without truly understanding methods of communication and interests within the local population. These items carried little meaning for a community that was more concerned with survival and defending its culture and identity; Reséndez concludes that "for the vast majority of the frontier inhabitants, neither the print media nor the schools went very far in promoting a sense of nationhood. For them, the most pervasive and perhaps the only indications of the existence of the Mexican nation were rituals and symbols" (Reséndez 1999, 162). Paredes describes members of the border community as familial and deeply dependent on one another, having created a rich and vibrant folklore and cultural identity: "They lived in isolation from main currents of world events. They preferred to live in small, tightly knit communities that were interested in their own problems . . . and their forms of entertainment were oral" (1963, 58).

The period between 1835 and 1934 was a time of great conflict in the border region and the most fruitful period of corrido production (Paredes 1958, 132). Given the events of this time, border conflict corridos were deeply rooted in an ambiguous sense of Mexican nationality and a constantly shifting political border. The typical border hero in the songs of this period is either an outlaw or a common man defending his right to his home, family, and freedom. The annexation of Mexico's northern territories by the United States through the Treaty of Guadalupe-Hidalgo in 1848 and later through the Gadsen Purchase imposed a new political boundary in the region that David G. Gutiérrez indicates "contributed both to a reinforcement of existing modes of individual and collective identification and a multiplication of new possibilities" (1999, 485).

The completion of Díaz's railroad just before the turn of the twentieth century brought many people from rural towns to the city for work. Migrants from most other ethnic regions of central and southern Mexico generally traveled to Mexico City instead of Monterrey (McLynn 2001). Monterrey was also home to a number of European immigrants, primarily German and Czech, who came to work on the railroads or as metalsmiths. Many were entrepreneurs who were lured by Díaz's concessions to foreign investors; they created independent businesses such as breweries, glassmaking factories, and cement companies (Meier and Ribera 1993, 108–114). During this time, Monterrey was a very modern and culturally sophisticated city that absorbed influences from European high society as well as from regional folk traditions brought by traveling laborers. The music of Monterrey itself represents a merging of rural styles as a result of the migration there of peasants and laborers from nearby towns and villages (e.g., Doctor Arroyo, Linares, General Terán, Bustamante, and China) as well as from other states in northern Mexico, such as northern Veracruz, San Luis Potosí, Guanajuato, Zacatecas, Durango, and Chihuahua.

Norteño culture and identity are both exclusive and multifaceted. To construct a history of norteña music in northern Mexico and follow its subsequent transformation as the music of solidarity, resistance, and modernity in the expanded Mexican diaspora across the United States and Mexico, it is important to understand the push-pull existence of the Norteño population during this period. European-style industrialization, North American expansionism, Mexican nationalism, and constant migration helped create a social and political system in which many had to struggle constantly against poverty, desperation, and an ambiguous sense of identity.

## Early Folk and Popular Music in Northeastern Mexico: 1860s–1920s

Though modern norteña music grew out of the border conflict described by Paredes, the music's instrumentation and stylistic features were representative of the multicultural nature of the border region itself. Norteña evolved from a merging of Mexican, European, and North American influences and styles and, though its historical roots lie in the northeastern Mexican territories (Nuevo León, Tamaulipas, and Coahuila), it now exists simultaneously on both sides of the border. Early folk orchestras and accordion–bajo sexto ensembles were predominantly instrumental. Corridos and lyric songs were already part of the rural repertoire of northeastern Mexico, but typically sung with guitar accompaniment. Songs from this region, collectively known as *canciones norteñas*, were sung in both sacred and secular contexts. The traditional repertoire of sacred songs includes hymns, praises, rosaries, prayers, and carols that are generally sung a cappella or are sometimes accompanied by the organ in church. Secular songs consisted of serenades—sung at dawn as a greeting to a neighbor or friend to express wishes for a birthday or happy event or as a declaration of love—and cantina songs, which are either boastful or about lost love (García Flores 1991, 10–12). Paredes, who located a number of comic songs from the region, notes that many love songs and songs about country life have a humorous tone; the Norteño often makes fun of himself as an uninformed migrant or a country bumpkin (1976, 134–135). Some of the songs Paredes has documented include "Dime Sí, Sí, Sí" (Tell Me Yes, Yes, Yes), "Carta Escrita sobre un Cajón" (Letter Written on a Wooden Box), and "El Crudo" (The Man with the Hangover). As we will see, self-deprecating humor—whether in depictions of the Mexican peasant up against the U.S. border patrol or of the undocumented immigrant in search of a green card—remains a distinctive element of the modern *norteña* song repertoire.

Aside from the corrido, the ranchera (country song) is the next most popular song form of the norteña ensemble. The ranchera was generally sung among workers or at informal gatherings of mostly men, was typically accompanied by the 3/4 waltz-time beat or the 2/4 canción-corrido rhythm on the guitarra sexta, and was probably based on the polka (García Flores 1991, 14). Another popular form was the bolero. By the 1930s, the Cuban bolero had made its way to Mexico City; it became a popular form throughout the country with the proliferation of recordings by Mexican singing stars such as Agustín Lara and Guty Cárdenas. However, many migrant workers from the state of Veracruz had traveled to Monterrey, where the bolero was already popular (as well as in the Yucatán) before making its way to Mexico City. Local scholars believe this song tradition was brought to the region by Veracruzan peasants who introduced the huapango dance rhythm, also widely played by orchestras and accordion–bajo sexto ensembles in the region. Many of these sacred and secular song traditions can still be found throughout the region today (García Flores 1991, 10–11).

Vocal music was not heard in the dance portion of weddings and celebrations or in the cantina settings of the *zonas de tolerancia* (red-light districts; see the Glossary) until the mid-1940s, when larger numbers of Mexicans were crossing the border for work. In Monterrey and other municipalities in the region, these bands not only represented governmental order and control but also were the primary means by which people gathered as a community. In a personal interview, the anthropologist and music researcher Raúl García Flores suggested that the first documented ensemble of this type was in 1835, in the town of Cadereyta, Nuevo León, roughly twenty miles southeast of Monterrey. This ensemble, La Banda de Música de Cadereyta Jiménez, still exists today as one of the region's premier youth orchestras. In the 1910s, official village and town military bands grew to about thirty members and included reed and brass instruments such as clarinets, flutes, saxophones, cornets, tubas, and trombones, along with other local instruments of Spanish derivation such as the *requinto* (a five-string guitar) and the *tambora* (a small hand-held drum) (Ayala Duarte 1995, 13–25).

European symphonic music and the salon dance tradition were embraced by the Spanish and Mexican elite during the nineteenth century, initially in Mexico City and later in Monterrey. German and Czech merchants and businessmen, lured by Porfirio Díaz's incentives for foreign investments, created a demand for European (particularly Italian) opera and popular salon music in Monterrey. A composite of petty-bourgeois European dance traditions—such as the Czechoslovakian polka; the mazurka; the Polish *redova*, which incorporated elements of the mazurka and the graceful *varsovienne*; the German/Viennese waltz; and the schottische, a Scottish highland dance that was popular in Germany—was played by small orchestras that included string instruments such as the violin, guitar, and mandolin.

By the middle of the nineteenth century, in the peasant *colonias* (neighborhoods) in and around Monterrey, small ensembles influenced by elite dance bands were becoming popular among migrating peasant communities. These ensembles featured roughly six to eight players and included various combinations of violins, guitar (or bajo sexto), cornet, clarinets, flutes, contrabass, and small drums (García Flores 1991; Alanís Támez 1994, 14). In addition to the polka, waltz, redova, and mazurka, their repertoire included Mexican huapangos, North American foxtrots, the cha-cha-cha, Cuban *danzón*, and Spanish flamenco (Ayala Duarte 1995, 28). There were also string ensembles of approximately eleven or twelve violins, guitars, and mandolins played by all-female student groups, such as La Estudiantina Allende. In most villages, a frame drum was hung from a tree to alert the community to a dance or other musical event (Alanís Támez 1994, 16–17).

These dance traditions also traveled with the peasant community to the small towns and villages in Nuevo León and Tamaulipas (for example, Montemorelos, General Terán, Hualahiuses, Linares, San Salvador, San Nicolas, and San Carlos). The ensembles typically featured two clarinets and a tambora (frame drum) made of wood and goat skin. These ensembles recall Spanish military "fife and drum" bands. There is also evidence that the *chirimía*, a double-reed woodwind instrument played in Spain and other European countries from the thirteenth to the seventeenth century, was paired with the tambora among largely indigenous communities. However, by the mid-nineteenth century the *chirimía* had disappeared in this region, though it is still found in other parts of Mexico, Guatemala, and Colombia (Stevenson 1952, 148). There are still a few such ensembles in the region today (García Flores 1991). Very much like the formal orchestras of their time, the small clarinet ensembles and slightly larger ensembles that also included string instruments (guitars, mandolin, harp, and violin) played popular European dance rhythms such as polkas, marches, waltzes, schottisches, and redovas, along with Mexican folk rhythms such as huapangos, *jarabes,* and pasodobles (Ayala Duarte 1995, 14–17).

Another clarinet and drum ensemble that was particularly popular among the indigenous people of the region is the *picota,* which originated in the San Carlos Mountains of Tamaulipas (Gómez Flores 1997, 24). (Locals also use this term to refer to a ritual dance characterized by high jump steps, turns, and sudden shifts in counter to the rhythm.) There is strong evidence that the clarinet and tambora ensemble originated in Nuevo León and traveled to the nearby state of Tamaulipas, where villages sprang up during the late 1600s in response to the Mexican government's soliciting people in Nuevo León to move there (Molina Montelongo and Quezeda Molina 1995b, 94–95). The performers of the clarinet and tambora ensembles were initially the *tlahualilos* or *tahualiles,* named for the *tlaxcaltecas,* an indigenous community that was brought in by the Spanish to work as laborers. They were taught to play these instruments by Spanish missionaries during the seventeenth century, and to this day these instruments are played among the local indigenous population (Molina Montelongo and Quezada Molina 1995b, 94). These tambora and clarinet ensembles in Nuevo León (particularly the villages of Cerralvo, Cadereyta, and Linares) were known as *tamborileros* (see Figure 2.5), as are the handful of family groups that remain today, performing primarily to announce the beginning of a village celebration or special event or for private parties and weddings (Molina Montelongo and Quezada Molina 1995b, 95). The first purpose of these groups was to alert community members to village gatherings and festivals and to take part in military or official government ceremonies, but over time these small ensembles became associated with the working class and imitated the repertoire of popular European-derived dances and local melodies that trickled down from the elite class. The regional historian Juan Alanís Támez said this about the tamborileros' role in the region: "In essence, the tamborileros represent a musical tradition that has instrumental limitations (one or two clarinets and a frame drum) and which you would not use to accompany singing; they are only for melodies that recall earlier times and are an important part of the cultural and musical identity of the northeastern national territory" (1994, 18, my translation).

The repertoire of European and regional Mexican dances played by tamborilero ensembles is, in part, a reflection of a constantly evolving and assimilating population in this part of northern Mexico. The movement of people from states

**FIGURE 2.5** Los Tamborileros de Linares (one of the most important clarinet and tambora groups in Nuevo León, which still exists today), circa 1953. Tamborilero (also known as *la picota* in the neighboring state of Tamaulipas) ensembles are typically associated with the indigenous population in northeastern Mexico.
(Photo from *A Tambora Batiente* [Monterrey, Nuevo León: Dirección General de Culturas Populares/ Unidad Regional Norte, 1997], cover.)

such as Veracruz, San Luis Potosí, Guanajuato, Querétaro, Jalisco, and Michoacán to the industrialized and cosmopolitan city of Monterrey and its surrounding towns and villages drastically reshaped and expanded the population in the late nineteenth and early twentieth century. In an interview I conducted with Raúl García Flores in 1998, he argued that the construction of the railroad, particularly in the North between 1880 and 1910, significantly transformed this region by bringing in hundreds of thousands of peasant laborers:

> At the end of the 1800s, the population dissipated and came to three primary industrial centers—Torreón [in Coahuila] for the cotton industry; Monterrey for cement, beer, glass, and other things; and Matamoros [in Tamaulipas], the port for ships—and the new train lines connected

these cities, and they began to grow at the moment they were connected to other parts of the country [Mexico]. What happened in the region was the migration of workers. During this period, Monterrey had three thousand inhabitants, and by the beginning of the twentieth century, seventy thousand people had come seeking work; in 1930 Monterrey had one hundred fifty thousand people and by 1950 there were five hundred thousand. (personal communication)

García Flores documented the names of numerous musicians who followed the workers or came to the border region to work themselves. Many of these musicians had trained in their hometowns in large student orchestras like La Banda de Música de Cadereyta Jiménez. In Monterrey, musicians performed in small and medium-sized orchestras at salon dances for the Mexican elite and European businessmen who had established and operated the numerous cement and glass factories, gasoline refineries, and breweries that had sprung up during this time. Some of these same musicians performed in small ensembles for the increasing number of peasants and laborers moving to the city to work in factories and in the service industry jobs that resulted from Monterrey's growth and continued industrialization (García Flores 1991). Tamborilero ensembles in the nearby villages were forced to compete, and by the early twentieth century, they were incorporating guitars, flutes, and violins (Molina Montelongo and Quezada Molina 1995a, 97).

Another important factor in the development of border music and society in the early twentieth century is the large wave of laborers from Monterrey, Torreón, Matamoros, and smaller villages in the region who migrated into Texas looking for work, both in the growing agriculture industry in the Lower Rio Grande Valley and in factories in urban centers like San Antonio, Corpus Christi, and Houston. Musicians also crossed the border, but they were workers themselves, and therefore it was difficult to assemble an orchestra or organize dances. Most performed informally, accompanied by guitar or violin, for other workers at the end of a long day in the fields. Additionally, this period saw a significant increase in the use of Mexican laborers to build railroads in other southwestern states. The restriction of Chinese and Japanese workers by Congress in the 1880s and early 1900s led to the active recruitment of Mexicans and prompted additional migration throughout the Southwest (Herrera-Sobek 1993, 35).[1] Mexican workers were largely responsible for the railroad construction in nearly all of the southwestern United States (Herrera-Sobek 1993, 35).

---

[1] Congress passed the Chinese Exclusion Act of 1882, which ended the immigration of Chinese laborers. The Geary Act of 1892 extended the 1882 exclusion policy. In 1907, Japan and the United States reached a "Gentlemen's Agreement" whereby Japan stopped issuing passports to laborers desiring to emigrate to the United States.

## Acordeón and Bajo Sexto:
## The Birth of a Border Tradition

By the late 1920s, a new instrument, the accordion, began appearing alongside, and eventually in place of, the clarinets in the tamborilero ensemble. The accordion was probably first heard in the port town of Matamoros, just across the border from Brownsville, Texas, where it was sold in local shops thanks to the vigorous marketing of initially one-row and then two-row diatonic button-accordion models made by the German firm Hohner, the leading accordion manufacturer of the time (Molina Montelongo and Quezada Molina 1995a, 97–98). For the migrant laborers crossing the border, the button accordion proved to be a less expensive and more portable instrument that could replace most of the brass and reed instruments of the folk orchestras and tamborileros.

García Flores also explained that he believes that the industrial revolution; the creation of the railroad network connecting the border to Mexico City; and the ensuing movement of laborers to Monterrey, northeastern Mexico, and across the border into Texas and other southwestern states led to the dissemination and popularity of the accordion. He found that during this period the local peasant and laborer population in northeastern Mexico viewed the accordion, which traveled with migrants returning home from Texas and the Southwest, as a completely modern instrument and a representation of wealth. With regards to its first appearance in northeastern Mexico, he recalled that "during the early days of norteña music, it [the accordion] was seen as an expression of identity. It was more as a show of wealth, that is to say, that the people didn't have much to eat, but they returned as if they had conquered the world, from Matamoros to Monterrey" (personal communication). Though the impetus for replacing brass and reed instruments in Mexican folk ensembles in the United States with the single accordion was largely economic, family members, friends, and neighbors associated the instrument with "el otro lado" (the other side), a place that offered modernity and the possibility of more money, work, and a better life. The late Monterrey-based folk musician and historian Filiberto Molina Montelongo supports García Flores's thesis in the following statement based on his own experience as a musician during the 1940s:

Cuando en su rancho se celebraba alguna boda, ocupaban orquestas del pueblo, que ejecutaban música que no era del agrado de los asistentes, pero se resignaban a bailar "al son que se les tocara." Pero llegó un día en que los músicos pueblerinos vieron que ya no tenían demanda, y en cambio el público le dio toda su aceptación a la música de acordeón. Como se dice ahora: "Era la nueva onda, era la moda" ... Debido a causas naturales como la sequía en verano y las heladas en invierno, hubo mucho crisis; y los campesinos optaron por irse a "las pizcas de algodón." Cuando regresaban, traían mucho dinero; buena ropa; botas vaqueros, sombreros tejanos y ganas de divertirse. (Molina Montelongo and Quezada Molina 1995a, 97–98)

When a wedding was celebrated on the ranch, the orchestra of the town was there; it played music that was not necessarily the taste of the attendees, but they were resigned to dance to "whatever song that touched them." But the day arrived when the town musicians saw that they were no longer in demand and that the public had instead given its complete acceptance to the music of the accordion. As they say today, "It was the new wave, the new fashion." It may have been due to natural causes like the drought in the summer and the frosts in winter, but there was a great deal of crisis, and the peasants opted to go "pick cotton." When they returned, they had a lot of money, good clothes, cowboy boots, Stetson hats and were looking to have a good time. (my translation)

Molina Montelongo also indicates that the accordion came to the region with strong associations with the campesino, who, through his hard work and worldly experience, returns with a distinct identity and musical genre all his own.

The Monterrey-based accordionist and songwriter Juan Silva, who has played with many popular norteña groups since the 1950s, also recalled in an interview the accordion's entry into the regional ensemble tradition and its almost immediate association with dancing: "When my father played in the 1920s and 1930s, the first instrumental duet was the accordion and drum; you could find these groups throughout the region. They sounded like the tamborileros; they were clarinet and tambora . . . like the ones from General Terán and Linares. But it was different with the accordion and tambora, and I'm referring to dancing. People didn't dance to the tamborileros, but they did to the accordion" (personal communication).

While the repertoire remained relatively constant, the accordion spread throughout the Mexican laborer community on both sides of the border. The introduction of the accordion in peasant ensembles in northeastern Mexico during the late 1920s and early 1930s coincided with the development of the radio and film industries in Mexico City and the availability of portable recording technology on the Texas side of the border. RCA/Victor first made recordings of Mexican and North American regional genres for release on its subsidiary, Bluebird. This label was established in the 1930s to cash in on the primarily rural and regional market. Sound recordists for the label began making excursions into Texas and other parts of the southern United States to record "regional roots music" or "race records"[2] such as African American blues, Anglo-American hillbilly-country, and some music to be sold in department stores like Woolworth's.

---

[2]This term was used between 1921 and 1942 to refer to recordings made in the United States particularly for black listeners. It was coined by Ralph Peer of Okeh Records, the first company to have a

Mexican accordionists living on the U.S. side of the border were recorded, in addition to such singers as the Houston-based Lydia Mendoza. One of the first accordionists recorded by Bluebird was Narciso Martínez. Born in Reynosa, Tamaulipas, Mexico, Martínez lived almost his entire life in San Benito, Texas, a few miles from his birthplace.

Though there were other popular accordionists in the region, such as Bruno Villarreal, Lalo Cavazos, and Pedro Ayala, Martínez's instrumental recordings were more widely played on Spanish-language radio programs on both sides of the border and were distributed among the local population (Peña 1983, 57). In a personal interview I conducted with Martínez in 1992, eight months before his death, he recalled hearing solo accordionists like Villarreal performing among friends and family; he also mentioned having heard smaller ensembles performing for workers near his home that featured the tambora, sometimes accompanied by the accordion, clarinets, and a guitar. When he began playing the accordion himself, he played solo and occasionally with a guitar and tambora. However, his early recordings featured the accordion, the tambora, and the bajo sexto.

Eventually, the tambora was dropped from the ensemble, and the majority of Martínez's recordings between 1936 and 1950 were as an instrumental duo (see Figure 2.6). The bajo sexto on these recordings was played by Santiago Almeida, who emigrated from the state of Durango with his family when he was a teenager. In a 1993 interview in his home in Sunnyside, Washington, the now-deceased Almeida said he considered himself a guitar player first but chose the bajo sexto because of its use in other Mexican orquesta ensembles and sometimes in tamborilero groups as an accompanying instrument (Almeida, personal communication). Though some Texas-Mexican accordionists had already begun playing in ensembles with the bajo sexto as well as other instruments, such as the saxophone, guitarra, tambora, and assorted wind instruments, it was the Martínez-Almeida recordings that made the pairing of the two instruments central to what would become the norteña ensemble style (later to be referred to as conjunto in Texas) (Peña 1983, 56). One element of the duo's popularity is that many of the songs they recorded were Martínez's own compositions, based on polka, waltz, mazurka, and redova dance rhythms. To be sure, most of the European-derived music played by earlier Mexican accordionists consisted of these dance types. Martínez, however, went beyond this; he absorbed the rhythms and the traditions of the European dances, but then created his own interpretations, often giving the songs Spanish names. In effect, he took the first steps in creating a truly Texas-Mexican tradition.

---

"Race Series." He adapted the generic term *the Race*, which was employed at that time in the black press. Other labels such as Vocalion, Columbia, and Victor established "race record" labels, many of which folded during the Depression. Eventually the term was dropped and labels began using more specific terms such as *blues* or *rhythm and blues*. Other regionally focused, rural genres such as "hillbilly" and "Mexican music" were also released on these labels. See Oliver 1984.

**FIGURE 2.6** Narciso Martínez (accordion) and Santiago Almeida (bajo sexto), circa 1948. (Photo courtesy of Arhoolie Records, CD 361.)

In 1940, Bluebird halted its recording expeditions in the rural South because of the economic strains placed on the record industry because of the outbreak of World War II. During the war years, recording was suspended to preserve shellac for military use. When RCA/Victor and other labels resumed recording again after the war, Spanish-language music producers looked to "exotic" Mexico for musicians who represented the "real thing," authentic, classic Mexican mariachi and trio ensembles. Yet recording activity in Texas did not come to a complete halt, as local labels such as Ideal—and later Falcon, Bego, El Zarape, Corona, Sombrero, Omega, Eco, Del Sol, and others—saw an opportunity to develop the local market. Texas-Mexicans had responded to Martínez's recordings and to the button accordion with enthusiasm, and there was clearly a market for an enterprising, regionally focused label.

In an interview in 1992, Martínez also recalled listening to the radio for the first time in 1936, the year in which he made his first recording, a polka titled "La Chicharronera" (The Crackling) for Bluebird. Over the years, this song came to be recognized as a classic among Texas-Mexican accordionists, partly because it introduced the accordion-bajo sexto core of the norteña ensemble and also because it became the primer for the polka, the rhythm of which was rapidly becoming the most popular in the border music tradition. The polka stood out as lively and—depending on the relationship between the accordion and bajo sexto—highly syncopated. In a tradition that was primarily instrumental, it was important to keep the audience dancing.

Traditionally, the norteña polka (*polka norteña*) has a simple binary structure with a 2/4 time signature, and the customary European (or rather, Bohemian) manner of playing emphasizes the first and third eighth notes of the measure, usually in the bass of the accordion. This produces a lively, highly regular dance step. But with Almeida's florid runs on the bajo sexto and Martínez's almost complete avoidance of the bass notes on the accordion, their early polkas were less structured and the melodies richly ornamented. Almeida's playing has its roots in the Mexican *bajo corrido* (running bass) playing style, traditionally associated with accompanying string instruments, particularly the bajo sexto, which sometimes was used to feature runs and passages in the subdivided rhythm.

The bajo sexto accompanying style was already in place before the twentieth century. In the small folk orchestra ensembles around Monterrey that featured the violin, clarinet, and flute, the bajo sexto took on the roles of both the string bass (providing the rhythmic accompaniment of the contrabass) and the guitar (providing fills and offbeats). The early bajo sexto style featured passing tones, scalar runs, solo countermelodies, and a consistent rhythmic backbeat, primarily played on the lower E string. Initially, the bajo sexto had six strings (E, A, D, G, C, F) and was tuned down from the traditional guitar (*guitarra sexta*), hence the name *bajo sexto* (lower six).

By the early part of the century the instrument's strings were doubled at an octave, making it a twelve-string guitar. Martínez and Almeida's pairing of the accordion and bajo sexto was an original concept, and Almeida's uniquely florid playing style—complete with tireless runs and passing tones—allowed Martínez to focus more on the right-hand melody. Martínez's originality lay in playing polkas with the feeling of the shifting rhythms of the huapango. Moreover, Martínez and Almeida would often leave the established rhythmic structure in order to explore melodic, rhythmic, and harmonic possibilities. In other words, they expected their listeners and dancers to "imagine" the rhythmic structure even while they were playing around or just behind it. Thus, while the 2/4 polka rhythm is there, it is not marked by the accordion and is only hinted at by the bajo sexto. In a way, this idea was already present in Mexican son traditions, particularly in the son *jarocho* tradition with its huapango rhythm and the percussive harp and *jarana,* a small, deep-bodied rhythm guitar. In essence, it is a characteristically syncopated interpretation of the German and Polish polka rhythm.

Martínez (together with Almeida) established the accordion and bajo sexto as the core of the early norteña tradition among migrant communities in the border region. This music was played and recorded only in southern Texas, specifically for members of the working-class community, and it served to bind the labor force together, linking families and friends from the Rio Grande Valley to San Antonio to Corpus Christi and as far north as Lubbock. As a result, the accordion would become a powerful symbol of Texas-Mexican working-class identity and the centerpiece of a distinctive regional North American music phenomenon. These songs were heard on radio stations on both sides of the border. However, García Flores explained that the Martínez-Almeida recordings were not as widely heard in Monterrey as they were on "border blaster" stations like XFEB in Río Bravo on the Mexican side of the border and on specialty Spanish-language programs on the Texas side (personal communication).

On the Mexican side, returning laborers demanded dance music featuring the accordion and bajo sexto, and local dance organizers and cantina owners were quick to accommodate them. Molina Montelongo recalled that the cantina and dance organizers began to abandon the six- to eight-piece ensembles for accordion and bajo sexto duos in order to compete for the money that the migrants brought back from their work in the fields on the U.S. side of the border. The businessmen of the *zonas de tolerancia* in the small towns of Nuevo León replaced the orchestra with the music of the accordion and bajo sexto to attract the "wetbacks" and earn their money (Molina Montelongo and Quezada Molina 1995a, 98).

Molina Montelongo also remembered the impact of radio in those early days, noting that the regional accordion and bajo sexto duo ensemble often performed live on local radio programs. However, he wrote that they had to compete with Mexico City recording stars like Guty Cárdenas, Agustín Lara, Pedro Vargas, Toña "la Negra," Chela Campos, Lupita Palomera, and many others who performed popular Cuban-inspired "urban" genres such as the bolero and canción romántica, or romantic song (Molina Montelongo and Quezada Molina 1995a, 97–98). They also competed with popular ranchera singers of the mariachi tradition, such as Lucha Reyes, La Torcacita, and Guadalupe "La Chinaca," who also had film careers, as well as with romantic trios "con guitarras" (with guitars), such as Los Panchos and Los Dandys (Molina Montelongo and Quezada Molina 1995a, 98). There was a great deal more Spanish-language music competition in Mexico than in Texas, and Martínez made little headway in the local market.

The accordion–bajo sexto ensemble's association with the *zonas de tolerancia* kept the music out of the mainstream. It was primarily heard live among campesinos in the villages and towns outside Monterrey and in the towns that bordered Texas. Towns like General Terán, Linares, and China were especially noted for their dances and musicians. Closer to the Texas border, Reynosa and Nuevo Laredo (both in Tamaulipas) were also popular stops for early norteña musicians. In this region today, local pioneering groups such as Los Alegres de Terán, Los Montañeses, Luis y Julián, and El Palomo y el Gorrión are honored in festivals and folklore programs, and popular recording artists, such as Los Invasores del Norte, Los Huracanes del Norte, and Los Cadetes de Linares, regularly perform in dance halls and concerts on both sides of the border; however, most of the other working local groups who are neither pioneers nor popular recording artists perform in run-down clubs on the outskirts of Monterrey and in small border towns where drugs, alcoholism, and prostitution thrive.

Many Mexicans migrated from northeastern Mexico to the Rio Grande Valley and then to San Antonio, Corpus Christi, Houston, and Chicago, and Martínez's recordings went with them. While many people made their homes in San Antonio, it was a "stopping-off" place for Mexican migrants moving to the Northwest and Midwest for work. It is estimated that during the late 1920s more than twenty thousand Mexicans passed through San Antonio each year on their way to other locations farther north. Recruitment of Mexican labor increased greatly during this period, and immigration of laborers from Eastern Europe was greatly discouraged in favor of cheaper Mexican workers (Meier and Ribera 1993, 120–127). At least half a million Mexicans settled permanently in San Antonio and along the border by the 1930s.

The movement of so many people farther north brought the music and recordings of Narciso Martínez to San Antonio and beyond. Martínez's recordings did not seem to travel much south of the border, though some older musicians in Monterrey do remember hearing them (personal communications with García Flores, Garza, and Villagomez). Later, while the ensemble sound was modernized with the addition of drums and electric bass, norteña maintained at its musical core the accordion and bajo sexto pioneered by Martínez and Almeida. Representing the merging of Anglo-European and Mexican cultures, these two instruments—the three-row button accordion in particular—have emerged as powerful symbols of regional Mexican and Mexican immigrant working-class identity on both sides of the border. Despite a history of conflicts between Mexicans and Anglo-Europeans in the border region, the musical core combination of bajo sexto and accordion represents the merging of two distinct music cultures that have come to symbolize the border life experience.

# 3

# Border Culture, Migration, and the Development of Early Música Norteña

## Migration, Border Crossing, and Mexican and Mexican American Identity

The growth in popularity of norteña music and new stylistic and thematic changes in the corrido song form are deeply aligned with the migration of Mexican workers into the United States. Mexicans' traveling to this country in search of work dates back to the mid-nineteenth century, when many laborers crossed the border to work in cattle ranches and on fruit farms in California (Gómez-Quiñones and Maciel 1998, 33–34). Since much of the Southwest had once been a part of Mexico, many Mexicans, particularly those from bordering states, considered themselves indigenous to this region and felt justified in crossing over (Gonzales 1999, 121).

### The Bracero Program

Until just before World War II, North American farmers and employers in the Southwest had been relying on cheap labor from Texas (Texas-Mexicans) and the northern Mexican states, thus extending the reach of Texas-Mexican and northern Mexican culture throughout the region (Gómez-Quiñones and Maciel 1998, 37). When the war began, farmers convinced the Immigration and Naturalization Service (INS) that the supply of workers was not sufficient, and in 1942 the INS enacted the Emergency Farm Labor Program, otherwise known as the Bracero (loosely translated as "unskilled laborer") Program; it allowed for the legal seasonal migration of Mexican workers into the United States to perform contract work on railroads and in agricultural enterprises in the Southwest, as well as in some locations farther north, such as Chicago (Calavita 1992, 32–36). The INS initially acted without the official approval of the U.S. Congress. The Bracero Program was never an act of law because the INS operated autonomously and at the urging of North American employers, especially in the agricultural industry. The program allowed U.S. employers to hire recruiters who traveled deeper into central Mexico to recruit workers, mostly in impoverished and rural areas (Fleshman 2002, 240)

During the twenty-two years of the program's existence, more than 4.6 million labor contracts were issued to workers. Large groups of bracero applicants came via train to the northern border, and their arrival altered the social and economic environments of many border towns. While some braceros returned to their hometowns during the off-season when their contracts had expired, a growing number settled in border communities on the Mexican side, making it easier to travel back into the United States when work became available again (Fleshman 2002, 241–242). Border cities like Ciudad Juárez (across the border from El Paso, Texas), Mexicali, and Tijuana (both bordering California) became hotbeds of recruitment and main gathering points for the agricultural labor force. From these border cities, it was much easier to make the crossing into the United States where jobs were more abundant. However, numerous restrictions and an overcomplicated process for legal entry made illegal crossing a popular and viable option for many workers (Gonzales 1999, 176).

## Changes to Immigration Laws

In 1964, the INS terminated the Bracero Program for three primary reasons: (1) complaints from unions that Mexican workers created too much competition; (2) greater mechanization of farming, particularly of cotton and tomatoes; and (3) evidence of human rights abuses by employers. The program also experienced negative publicity, particularly after Lee G. Williams, the U.S. Department of Labor officer in charge of it, described it as a form of "legalized slavery" (Gómez-Quiñones and Maciel 1998, 40–41). The end of the Bracero Program saw the beginning of the increases in illegal immigration that continue today (Gonzales 1999, 176). When the program ended, Mexican workers were no longer allowed to travel freely across the border for work. Migration patterns had been firmly established, however, and farmers still wanted workers. Similarly, Mexican workers still needed work; in fact, many more were desperately seeking employment since the Mexican government had shifted federal assistance for subsistence farmers to corporate farms instead. Many rural farmers and laborers sought jobs in the newly emerging U.S.-owned border factories (maquiladoras) or took their chances by traveling illegally to the United States (Gonzales 1999,

176). Because there was never an official law regarding Mexican migration, the U.S. government was and still remains ambivalent about the legal migration of workers (as witnessed by the current debate on immigration law).

The political scientist and labor expert Manuel García y Griego has said that the Bracero Program "institutionalized" the use of Mexican labor in North American society (1996, 45). North American employers and the marketplace, particularly in the agriculture industry, came to depend on the constant flow of cheap labor. In fact, many undocumented workers who traveled to the United States after 1964 often worked for the same employers they worked for previously under legal contracts (García y Griego 1996, 71). In effect, even more undocumented workers entered the United States as a result of the government's new policy of passive labor acceptance, combined with a progressively more restrictive legal immigration program (Gutiérrez 1999).

In 1986, the U.S. government passed the Immigration Reform and Control Act (IRCA)—also known as the Simpson-Rodino Act—which increased funds for the United States Border Patrol, penalized employers for hiring unauthorized workers, and provided amnesty to long-term, undocumented residents (Fleshman 2002, 244–245). However, illegal migration continued, and the crackdown on employers, which encouraged frequent visits by INS agents to workplaces, only forced Mexican migrants to fan out across the United States in an effort to seek out new employers in both rural and urban areas previously unknown to INS agents. Mexican workers began relocating in communities where they accommodated new demands for skilled and unskilled labor in service industries, manufacturing, construction, and other areas.

The U.S. government responded with very strict militarization of the border in the 1990s, making it even more difficult for workers to return to Mexico to visit family or to work seasonally (Fleshman 2002, 250). In 1994, after a long campaign peppered with racial rhetoric, California voters passed Proposition 187, a referendum rendering undocumented immigrants ineligible for all state public services, including schools and hospitals. Though some provisions of Proposition 187 have since been ruled unconstitutional, the campaign to pass the law opened the door for politicians to push through stricter immigration enforcement legislation (Fleshman 2002, 250–251). This legislation included a February 1994 strategic plan created by the Attorney General Janet Reno and the INS Commissioner Doris Meissner, which blocked off the undocumented immigrants' preferred routes of entry, such as San Diego, California, and El Paso, Texas, forcing travelers to cross through more difficult terrain, where the Attorney General believed the INS had a tactical advantage.

In 1996, Congress passed the Illegal Immigration Reform and Immigrant Responsibility Act to further aid Reno's plan by requiring the border patrol to hire and deploy one thousand new agents and three hundred new support personnel every year from 1997 to 2001 (Fleshman 2002, 251). Thus, border crossing has become much more dangerous, and the death toll of illegal migrants has risen each year since the 1994 enforcement plan.[1] In spite of these dangers, rather than navigating through the now lengthy and arduous process of legal entry into this country, crossing the border illegally was and still is the only viable option for workers who must face the reality of feeding their families when there is no work to be found in their own country. The U.S. policy toward Mexican immigration has been what the sociologist Julián Samora described in his exhaustive survey of undocumented workers from the 1920s to the 1970s as "an extensive farm labor program" that represents a "consistent desire for Mexicans as laborers rather than as settlers" (1971, 57). Today, little has changed except for the fact that this "program" encourages illegal travel and entry. Therefore, it becomes even more important for the Mexican migrant community to find creative mechanisms to remain connected to their culture and their families.

## Community and Identity through Music

One such mechanism is norteña music. A history of increasingly dangerous, undocumented migration and immigration set the stage for the growth of a modernized version of the border norteña music tradition and the development of a transnational music industry. By the late 1960s, norteña emerged as a cross-cultural phenomenon uniquely tied to travel to the United States and to the experience of work and as a means of connecting the regions, communities, and families of people who cannot easily return to their regions and towns of origin. But why norteña music? With so many people now traveling from regions much farther south of the U.S.-Mexico border and with several of those regions boasting unique musical traditions (e.g., son *jarocho*, son *huasteco*, son *arribeño*), why has norteña dominated the tastes of the Mexican working-class immigrant community as a whole?

Though there are many reasons (which will be discussed later in this chapter) for norteña's rise in popularity among traveling immigrants, there are two primary ones. The first is the music's early association with an autonomous northern Mexican community that harbored ambiguous feelings about its Mexican identity and its early encounters with North American society and migrant travel. The anthropologist Arjun Appadurai has argued that the current global processes of migration lead to a "deterritorialization" of the nation-state that allows for the traveler to emphasize "history" over "place" (1996, 192–196). Norteño music and

---

[1] Among many charts of deaths of undocumented immigrants along the border, statistics on border deaths from San Diego to Brownsville are most startling. Sixty-one deaths were reported in 1995, and by 2000 there were 499. However, the tightening of security on the Arizona border has pushed illegal crossings to parts of Texas and San Diego in particular. The figure for 2005 was down slightly, to 472, and is expected to remain at or close to this level in coming years. Data from Berestein 2006.

culture represent a unique Mexican identity that has been shaped by isolation, political and social autonomy, working-class ideology, and travel made difficult by U.S. immigration laws and related cross-cultural social and political conflict. Like the Norteño, new border immigrants and migrant travelers to the United States participated in the development of a society that held no clear allegiance to Mexico or the United States but rather to the experience of living and traveling between both worlds. Such experiences became part of a Mexican migrant folklore and identity where everyone who traveled or had family members who traveled had some story to tell about the experience of crossing the border or living and working in a new and foreign culture. Norteña music provided a musical format for constructing a distinct Mexican migrant history and identity, particularly for the undocumented worker.

The second reason for the popularity of norteña music among Mexican immigrants is the maintenance of the corrido. The topical narrative ballad form traditionally found throughout Mexico had been transformed in northern Mexico and the borderlands by the 1920s. Early song topics were largely in response to the historical events affecting Norteños, such as Anglo-American encroachment, the border Mexican's subsequent role as second-class citizen, and a long history of crossing the border in search of work; the lyrics often told of intrepid border residents such as revolutionary bandit heroes who—like Pancho Villa and Gregorio Cortez—gained fame and respect by taking the law into their own hands. Though many of these early corridos were sung by mariachis and border guitar and voice duos, the primary musical vehicle for both traditional and newly composed corridos by the 1940s was the norteña ensemble that featured the accordion, bajo sexto, and tololoche (double bass).

In writing about the immigrant experience as it is documented in corridos among Mexicans in California, María Herrera-Sobek has noted that songs on the theme of border crossing and the migrant experience increased after the end of the Bracero Program (1993, 192). She attributes this increase to the use of these songs (many written in traditional corridor form) in campesino theater productions and as a form of protest, particularly by the Mexican American farmworker rights leader César Chávez and other Chicano activists. Chicano composers did write some songs to inspire protestors and leaders with descriptions of hardships, unfair treatment of laborers, and racial prejudices. However, many more corridos composed after the program's end and continuing to the present were written by less-assimilated immigrants and intended as a means of sharing the experiences and difficulties of living and working as a migrant—often illegally—and of educating their fellow travelers (and family members back home) and creating a collective sense of solidarity among communities now increasingly scattered across the United States. The simultaneous development of a transnational recording industry and touring network as a means of connecting emerging immigrant communities across the United States to Mexico also contributed to the corrido's surge in popularity and longevity. The increased popularity of norteña corridos in the 1960s had less to do with a newly formed Chicano identity and presence than it did with the increased travel of largely undocumented Mexican immigrants who were beginning to spread out across the United States and outside the Southwest. Not only did these songs speak of this experience but they also linked communities across a rapidly expanding Mexican diaspora.

Along with the large influx of workers crossing the border, the mid-1960s marked the beginning of an extensive touring circuit for artists who tended to follow these new Mexican arrivals wherever they went for work. Norteña musicians traveled not only to Texas and the Southwest but also to rural and urban locations farther north and across the United States, such as Chicago, Washington's Yakima Valley, northern California, and Las Vegas. Most norteña groups were located in Monterrey and Mexican towns bordering Texas, such as Reynosa, Matamoros, and Nuevo Laredo. Some were based just across the border in Laredo, Brownsville, Harlingen, and McAllen. By the mid-1960s, much of the recording and promotion of norteña music had shifted from the border region to Monterrey (Disa, DLV, Del Valle Records). However, by the late 1960s, independent record labels with larger distribution networks were located on the U.S. side (and farther away from the border), such as Fama (now Fonovisa) in San José, California; Hacienda and Freddy Records in Corpus Christi, Texas; and Joey International in San Antonio, Texas. All these labels still exist today, and they inspired the development of a cross-cultural music industry. The independent recording labels that focused primarily on norteña music and an emerging touring network of artists were, in fact, separate from the Texas-Mexican and Chicano music industry that was already in place in Texas and California by the mid-1960s.

Texas-Mexican, or tejano, conjunto music features the same core instrumentation as norteña: accordion, bajo sexto, and electric bass (drums were added by the mid-1950s). Also, like norteña, this regional genre emerged among working-class Texas-Mexicans and Mexican migrants, primarily from bordering Mexican states, who had traveled to Texas and the Southwest before World War II and had adopted a local Tejano identity. By the 1960s tejano music had taken on influences from North American popular music styles such as country music, jazz, and big band. Manuel Peña writes that, after the Second World War, tejano conjunto was also influenced by an emerging Chicano middle class that "openly considered the poor and/or unacculturated Mexican immigrant an impediment to the Mexican American's upward mobility in American society" (1981, 291). By the 1960s tejano conjunto and a more Americanized popular genre, orquesta tejana, were directly associated with the Chicano and Tejano population. These genres were celebrated throughout the Southwest as forms of artistic expression associated with the upwardly mobile Mexican American and Chicano society there.

In order to establish their presence socially, economically, and politically in the region, Chicanos moved away from their Mexican working-class identity, cultural values, and the migrant experience that, Peña asserts, stalled their chances for full acceptance in North American life (Peña 1981, 291). In so doing, the largely regionally based tejano record labels, touring circuit, and audience grew estranged from the rapidly growing norteña music industry and the largely poor and undocumented Mexican community associated with it. Similarly, by the mid-1960s, Texas-Mexicans and Chicanos had ceased traveling the migrant circuit for work and there was less demand for conjunto groups; only a handful of more established tejano conjunto musicians like Tony de la Rosa, Los Guadalupanos (featuring accordionist Mingo Saldívar), and Little Joe y la Familia were able to travel and only to select towns and cities with visible Tejano and Chicano communities. These musicians traveled less often and to fewer migrant communities outside Texas (though many tejano artists like Flaco Jiménez were invited to folk festivals throughout the United States and Europe as representatives of regional American "roots" music). Orquesta tejana—with stylistic elements based on a combination of tejano conjunto, North American big band swing, rhythm and blues, Latin jazz, and the symphonic dance bands originally associated with the Mexican elite—began to dominate the Texas-based (and regionally focused) recording industry in the 1960s and 1970s, placing the accordion-based conjunto ensemble in the role of regional Mexican American "folk" music. The popularity and eventual domination of the more polished and professional orquesta allowed the Tejano and Chicano population the opportunity to move away from its working-class past, which was connected to a conflict-ridden and impoverished border culture.

The now "folkloric" conjunto musician, with accordion in hand, stood as a reminder of this community's lower status in North American society. A professional orquesta tejana touring circuit—featuring artists like Beto Villa, Little Joe y la Familia, Rubén Ramos and the Mexican Revolution (he later changed the group's name to the Texas Revolution), Don Tosti, and others—focused primarily on cities and areas where there were significant Tejano and Chicano populations with emerging middle-class communities (such as Fresno and Los Angeles, California; Albuquerque and Las Cruces, New Mexico; Denver, Colorado; San Antonio and Houston, Texas; Tucson, Arizona; and Yakima Valley, Washington). The Mexican American orquesta (a predecessor to the música tejana, or tejano, popular music phenomenon that would emerge in the early 1980s) is described by Peña as a product of the transformation of Mexican American society that began in the 1930s and accelerated after World War II (1999b, 22–23). As a hybrid popular music style, it was associated with a new, upwardly mobile community of North Americans of Spanish and Mexican descent whose parents and grandparents were primarily from southern Texas and Mexico's northern region.

This community, Peña says, was in the process of completing the transformation of its cultural identity and establishing a stronger political presence (1999b). The community was increasingly bicultural and bilingual, having constructed a society that was both actively assimilating into North American society and extolling its Mexican and Spanish roots, even though the historical and cultural references were often based on myth and imagination. It is not surprising, then, that the modern orquesta genre—complete with the extravagance of a larger ensemble of brass instruments and keyboards—inspired a well-organized performing network, an independent recording industry, and a growing stable of recognized bandleaders that would be presented as a symbol of both prosperity and possibility during the Chicano Movement of the late 1960s and early 1970s. Chicano leaders (journalists, intellectuals, literary writers) and tejano musicians like Little Joe y La Familia joined with farmworker rights activists to raise national awareness of the poor conditions of Mexican laborers, thus giving a political voice to immigrant laborers of Mexican and Latino descent in this country. Chicano musicians, poets, and theater groups recast border conflict corridos as protest music, paralleling similar trends such as the *nueva canción* (new song) movement, which began in Chile (and which was called *nueva trova* in Cuba) and spread throughout Latin America.

On a social level, however, Chicano and Tejano music and culture seemed to exclude the newer and much larger stream of Mexican immigrants, particularly the undocumented and increasingly more indigenous populations who were now traveling from the impoverished slums of Mexico City or from rural and isolated regions of central and southern Mexico. Within the Chicano and Tejano community, issues of identity and ethnicity were hotly debated, and there were disagreements about how much the United States should restrict immigration and travel by undocumented Mexicans. A more militant wing of socialist Chicanos advocated for amnesty for all undocumented Mexicans in the United States and denounced the border as oppressive and controlled by imperialistic motivations. The majority of Mexican migrants and immigrants traveling during this time maintained stronger connections to their homeland, preferred to speak the Spanish language, and were more focused on finding work and supporting their families. Though these new traveling Mexicans benefited somewhat from the advances of the Chicano Movement, which itself had been fueled by the farm labor movement and brought about improved working conditions, better pay, and awareness among North American employers in the area of economic and racial discrimination in the Southwest, their need for work and their desire to remain connected to their hometowns and regions of origin in Mexico meant that few actually participated directly in the movement or its ideology. The protest songs and campesino theater groups about which Herrera-Sobek (1993) writes were part of a Chicano culture and society that stood against an aggressive U.S. immigration policy while advocating a modified assimilationist strategy.

In contrast, new migrating Mexicans, now traveling beyond the Southwest to jobs farther north, were not fully and collectively engaged in a formal immigration rights struggle (primarily because of their undocumented status), and they did not tend to integrate into Chicano society. In research conducted among working-class Mexican immigrants, the folklorist and anthropologist José Limón notes a tendency among more recent arrivals to refer to themselves as "mexicanos" or "mexicanas" (1981, 222). Once an ethnic-class slur, Limón writes, the "Chicano" identifier was appropriated by "middle- and upper-class, U.S.-born Americans of Mexican descent" (1981, 205). The Chicano historian Mario T. García further distinguishes types among the Mexican community in the United States: the Mexican American who is focused on integration and acculturation, the Chicano who advocates an ethnic revival with Marxist tendencies, and the Mexican national who sees the United States as an extension of Mexico and a collective identity that is loosely defined by nationality or citizenship (1996, 112–113). This third group makes up the bulk of the Mexican immigrant population in the United States, which has more than tripled since the end of the Bracero Program in 1964.[2] The majority of these arrivals prefer to speak Spanish and maintain regional folk traditions and religious practices, allowing them to freely accept or reject elements of North American culture, unlike their Tejano and Chicano counterparts prior to the beginning of the Bracero Program in 1942. David G. Gutiérrez has noted that, though Mexican immigrants and migrants often maintain elements of a Mexican identity, they also remain "ambivalent" toward the concept of a nation-state and a "national" community promoted by the "ruling elites" on either side of the U.S.-Mexico border (1999, 517).

It is this segment of the U.S.-based Mexican population that has provided the bulk of the audience for norteña music since the late 1960s and early 1970s. Norteña's popularity among this expanding immigrant population is, in part, due to the development of a touring network of artists that followed migrants throughout the United States. It is also due to the maintenance of the corrido tradition, which represented a connection to Mexican history and culture. The topical nature of narrative song form and its traditional focus on border conflict and travel allowed for the proliferation of new songs based on both real and fictional accounts of Mexican immigration. The popularity of these songs, as well as of other song genres from Mexico such as rancheras, canción-corridos, and cumbias, which were being incorporated into the norteña repertoire, led to the expansive reach and popularity of a multimillion-dollar recording and touring industry.

---

[2] The U.S. Bureau of the Census reports that the Mexican immigrant population grew from 4.5 million in 1970 to 8.7 million in 1980 to more than 17 million by 1997. Of the 17 million figure of 1997, it was reported that nearly 7 million were born in Mexico. Data from "Hispanic and Asian Populations Increasing Faster than Overall Population," U.S. Census Bureau News, June 14, 2004, http://www.census.gov/Press-Release/www/releases/archives/race/001839.html (accessed April 19, 2005). An AP article entitled "U.S. Undocumented Population Surges," March 21, 2005, which appeared in several newspapers and magazines throughout the United States, reported that the overall U.S. foreign-born population, regardless of legal status, was 35.7 million in 2004. Those of Mexican descent again constituted the largest group, more than 11 million, or 32 percent. See http://wireservice.wired.com/wired/story.asp?section=Breaking&storyId=1007631 (accessed April 20, 2005).

## Early Independent Recording and Radio in the Texas-Mexican Border Region

Norteña music—with its history of real and imagined heroes and experiences associated with the border; its themes of hard work, danger, and defiance; and its deep connection to a displaced and marginalized community—is the story of a modern Mexican diaspora in the making. Norteña songs (primarily corridos) initially documented the intensity of demographic and cultural change in the U.S.-Mexico borderlands, a change that has spread throughout the Mexican diaspora, where questions of personal and collective identity and affiliation are especially volatile. It is the primarily undocumented Mexican immigrants who have supported and continue to support the growth of a norteña music industry and network of touring artists that, for them, parallel their own transnational experiences of travel to the United States. Today, these individuals live in a more ambiguous, dangerous, and continuously expanding Mexican diaspora that allows for a larger set of local affiliations and subcultures that can be reinterpreted and redefined on the basis of their own experiences. While researchers such as George Lipsitz (1994), Néstor Canclini (2000), and Juan Flores (1993) have pointed to the dynamism of border zones as a crucible for new expressive art forms, it is increasingly apparent that such zones need not be actual geographic boundaries but can also include the experiential border created and invoked in the songs of norteña.

Recording, extensive travel by artists, and the establishment of Mexican communities and enclaves throughout the United States are the primary ways norteña music has not only gained in popularity but also contributed to the formation of solidarity and collective identity, predominantly within an expanding Mexican immigrant population. The record industry, like the music itself, was tied simultaneously to the northward migration of Mexican workers into the United States and to the development of a separate Texas-Mexican and Chicano society. After World War II, the exodus of the RCA/Victor subsidiary Bluebird Records left the door open for the establishment in 1946 of Ideal Records, the first Mexican American–owned independent record company in southern Texas (Peña 1999a, 96–97; 1999b, 75). Mainstream North American labels looked to Mexico City for "authentic" Mexican music, such as mariachi and recordings by popular singing stars that were being promoted in Mexican films and would likely sell to a crossover market. These labels were no longer interested in the regional music produced by Mexican Americans and Mexican immigrants and left an already established regional Spanish-language music market open for local, independent record entrepreneurs to step into.

Ideal's co-owners, Armando Marroquín and Paco Betancourt, set their sights on the local Texas-Mexican community, whose purchases of Bluebird recordings by artists such as Narciso Martínez and Lydia Mendoza provided an active (and lucrative) market for regional Mexican American music. However, almost from

FIGURE 3.1   Beto Villa and his "small" orchestra in the late 1940s. Though the piano accordion shown here is not typical of that used by norteña and Texas-Mexican conjunto ensembles, Villa occasionally used it to project a more "sophisticated" and "modern" image and sound. Villa used the button accordion (played by Martínez, Longoria, and La Rosa) on many recordings as well. (Photo courtesy of Arhoolie Records.)

the very beginning, the artists the entrepreneurs cultivated and promoted were, like themselves, Mexican Americans born and raised on the U.S. side of the border and aspiring to be middle-class. Aside from early recordings by the conjunto accordionist Narciso Martínez, the feature artists Ideal cultivated were more "sophisticated," because they incorporated the instrumentation, musical influences, and repertoire of North American big bands such as Glenn Miller and Tommy Dorsey, as well as popular Afro-Cuban dance bands of the time, such as Xavier Cugat and His Orchestra and Machito and His Afro-Cubans. The popular saxophonist and early orquesta bandleader Beto Villa, originally from Falfurrias, Texas, began recording for Ideal in 1947 (see Figure 3.1). He also accompanied the singing sister duo Carmen y Laura (a Mexican American version of the Andrews Sisters) and the local romantic ballad singer Chelo Silva.

Peña has described Villa as the "father of modern orquesta tejana" whose music successfully forged a modern "hybrid" sound that allowed Mexican Americans to both assimilate and maintain "powerful associations to a nutrient ancestral 'heritage'" (1999a, 133). Peña suggests that, though Marroquín was a resourceful business manager for the label, he was also aware of a "Tejano cultural network" within the confines of an ethnic regional music market that he fully understood and cultivated (1999b, 76). Between 1950 and 1956 Marroquín also organized several tours throughout the Southwest and Chicago for Villa and Carmen y Laura (Carmen was Marroquín's wife) that expanded the reach of this music throughout the Southwest as well as in Mexican American communities in Chicago, Kansas, and Utah. In a taped interview with Hector Galán, the director of two documentaries about Texas-Mexican music (*Songs of the Homeland* and *Accordion Dreams*), a seventy-five-year-old Carmen Marroquín describes how she and her husband were pioneers not only in recording Spanish-language music in the United States but also in establishing a touring network that brought the label's artists to Spanish-speaking migrant communities throughout the Southwest, and eventually to other states, in order to boost sales of the label's recordings:

We opened the gate, we opened the road for everybody. When we started the Ideal Recording Company we had to have exposure and the only distributor we had was Rangel, in San Antonio. So after that we got a distributor in El Paso and in Los Angeles. Everything was very, very limited, there was nothing, there were no halls, no promoter, no Spanish-language radio—there might be a one-hour program, but that was it. But no radio stations in Spanish, nothing like that. So when we started, we wanted to be heard, and we wanted to sell and we knew we had to go and work. We got a map, and we said we'll go here and here and here. The first place we went to was Del Rio [Texas] and from there we went to West Texas, Fort Stockton, I mean Fort Davis, Pecos, El Paso, Martha. From there we went to New Mexico and then Arizona and California. That was our first route. Once we got to these places we had to approach people to make the dances and we had to ask the clubs to sponsor us. Because few towns had halls, we used to go to the school gyms. We did that the first time out. The second time we went further and further (laughs). It was like that all the time and we usually went in the summers. So we opened the path from Del Rio, California, Utah, Kansas, Illinois . . . all those places. You know, I was very surprised, I knew there were Mexican people in Los Angeles and in Chicago, but I never dreamed I would see Mexican people in Salt Lake City. And, you know, people went wild. When we got on stage they started throwing money at the stage. They were thirsty, you know, for hearing something in Spanish.[3]

Ideal, however, did not completely abandon the working-class, accordion-based conjunto—also referred to as "norteña" by some members of the population who still associated it with the border—at least not right away. In fact, Marroquín recorded a new generation of accordionists, such as Valerio Longoria, Conjunto Bernal, and Tony de la Rosa, who were looking to modernize and in some ways Americanize the traditional polkas, waltzes, and huapangos played by

---

[3] Carmen Marroquín, interview by Héctor Galán, May 7, 1996(?), transcript no. 135 from videotape, Galán Incorporated Television and Film, Austin, Texas.

**FIGURE 3.2** Tony de la Rosa. By the early 1950s, La Rosa had stepped into the role of pioneering accordionist Narciso Martínez as house accordionist at Ideal Records (the first label in the United States owned and operated by Mexican Americans). (Photo courtesy of Arhoolie Records.)

working-class, accordion-based ensembles. Longoria had released his first recording on the San Antonio-based Corona Records label (which later became Río Records) in 1947. It was a song titled "El Rosalito," which featured Longoria singing a canción romántica and playing the accordion. However, at Ideal, Longoria's primary job was to accompany singers and to "blend in" with the orquesta tejana, as Martínez had done before. Marroquín had settled on a more "symbolic role" for the accordion—as part of larger orquesta ensembles or occasionally accompanying featured vocalists such as Carmen y Laura and Chelo Silva.

By the early 1950s, Tony de la Rosa took over as the house accordionist for Ideal Records, but he left in 1955 to form his own group (see Figure 3.2). As a second-generation Texas-Mexican, La Rosa had a style that was as much influenced by Martínez's early recordings as it was by other regional North American musical elements. As a teenager and an accomplished guitarist, La Rosa realized he could earn money playing in local "Texas swing" bands. In a personal interview, he spoke of his early exposure to what he described as the "hillbilly music" of Bob Wills, the local German/Czech country swing band leader Adolph Hofner and his Pearl Wranglers, and the East Texas Cajun/country swing fiddler Harry Choates. La Rosa, who admired the Texas country fiddle style, told me in a 1991 interview that he tried to imitate that sound on his accordion:

> I would listen to the Spanish program and that's where I heard my first accordion, and it was Narciso Martínez—the very, very first. I call him the "Daddy of Accordionists," you know. And there's a lot of other people involved in it, but my strong point was country. It used to give me a go within myself. It was during the time of Bob Wills, Gene Autry, Roy Rogers, Roy Acuff, and Cajun, you know, Harry Choates, The Texas Top Hands, Adolph Hofner, quite a few of these people, they were traveling around the state and I saw them all. There's a whole bunch of 'em . . . Lefty Frizzell . . . all that western stuff. My music was a mixture of all that. I listened to the melody of the violin, both in western-style country and Cajun country, and I played polkas on my accordion in that way. (personal communication)

Tony de la Rosa, who passed away in 2004, hailed from Riviera, Texas, just south of Corpus Christi and was the first to include drums and electric bass in recordings (not for Ideal). As a result, the consistent backbeat was slowed down to a "dance hall glide," providing a solid pulse that emphasized the offbeats. The addition of drums and the electrification of instruments "settled down the tempo, especially on polkas, freeing the accordion and bajo sexto from attending to melody, harmony, and rhythm and allowing them to explore new modes of articulation" (Peña, 1985, 87). La Rosa established the conjunto "dance hall" sound that would set the standard for all Texas-based ensembles to come. These features would also distinguish the accordion-led conjunto ensemble from those that were located closer to the Mexican border and in Mexico proper. Ideal Records was located in Alice, Texas, roughly two hours north of the Texas-Mexican border, and the artists on its label were primarily marketed to Spanish-language radio in urban centers in Texas such as San Antonio, Houston, and Corpus Christi, and later communities throughout the Southwest and, eventually, the Midwest. Ideal Records and its artists would pioneer a distinctly modern Mexican American (i.e., Tejano and/or Chicano) music industry.

Until the late 1950s, *conjunto* and *norteña* were used interchangeably to refer to any ensemble featuring the accordion and bajo sexto. The popularity of La Rosa's "dance hall" sound, with its influences from Texas swing and country music and a more prominently featured accordion, required that a distinction be made. Texas-Mexicans referred to La Rosa's sound as *conjunto,* a term probably taken from the group's name, Tony de la Rosa y Su Conjunto (Tony de la Rosa and His Group). This music also mirrored a desire among Tejanos to distinguish themselves from the migrating Mexican population while not completely assimilating into the local Anglo-American population. Public dances and radio airplay of Texas-Mexican artists like La Rosa and Longoria encouraged the development of a separate tejano music industry during this period (Hagan, Dickey, and Peña 1979, 66–67). Like the music of local country and western swing bands, conjunto was performed in dance halls where upbeat dance rhythms like the polka, schottische, redova, and huapango were emphasized and fewer corridos were played. If Tejanos played corridos in these dance halls, they were set to a 2/4 polka rhythm and sung at a faster pace (Hagan, Dickey, and Peña 1979, 67).

However, ensembles located in the border region, where the accordion and bajo sexto served to accompany the corrido and other song forms, maintained the name *norteña*. During this period most conjunto groups, including La Rosa's, played primarily instrumental polkas, schottisches, and redovas (except the accordionist Valerio Longoria, who also sang boleros and canciones románticas). But the norteña groups' focus on song forms—especially the topical corridos and canción-corridos, which contained few repetitions and featured a story-like narrative—required fluent knowledge of Spanish, which many Tejanos and Chicanos had lost or were losing as they assimilated. Moreover, since these songs were written by immigrants themselves, they were often filled with Mexican slang as well as words and phrases from specific regional dialects not known to Texas-Mexicans who had never lived in Mexico or who had been living in the United States for many years.

Falcon Records, a second independent Mexican American–owned label, which opened for business in 1947, just one year after Ideal, also began recording and distributing records in the region. This label, founded and owned by Arnaldo Ramírez, a former disc jockey and a future mayor of the border town Mission, Texas, focused its efforts on developing a stable of local recording artists from both sides of the border. Many of these artists were undocumented Mexican migrants themselves who played the type of norteña music that appealed initially to an expanding and now more regionally diverse immigrant border community. During the early 1940s, Ramírez purchased two radio programs on the Reynosa, Tamaulipas–based "border blaster" station XEAW.[4] One of Ramírez's Spanish-language programs, *La hora del soldado* (The Soldier's Hour), was dedicated to

[4]In 1930, radio station XED, the precursor of XEAW, opened for business and began broadcasting at a power of 10,000 watts. Studios were located in the McAllen Hotel in McAllen, Texas, and in Reynosa, Tamaulipas, just a quarter of a mile south of the U.S.-Mexico bridge. To avoid licensing problems from the FCC, the transmitter was located in Reynosa, making the station the most powerful in Mexico. The station was owned by International Broadcasting, a Mexican corporation, with four Texans from McAllen and one Mexican citizen as founding partners. XEAW was one of several megawatt "border blaster" stations, set up just across the Mexican border to evade U.S. regulations while beaming programming across the United States and into Canada. (See Fowler and Crawford 2002, 146–147.)

Mexican American soldiers serving in World War II. The station, which was aimed toward the United States and could be heard as far north as Nova Scotia, Canada, featured hillbilly music, Mexican corridos, evangelists, astrologers, and an unending stream of hustlers and promoters selling everything from "genuine simulated diamond rings" to medicines that could not be legally advertised over the airwaves in the United States (Fowler and Crawford 2002, 146–148).

In 1943, XEAW was closed in a political deal by Mexican authorities, and its frequency was given to a radio station in Monterrey, Nuevo León. However, Ramírez realized he had a sizable audience for his Spanish-language programs on both sides of the border and established Falcon's recording studio in McAllen, Texas, just two miles from the U.S.-Mexico border. Ideal's studio, on the other hand, was located about two hours north of the border and on the road to San Antonio (which eventually became a primary hub for the tejano recording industry). The location of these two studios is a good indication of the communities for whom their recordings were destined.

Ramiro Cavazos, a former member of the border-based norteña group Los Donneños (a contemporary of Los Alegres de Terán, which also recorded for Falcon), recalled in an interview that his experience resembled that of many of the artists who recorded on Falcon and the other local labels that came on the scene during the 1950s and 1960s (personal communication). Cavazos and his musical partner, Mario Montes, were Mexican migrant laborers who came to Texas for work in the 1940s, but as seasonal workers they remained close to the border and often traveled between the border town of Donna, Texas (the inspiration for their name), and Mexico, eventually developing a following on both sides of the border:

> I was picking cotton and, in the evening, playing in a restaurant and making money. One day I met another musician, Mario Montes, who was working in the fields picking fruit. I left work and rode my bicycle around and saw him playing on the curb with another guy and I checked them out. And I had a guitar and they asked if I played the accordion, and I said a little. And he said, "Do you know how to play the guitar?" And I began to play and he said that I played beautifully, and, well, afterwards we began to play together. I was from Los Ramones, Nuevo León, by the Rio Grande, and he was from Monterrey, but we knew each other because of the work near Donna. (personal communication)

David G. Gutiérrez has found that the majority of Mexican migrant and immigrant workers who came into the United States after World War II were not able to improve their economic position by moving from low-skilled occupations to skilled blue-collar jobs of higher status and better pay, as many of their Chicano/Tejano predecessors had done (1999, 507). Population and migration analysts like Jorge Chapa (1990) and Elaine M. Allensworth (1997) support this finding with statistics showing that the socioeconomic prospects for ethnic Mexicans in the United States stagnated in the mid-1970s and, by the end of that decade, fell into a steep decline that continued into the 1990s. This fact, in addition to tighter restrictions on immigrants, which force many to migrate illegally, has kept the Mexican national immigrant community marginalized, forging a gap between them and the majority of the Chicano/Tejano population.

Each of the two rival labels, Ideal and Falcon, would concentrate its interests on one of the two emerging Mexican American communities in the border region: Ideal marketed to the bilingual and increasingly well-educated sons and daughters of Texas-Mexicans (or Tejanos), who had a long history in the region; Falcon focused on the expanding border-based and constantly traveling Mexican migrant laborer community. This latter population was rapidly growing and transforming the border region with new migrants from nonbordering Mexican states, the majority as participants in the Bracero Program. After the program ended, many more Mexican workers continued to travel, though largely undocumented, as a result of chronic unemployment, currency devaluation, government corruption, and a myriad of other social and political problems that plagued Mexico. The distinctions between these two communities—a more established, bilingual, and assimilated Tejano/Chicano community and a constantly traveling, Spanish-speaking marginalized Mexican migrant/immigrant community—led to stylistic and contextual distinctions between the tejano (conjunto and orquesta) and norteña musical genres.

Unlike the dance hall–oriented tejano conjuntos or the big band, Latin jazz sophistication of orquesta tejana ensembles, norteña artists remained true to the traditional corrido song form—though they would later move away from historic border themes of Anglo-Mexican conflict and pistol-packing bandits and revolutionaries. New corridos would tell stories that dealt with contemporary and more politically relevant issues such as economic struggles, social alienation, oppression (not only by Anglo bosses but also by the Mexican American border patrol and by Chicano culture), displacement, "undocumented" status, drug-smuggling bandits, lost love, the breakdown of the family, and border-crossing exploits. While norteña music was also performed in dance halls and at community celebrations such as weddings and festivals, the songs were primarily text-driven and spoke directly to the immigrant experience. Additionally, the introduction of electric bass and drums and the emergence of stylistic nuances that were associated with dominant regional sending populations—for example, the occasional use of the saxophone by groups from Nuevo León and Tamaulipas and the tuba-like electric bass sound of groups from Sinaloa—led to the modernization and growing cross-cultural popularity of norteña.

By the mid-1970s, norteña began to dominate its accordion-driven counterpart, tejano conjunto, thanks to wider record distribution and a more expansive touring network throughout the United States and in Mexico. In addition, the militarization of the border made travel for undocumented workers back to

Mexico much more difficult than in the 1940s, 1950s, and 1960s (Gonzales 1999), so recordings by norteña artists were in demand among Mexicans in the United States who wanted to remain connected to their "Mexican" roots while listening to songs that told stories that resembled their own experiences (Raúl García Flores, personal communication). Similarly, migrants' families in Mexico wanted to share in the experience of their loved ones, and by the late 1980s, norteña music emerged as a vehicle for solidarity and collective imagination. The dissemination of norteña music and the proliferation of artists willing to travel to communities on both sides of the border led to a well-oiled industry aimed at a rapidly expanding Mexican diaspora that grew even as the United States set out to close the border to traveling workers.

## The Emergence of Norteña Style: 1920s–1940s

García Flores found that from the early 1930s makeshift flute and string ensembles imitating the *orquesta típica*—an elite format very popular between the mid-1880s and the early 1930s—were popular among communities of poor migrants living on the outskirts of Monterrey and, later, farther north and closer to the U.S. border (personal communication). These groups were an outgrowth of the larger brass band ensembles associated with military and civil functions in villages and towns, and their repertoire included many of the same instrumental polkas, schottisches, and waltzes that the ten- to fifteen-piece bands played at "official" governmental presentations or festivals and that working-class tamborilero duos and trios also played. Typically, boys were recruited very young to play in village orchestras, a practice that still exists in many rural Mexican villages. In essence, the village orchestras were an extension of the tamborilero ensemble, which had its musical limitations and was more directly associated with rural, largely indigenous, laborer communities. These ensembles were an outgrowth of the urban and rural economic and social classes coming together as rural-to-urban migration was changing and expanding the region. One of the most popular of these ensembles was Los Montañeses del Álamo (the Mountaineers of Álamo), whose European-derived salon music featured flute, violin, contrabass, and guitar. Later, the group added the saxophone (as is illustrated in Figure 3.3), probably in response to the success of Latin dance bands popular in Mexico City and the United States during this period. On occasion, the group substituted the guitarra sexta, an instrument believed to have been brought to the region by migrants from the northern state of Durango, for the twelve-string bajo sexto.

Los Montañeses was founded in 1926 by the bajo sexto player Pedro Mier and featured a violin, played by Isidoro Leija, a migrant musician from San Luis Potosí, a northern state bordering Nuevo León. By 1931 the group had expanded to include flute and tololoche, and seven years later it was bigger yet (Alanís Támez 1994, 24–25). The group hailed from the village of Las Albas, Nuevo León,

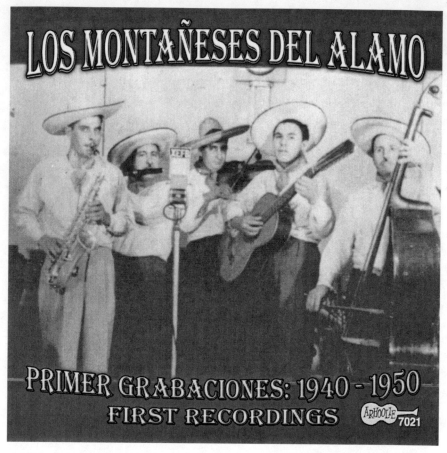

**FIGURE 3.3** Los Montañeses del Álamo, one of the first regional norteña recording groups, performing live on the Monterrey radio station XEFB during the mid-1940s. (Photo courtesy of Arhoolie Records.)

a poor laborer community located in the municipality of Santiago, in the foothills of the Sierra Madre mountains, just forty-five minutes southeast of Monterrey. During the 1930s, a large number of migrant workers from other regions of northern Mexico had begun to populate villages and municipalities around Monterrey. Los Montañeses played at weddings and *quinceañeras* (girls' fifteenth birthday celebrations) as well as in local cantinas in this community (Alanís Támez 1994, 23–25).

By 1938, the ensemble included Mier's sons, Nicandro and Jaime, and the group had a steady gig at the El Álamo resort, a weekend destination for wealthy families from Monterrey (Alanís Támez 1994, 24–25). This was also the year that surviving family members say Los Montañeses made its first recording for Discos Peerless (Alanís Támez, personal communication). However, Chris Strachwitz of

Arhoolie Records in California, the label that has been documenting and reissuing the group's music, claims that the first recordings were actually made two years later in 1940.[5] The group's recording spread its popularity throughout the region, and as its sound evolved, it added to its repertoire more contemporary dance genres such as tangos, habaneras, and North American foxtrots. This was largely in response to the demands of the more "elite" audience at El Álamo, though Los Montañeses continued to play at family parties, weddings, and other community functions for their original working-class, rural audience, The group assumed a highly visible role among the community, along with many tamborilero groups. However, it was Los Montañeses' instrumentation, nonindigenous personnel, large musical repertoire (which included instrumentals as well as songs), position as "professional" entertainers (rather than folk musicians), and access to early radio and recording opportunities that allowed them to emerge as the first commercially successful group in the region, an accomplishment that the largely indigenous tamborileros could not attain. However, many local scholars and cronistas, such as Alanís Támez, confirmed the importance of the more rural tamborileros as well as the popular Los Montañeses in the formation of a regional norteña style. He wrote, "Entre los tamborileros y los Montañeses del Álamo, existe como similitud, únicamente el repertorio musical de polkas y redobas; el violín, flauta, contrabajo, bajo sexto, y más tarde el saxofón, habrían de revolucionar en el ámbito musical, logrando significar la imagen fiel, de esta expresión artística regional, traspasando las fronteras de Nuevo León, Coahuila y Tamaulipas" (1994, 18).[6]

In his first book, *The Texas Mexican Conjunto: Music of a Working-Class People*, Peña (1985) describes small ensembles in southern Texas border towns during the 1930s that featured various combinations of flutes, violins, and guitars. This instrumentation is similar to that of Los Montañeses, which is considered by many northern Mexicans to be one of the earliest and most influential representatives of northeastern regional Mexican music and a prototype of the modern norteña ensemble (personal communications with García Flores, Alanís Támez, and Guillermo Berrones). The group's regional popularity, dating back to the late 1920s, indicates their possible influence on these folkloric ensembles among migrant communities along the border.

One reason that Los Montañeses' popularity was so widespread was that they were the first regional folk ensemble heard on radio in the border region. In order to drum up more business for his resort, the El Álamo proprietor, Don Alfonso

---

[5]"Los Montañeses del Álamo," liner notes to the CD *Primeras Grabaciones: 1940–1950*, Los Montañeses del Álamo, Arhoolie Records, 2002.

[6]"Between the tamborileros and Los Montañeses del Álamo, which shared a unique musical repertoire of polkas and redovas, the violin, flute, contrabass, bajo sexto, and, much later, the saxophone, together [they] have revolutionized the musical limits, managing to represent a faithful image of this artistic regional expression that traveled across the borders of Nuevo León, Coahuila, and Tamaulipas."

M. Salazar Támez, sponsored the group's radio appearance (Alanís Támez, personal communication). Monterrey is distinguished as the birthplace of Mexico's first radio station, which was established on October 9, 1921, by the pioneering Mexican radio engineer Constantino de Tárnava, almost a year and a half before the first radio station in Texas was created in Houston on March 22, 1922 (Sosa Plata 2002). In addition to offering news and weather reports, Tárnava featured artists such as the Colombian poet Leopoldo de la Rosa and the Cuban journalist Eutiquio Aragonés. Tárnava also invited local orchestras and symphonies like the Orquesta Sinfónica de Monterrey, classical pianists, violinists, vocalists, and jazz/foxtrot ensembles such as the Monterrey Jazz Band, which were popular among the city's elite society, to perform live from his parents' living room, where his experimental station was located. Later, in the late 1930s, in an effort to reach out to the migrant communities in surrounding villages, he invited Los Montañeses. By 1938, Tárnava was broadcasting at a thousand watts under the call letters XEH and using the slogan "XEH, la más grande" (XEH, the greatest), later changing it to "La voz de Monterrey desde 1921" (The voice of Monterrey since 1921) (Ayala Duarte 1995, 64–65). He was broadcasting via remote control to twenty-eight stations in the region, and in 1940 he played his first recorded disc on the air. It was an advance copy of a Los Montañeses release from RCA Victor's Mexico City branch. However, since the group's first recordings were made from live broadcasts, it is likely that these recordings were originally made from Tárnava's own live studio broadcasts (Sosa Plata, 2002).

During their long history in northeastern Mexico (which continues today), Los Montañeses changed very little of their style, except to add saxophone in the early 1940s (an influence of popular Mexican and U.S.-based Latin jazz dance bands). The saxophone has remained central to the group's sound and since the 1980s has been paired with the accordion, partly because of that instrument's popularity in modern norteña groups in the region. The group continued to record for Peerless Records, retaining a link to the nineteenth-century folk music of the region and helping to maintain that music's popularity. One interesting note is that Pedro Mier's brother, Jaime Mier, traveled to Texas to participate in recording sessions with the singer Carmen Marroquín (of Carmen y Laura) for Ideal Records.

Another important figure in the early development of modern norteña music in Mexico was the accordionist Antonio Tanguma, who also made his first recording for Peerless in 1938 (the same year the first recording by Los Montañeses is believed to have taken place), though he had been performing in Monterrey and the border region for over a decade. Tanguma's recording was a redova (also known in this region as *vals bajito*) called "De China a Bravo" (From China to Bravo). The redova is basically a fast waltz played in the accordion's lower register. Though this was an instrumental composition, Tanguma's title is likely the earliest association of rural accordion music with the experience of migration and traveling for work. As Tanguma states, he composed this redova many years earlier while traveling between his hometown of China, Nuevo León (sixty miles northeast of Monterrey) to the border town of Río Bravo, which overlooked the Río Grande and was just across from McAllen, Texas. "En realidad mis primeras composiciones las traje siempre en la mente, porque cuando trabajaba en la labor, me inventaba tonadas y las repetía silbando," Tanguma tells the cultural historian Celso Garza Guajardo. "En 1938 terminé la primera pieza, 'De China a Bravo.' Ese nombre, yo no se lo puse, pero como la pasaba viajando de China a Bravo, así se le fue quedando" (Garza Guajardo 1993, 18).[7]

As a migrant worker who crossed the border into Texas on numerous occasions to work in the fields and, at times, play in local cantinas or parties, Tanguma performed in places like Laredo and Corpus Christi. Prior to his death on December 25, 1989, Tanguma told the story of how he acquired his first accordion in 1927 by crossing the Rio Grande to find work in Texas. After making his first twelve dollars, he bought his accordion in Laredo. He later recalled how he traveled to Corpus Christi and played solo for dances, eventually earning enough money to buy several other accordions to bring back to Mexico, specifically to China and General Terán, to sell to other musicians (Garza Guajardo 1993, 17–19). His memories of bringing accordions to these cities suggest that accordions, which were scarce in northern Mexico, were likely brought into that country by migrant workers traveling back from Texas. Tanguma was known as a solo accordionist and was often enlisted to perform with groups like Los Montañeses or local tamborilero ensembles. Tanguma rarely performed with a guitarist or bajo sexto player, as Narciso Martínez did, unless he was asked to do so for recordings or at dances (Garza Guajardo 1993, 22–27). His own compositions, mostly redovas, schottisches, and polkas, were written for the accordion, and he played both treble and bass parts, unlike Martínez and other Texas-based players of that time. However, in later recordings, he was often accompanied by the tololoche, which played simple accompanying patterns. Tejano accordionists of this time, such as Martínez, Santiago Jiménez, and Tony de la Rosa, were typically paired with the bajo sexto, which provided both the bass line and harmonic accompaniment, allowing the accordionists to focus on the melody in the treble side of the instrument (Peña 1981, 284–285).

Tanguma wrote and recorded sixty original compositions, many of which are now considered classic folk songs and are the basis for a folkloric dance tradition that is practiced today in schools, colleges, and community centers throughout northeastern Mexico (Garza Guajardo 1993). Ironically, many of Tanguma's compositions—such as "Monterrey Polka," "Evangelina Polka," and "El Cerro de la Silla" (the title of this last song refers to the saddle-shaped mountain that

---

[7]"In reality, my first compositions were always created in my mind, because when I worked in the fields, I invented the tunes and later could whistle them exactly. In 1938 I finished my first piece, 'From China to Bravo.' I didn't really give it that name, but since I was traveling from China to the Río Bravo, the name just stuck."

overlooks Monterrey)—are also part of the repertoire of traditional tejano con-junto accordionists. However, most of the accordionists I have spoken with who play Tanguma's compositions (aside from Martínez) were unfamiliar with the composer of these songs and referred to them as "folk songs from Mexico." Northeastern Mexicans, particularly in Nuevo León, regard Tanguma as a local hero and the father of música norteña. Even today, there are celebrations and festivals honoring his contributions to local culture and music, and a bronze statue of the accordionist stands in Monterrey (Garza Guajardo 1993). After his 1938 recording, Tanguma rarely traveled to the United States for work. He mar-ried soon after and remained in Monterrey, though, like Martínez, he was unable to make a living as a musician and had to take other jobs as well. Los Montañeses, on the other hand—who rarely performed with the accordion—maintained their status as "professional musicians," probably because of their connection to elite Mexican society in Monterrey. In fact, the group still performs today as a folkloric ensemble and is composed of some members of the Mier family along with other professional musicians.

As a solo accordionist, though, Tanguma was an anomaly. The same can be said of Los Montañeses. Though many local musicians and music historians con-sider these artists pioneers of norteña music, the next generation of musicians did not continue either instrumental tradition but rather forged a fusion of the two. Furthermore, continued travel across the border, the development of a Texas-Mexican recording and touring circuit, and a growing and increasingly nation-alistic Mexican music and film industry greatly influenced the next phase of the development of early norteña music. The Tanguma and Los Montañeses record-ings in the late 1930s reflected the need for the post-revolutionary government in Mexico to include regional traditions, culture, and values in the identity it shaped for the country. In his book on Mexican nationalism and business culture in the 1930s and 1940s, the historian Julio Moreno (2003) maintains that, for politicians and business executives, incorporating a romanticized interpretation of a rural and "traditional" lifestyle into modern industrial capitalistic development allowed for an all-inclusive definition of Mexican identity that was presented to both North American investors and the world community. The government wanted to present to the world, as well as to its own people, a unified Mexico that duti-fully carried out revolutionary ideals and took pride in its varied regional cul-tures, giving them national and international attention. However, García Flores pointed out in an interview with me that the Mexican government also noted the importance of recognizing regional diversity and allegiances that were main-tained by migrants traveling to Mexico City. One lesson learned from the Revolu-tion was the importance of incorporating regional (as well as indigenous) dif-ference into a cohesive Mexican national identity (personal communication).

In the late 1930s and early 1940s, the recordings of Tanguma and Los Mon-tañeses were two examples of early norteña style and culture, embodying the region's individualistic identity and its unique and steadfast assimilation of European and North American instrumentation and dance rhythms (e.g., polka, schottische, redova, mazurka, waltz, and foxtrot). No other region in Mexico had adopted the accordion or these dance traditions as its primary folk music repertoire. The majority of research and writing about regional folk music in Mexico was (and still is) focused on the string-based son ensemble traditions, in particular, son *jarocho*, son *huasteco*, and son *jalisciense* (the basis of the modern mariachi tradition). However, by the 1940s, Mexico had a keen interest in the border region in response to increased travel of immigrants and expanding North American investment. Interest in recording authentic música norteña developed among major labels in Mexico City, particularly Latin divisions of many North American–owned companies such as Capitol, Peerless, Decca, and Columbia (Rogelio García, personal communication). Yet label executives considered the purely instrumental sound of Los Montañeses and Tanguma dated because the 1940s saw a surge of popular singers like José Alfredo Jiménez, Jorge Negrete, and Pedro Infante, who had relocated from different cultural regions to Mexico City. Label executives also thought the instrumental sound of Los Montañeses and Tanguma was insufficiently "mexicanized." Moreno Rivas explains that in the 1940s, producers were looking to "modify" regional music and to update it for radio and film (1979, 188).

As part of the process of modernization, particularly in Mexico City, the capital was grossly expanded by rural-to-urban migration. The maintenance of regional songs (as a part of cultural identity) was important in the urbanization process. However, in this context they were transformed to coincide with the rapid industrialization and modernization experienced by the city and the country (Moreno Rivas 1979, 188–189). The invention of the microphone allowed for a more intimate experience between audience and performer, and the film industry helped bring urbanized regional singing stars even closer to the public. The popular brass and string sound of modern mariachi music (which was itself an amalgamation of folkloric and popular styles) had exploded in Mexico City in the 1920s and 1930s but was now considered loud and folksy in comparison to the canciones románticas of singer/composers like Agustín Lara, Pedro Infante, and popular vocal trios (inspired by Cuban groups like Trío Matamoros) such as Los Panchos and Los Dandys. These groups also enjoyed great success in the United States as representatives of modern Mexican music (Moreno Rivas 1979, 158–162). The popularity of romantic crooners like Bing Crosby and Fred Astaire penetrated the popular music consciousness in Mexico as well. Thus, when Mexico City recording executives returned to northern Mexico looking for regional music to fit their "nationalistic" and "urban" criteria, they discovered the music of Los Alegres de Terán, an accordion-based duo already known in the border region for updating the regional norteña ensemble sound.

## Música Norteña: From Folk to Modern

The duo of Tomás Ortiz and Eugenio Abrego, known as Los Alegres de Terán, was already popular in the border region for fusing traditional and newly composed corridos and canciones rancheras with the accordion and bajo sexto guitar (later accompanied by tololoche). The duo was known to the border community because they had traveled between the town where they met and started the group—General Terán in the state of Nuevo León—and McAllen, Texas, where they worked as both laborers and musicians. On the Mexican side of the border, local researchers and music fans speak of General Terán as an unusually active center for music, particularly for the new accordion-based ensembles (personal communications with García Flores, Rogelio García, Julián Garza, et al.). There are reports of the popularity of accordion and bajo sexto duos in the cantinas of General Terán in the 1930s, where patrons and musicians sang traditional and popular songs of the day to polka, waltz, mazurka, and huapango dance rhythms (personal communications with Carlos Salazar, García Flores, and Cavazos). One of the very first groups to record for the Falcon label, Los Alegres de Terán had amassed a following in the border region, particularly among laborers in the Rio Grande Valley and in bordering Mexican towns. In 1948, the same year they recorded for Falcon, they also recorded for the Monterrey-based Orfeo Records, and, in addition to promoting the group in Mexico City, Orfeo made the record available to radio stations in Monterrey and throughout Nuevo León, Tamaulipas, and Coahuila. Falcon also recorded another similarly styled vocal duo with accordion, Los Donneños, which featured Ramiro Cavazos and Mario Montes. Though Los Donneños were also quite popular in the border region, Los Alegres de Terán traveled more often between Mexico and Texas.

The singing male duo tradition had a long history in the region, and, in fact, some of the first recordings of Mexican music made by Bluebird and Columbia were of border-based guitar and vocal duos like Jesús Maya y Timoteo Cantú (who also recorded as Maya y Cantú) and Pedro Rocha y Lupe Martínez (Rocha y Martínez). Los Alegres de Terán (their first recording was originally released under Abrego y Ortiz) and Los Donneños were the first to popularize the accordion ensemble with vocals on recordings of norteña music in the border region (personal communications with García Flores, R. García, and Cavazos). Los Alegres' addition of vocals was likely influenced by Mexican singing stars of the time, such as Jorge Negrete, Luis Aguilar, and Miguel Aceves Mejía, who also popularized regional songs as a means to connect with migrant Mexicans living in large cities like Mexico City and Monterrey and who were regularly promoted on Mexican radio and in films.

Though Ortiz and Abrego lived part of the year on the Texas side of the border, their popularity on the Mexican side spread widely, and they became some of the most influential representatives of modern norteña music (personal communications with Cavazos and García Flores). They are one of the few early norteña groups known to most Mexicans. However, the duo's popularity derived not so much from basic instrumentation of accordion and bajo sexto—though it was indicative of the ensemble tradition being established in the region (and not found in other parts of Mexico)—as from their *dueto* (duo) singing style and the many corridos and canciones románticas they composed (which have since been recorded by numerous norteña groups). Unlike that of Los Montañeses and Antonio Tanguma in Mexico and that of Narciso Martínez and Valerio Longoria in Texas, the popularity of Los Alegres de Terán was driven by the melodic and harmonic sophistication that resulted from the combination of a well-established regional tradition and the new accordion-bajo sexto ensemble sound popular among traveling migrants on both sides of the border. The traditional sung dueto of the region generally featured a guitarra sexta or bajo sexto along with a vocal line sung by two vocalists in parallel thirds in a strophic and exhaustive "running" narrative style (Paredes 1993, 236–238). In his book of border songs, *A Texas-Mexican Cancionero*, Américo Paredes emphasizes how the simplicity of this singing style and the guitarra sexta accompaniment allow the listener to focus on the unfolding storyline of the narrative corrido (1976, 64). He writes that "the most specialized of our border singers were far from being sophisticated musicians. The chords and the melody line are the simplest and most necessary ones for accompaniment. The fewer musical butterflies, the more genuine and honest the performance will be" (Paredes 1976, xxiv).

One of the earliest "border conflict" corridos, "Gregorio Cortez," tells a story that takes place in southern Texas in 1901. It narrates the famous search for a Mexican ranch hand (Cortez) who murdered a sheriff who, moments earlier, had murdered Cortez's brother Ramón (Paredes 1976, 31). The transcription shown in Figure 3.4 is of the first recording of this corrido by Rocha and Martínez in 1929 on RCA's Vocalion label. (It has been performed on numerous occasions since the turn of the twentieth century and has many variants.) Paredes writes that this corrido is "sung a bit more slowly than the average corrido, with the basses on the guitarra sexta strongly accented" (1976, 64). However, this recording is typical of corrido performances before the mid-1940s. In it the poetic and rhythmic structure is focused on the recurring music of each stanza, which allows for the unfolding of the story. The guitar accompaniment alternates between E7 and A in a waltz-like rhythm throughout with a two-measure interlude between each stanza. Like most traditional border corridos, "Gregorio Cortez" has no refrain and the lyric content of each stanza is new (McDowell 1981, 56).

This corrido is sung in a series of four-line strophes. Each line contains eight syllables, and the last word of even-numbered lines is controlled for the purposes of rhyme or assonance. This is typical of Spanish poetic meter (also known as the romance or ballad meter), in which the final stress of each line is always on

FIGURE 3.4 Transcription of "Gregorio Cortez," mm. 1–19. Author unknown (probably written in 1902). As performed and recorded by Pedro Rocha (guitarra sexta, voice) and Lupe Martínez (first voice). The approximate starting tempo (♩.) is 52. In measure 4, the tempo accelerates and is faster throughout the song.

(Originally recorded in San Antonio, Texas, in October 1929 for Vocalion Records and now available on *Mexican American Border Music, Vols. 6 and 7: Corridos y Tragedias de la Frontera* [Arhoolie/Folklyric CD 7019/7020].)

the last, penultimate, or antepenultimate (third to last) syllable (Lauer 2002). In some cases, an unstressed syllable at the end of a line is counted as two as a means of lengthening a poetic line, as in line 3 in the next example (McDowell 1981, 57). As in many Spanish songs, the sung accents are also imposed by the rhythm and are regular, always falling on the second, fourth, and seventh syllables in a rhythmic pattern in keeping with the corrido's triple meter (*En el condado del Carmen*). The act of prolonging or accentuating these three syllables of the lines throughout this corrido produces "the perception of a repetitive grouping" (Fraisse 1982, 149). However, McDowell argues that the prolongation of random syllables within the verse line is associated with musical rather than poetic considerations. While this feature is in keeping with Spanish poetic devices such as *diéresis* (lengthening of a poetic line), McDowell is correct in finding some musical logic in this device: Each musical phrase in "Gregorio Cortez" begins with a quick upbeat, followed by a prolonged downbeat. This opening gambit gives the melody its distinctive jauntiness and clearly defines the boundaries of musical phrases within the corrido (1981, 69).

The lyrics of "Gregorio Cortez" are shown in Figure 3.5. The assonant rhyme (*rima asonante*) occurs when the last stressed vowels of all the even-numbered lines (*versos pares*) rhyme, leaving the odd-numbered lines (*versos impares*) unrhymed. Also, only strong vowels (*a, e, o, i, u*) count as vowel rhymes and weak vowels (like the unaccented *i* or *u*) in diphthongs are ignored (Lauer 2002). Therefore, in the third stanza the word *después* rhymes with *Cortez* since *ez* is pronounced as *es* in Spanish in the Americas. In the last line of the first stanza, the accent on the fourth syllable is stronger because of a double beat that occurs on the second syllable in the previous three lines. The basic syllabic structure is illustrated in the first stanza that follows.

In the first two quatrains, we can almost immediately see one of the most distinctive corrido practices, which is to create action and to get the song moving from the very beginning. The three primary stresses that are coupled with extended long syllables are found in the second line (*miren lo que ha sucedido*)

---

### Gregorio Cortez

| | |
|---|---|
| En el condado del Carmen<br>1  2  3  4 5  6   7   8 | In the county of Carmen |
| miren lo que ha sucedido<br>1 2  3   4      5 6 7 8 | look what has happened |
| murió el Cherife Mayor,<br>1  2      3  45  6 7/8 | the head sheriff has died |
| quedando Román herido<br>1  2   3   4   5    6 7 8 | and Román has been wounded |
| | |
| Otro día por la mañana | The next morning, |
| cuando la gente llegó, | when people arrived, |
| unos a los otros dicen: | they said to each other: |
| "No saben quien lo mató." | "Nobody knows who killed him." |

*(continued on next page)*

FIGURE 3.5  "Gregorio Cortez." Author unknown (probably written in 1902). (From *Mexican American Border Music, Vols. 6 and 7: Corridos y Tragedias de la Frontera* [Arhoolie/Folklyric CD 7019/7020]. English translation of lyrics from CD liner notes courtesy of Arhoolie Records.)

## Gregorio Cortez *(continued)*

Se anduvieron informando,
como tres horas después
supieron que el malhechor
era Gregorio Cortez.

They investigated
and about three hours later
Gregorio Cortez was the
wrongdoer.

Insortaron a Cortez
por toditito el estado:
"Vivo o muerto que se aprehenda
porque a varios ha matado."

A warrant for Cortez's arrest
was issued throughout the state:
"Bring him in dead or alive;
he is wanted for murder."

Decía Gregorio Cortez
con su pistola en la mano:
"No siento haberlo matado,
al que siento es a mi hermano."

Gregorio Cortez said,
with his pistol in his hand:
"I'm not sorry for killing him,
my concern is for my brother."

Decía Gregorio Cortez
con su alma muy encendida:
"No siento haberlo matado,
la defensa es permitida."

Gregorio Cortez said,
with his soul ablaze:
"I'm not sorry for killing him,
self-defense is justifiable."

Venían los americanos
que por el viento volaban
porque se iban a ganar
tres mil pesos que les daban.

The Americans were coming
as fast as the wind,
because they would earn
a reward of 3,000 pesos.

Tiró con rumbo a González,
varios cheriffs lo vieron,
no lo quisieron seguir
porque le tuvieron miedo.

He fled toward González.
Several sheriffs saw him
but they didn't want to pursue him
because they were afraid.

Venían los perros jaunes,
venían sobre la huella,
pero alcanzar a Cortez
era alcanzar a una estrella.

The hound dogs were coming,
following his trail,
but catching Cortez
was like reaching for a star.

Decía Gregorio Cortez:
"¡Pa' qué se valen de planes,
si no pueden agarrarme
ni con esos perros jaunes!"

Gregorio Cortez said:
"Why do you even try,
you can't even catch me,
with those hound dogs!"

Decían los americanos:
"¿Si lo vemos qué le haremos?
si le entramos por derecho
muy poquitos volveremos."

The Americans said:
"What shall we do if we find him?
In an open confrontation
only a few of us will make it back."

*(continued on next page)*

**FIGURE 3.5** *Continued*

## Gregorio Cortez (continued)

| | |
|---|---|
| En el redondel del rancho<br>lo alcanzaron a rodear,<br>poquitos más de trescientos<br>y allí les brincó el corral. | By the corral of the ranch<br>they surrounded him.<br>There were more than 300 men,<br>but he jumped through their ring. |
| Allá por el Encinal,<br>asegún por lo que dicen,<br>se agarraron a balazos<br>y les mató a otro cherife. | Around El Encinal,<br>according to what they say,<br>they had a shoot-out<br>and he killed another sheriff. |
| Decía Gregorio Cortez<br>con su pistola en la mano:<br>"No corran rinches cobardes,<br>con un solo mexicano." | Gregorio Cortez said,<br>with his pistol in his hand:<br>"Don't run, you cowardly Rangers,<br>from one lone Mexican." |
| Giró con rumbo a Laredo<br>sin ninguna timidez:<br>"¡Síganme rinches cobardes,<br>yo soy Gregorio Cortez!" | He turned toward Laredo<br>without any fear:<br>"Follow me, you cowardly Rangers,<br>I am Gregorio Cortez!" |
| Gregorio le dice a Juan<br>en el rancho del ciprés:<br>"Platícame qué hay de nuevo<br>yo soy Gregorio Cortez." | Gregorio says to Juan,<br>at the ranch of the cypress:<br>"Tell me, what's new,<br>I am Gregorio Cortez." |
| Gregorio le dice a Juan:<br>"Muy pronto lo vas a ver,<br>anda háblales a los cherifes<br>que me vengan a aprehender." | Gregorio says to Juan:<br>"You will soon find out.<br>Go and call the sheriffs,<br>tell them to come and arrest me." |
| Cuando llegan los cherifes<br>Gregorio se presentó:<br>"Por las buenas sí me llevan,<br>porque de otro modo no." | When the sheriffs arrived<br>Gregorio turned himself in.<br>"You can take me only on my<br>own terms and no other way." |
| Ya agarraron a Cortez,<br>ya terminó la cuestión,<br>la pobre de su familia<br>la lleva en el corazón. | They caught Cortez<br>and the case is closed.<br>His poor family<br>is always in his heart. |
| Ya con esta ahí me despido<br>con la sombra de un ciprés,<br>aquí se acaba cantando<br>la tragedia de Cortez. | I now take my leave,<br>by the shade of a cypress tree.<br>Here I end the song of<br>the tragedy of Cortez. |

**FIGURE 3.5** *Continued*

and give the listener the sense that the narrator is actually present at the scene of the crime, which heightens the tension of the corrido from the beginning. "Look at what has happened" is the translation of this line, which prepares the listener for the next line and the next strong and extended long syllable at the beginning of it: *murió el cherife mayor,* which speaks of the death of the county sheriff. In fact, we are given a brief summary of the crime that Gregorio Cortez supposedly committed in the first four quatrains before his name is mentioned. The counterpoint and syncopation that occurs between the verse and rhythm places the listener alongside the narrator, in the heart of the action. Each line of eight syllables contains the same melodic figure that ascends from the lowest note in the range and descends within a third of the final note. This figure is repeated in each melodic line.

The vocal style of both singers is an impersonal, emotionless tone, since the singer of corridos during this time was not typically the composer and was regarded more as a storyteller and historian than as a musician. Border corridos are generally sung in parallel thirds with the second voice singing relatively high in its vocal range, a feature that today's singers of corridos emphasize and embellish. By the 1930s and 1940s, border singers would be influenced by popular singers of romantic ballads and rancheras, and they began to develop a more emotional style (expressed in vocal delivery and instrumental effects), though still maintaining the traditional dueto form. In later years, as the corrido absorbed influences from film and other mass media and began to be accompanied by a wider range of instruments—such as the accordion, saxophone, electric bass, and drums—the relationship between musical and poetic considerations became more complex and intertwined, as is evident in the Los Alegres example that follows later in this chapter.

Like Rocha and Martínez, Los Alegres de Terán (see Figure 3.6) remained true to the working-class regional dueto vocal style, but added melodic and harmonic depth to the overall performance by including an accordion introduction that lasts four measures (the length of two lines of the six-line stanza) and by replacing the guitar with the bajo sexto and later adding the tololoche. Since some accordion ensembles in General Terán often featured the tololoche, it is likely that the idea (and the instrument) traveled from Mexico to the border region and later into southern and central Texas. There is documentation that the instrument traveled from Monterrey to nearby regional towns like General Terán as part of nineteenth-century *orquestas típicas* (Ayala Duarte 1995, 50–53).

## Los Alegres de Terán:
## "Los Padres de la Música Norteña"

Los Alegres de Terán have often been referred to as "los padres de la música norteña" (the fathers of norteña music), in part for their most memorable

**FIGURE 3.6** Los Alegres de Terán in a photo from their CD taken in the early 1950s. Tomás Ortiz (bajo sexto and first voice) and Eugenio Abrego (accordion and second voice) with an unknown tololoche player. (Photo courtesy of Arhoolie Records, CD 9048.)

contribution to the development of the modern norteña sound: the pairing of the accordion, an instrument of migrant laborers that linked Mexico to "el otro lado" (in this case Texas), with vocal music. In the late 1930s and early 1940s, this was a novel idea; vocal music was typically accompanied by the guitar only. On both sides of the border, the accordion–bajo sexto combination was restricted to instrumental music for dancing. Similarly, other instrumental ensembles such as tamborileros and small orchestras never featured vocal music. Julián Garza is a well-known composer of corridos and canción-corridos from the early 1960s to the present and a member of the Monterrey-based norteña group Luis y Julián. In an interview, he recalled the impact these elements had on Los Alegres' career and the development of a popular norteña ensemble sound.

"Hasta que Los Alegres de Terán empezaran a tocar y grabar, era raro oír alguien canta con acordeón. Recuerdo a acordeonistas como Narciso Martínez, Antonio Tanguma y Pedro Llerena que tocaban huapangos, polcas y redovas, pero de forma instrumental . . . no cantaban. Los Alegres fueran los primeros a cantar con la acordeón y llegaron a ser muy famosos"[8] (personal communication).

The following transcription is of the first stanza of one of the duo's earliest recordings, a canción-corrido written by Tomás Ortiz and entitled "Carta Jugada" (Played Card), which they recorded for Falcon in 1953. It features accordion and bajo sexto, though the group was performing regularly with the tololoche by the mid-1950s. Peña has defined the canción-corrido as combining the lyrical features of the typical *canción mexicana* (canción romántica or canción ranchera) with some of the narrative features of the corrido (1999a, 70). However, one might also consider it a modern variant of the corrido, which features at least three components of the traditional narrative border ballad song structure as described earlier. The advent of commercial recordings also necessitated the shortening of narrative corridos into Tin Pan Alley–like song form with alternating repeated musical sections (AABAB).

"Carta Jugada" reveals some of the stylistic nuances employed by the group to update the traditional border corrido form, rendering it more musically expressive. The example opens with an instrumental introduction that features Ortiz playing the accordion in a descending scale from d1 to a2. Ortiz also executes short melodic phrases on the accordion in the flowing, legato style that was initially popularized on early recordings by Narciso Martínez on Bluebird and Ideal. Abrego accompanies Ortiz, playing the bass line on the bajo sexto, alternating between the tonic g and d on accents one and three, and strumming the offbeats.

However, in order to give focus to the narrative text of the song, short accordion fills are played after the first two lines of each of the six-line stanzas. Though most traditional border corridos featured four-line strophes, some had six lines (in corridos with mostly four-line strophes), and this would become a common feature of the modern canción-corrido. A longer accordion fill, based on the song's melody, is played after the final extended stress of the last word of the stanza (i.e., amor, amar, pensar, regresar, pensar). The musical elaborations on the canción-corrido form represent the group's most significant contribution to the modernization of norteña style. This song form omits the address, farewell, and other details such as date, time, and place, though it maintains the basic song structure and rhyme scheme of the traditional cor-

---

[8]"Until Los Alegres de Terán began playing and recording, it was rare to hear an accordion with singing. I remember listening to accordionists like Narciso Martínez, Antonio Tanguma, and Pedro Llerena playing huapangos, polkas, and redovas, but it was always instrumental, no singing. Los Alegres were the first to bring the accordion and singing together, and they became very famous."

rido: eight syllables in each line, three-stress rhythmic pattern, assonant rhyming on even-numbered lines, and the lengthening of poetic lines, in which the last word of even-numbered lines is controlled for the purposes of rhyme or assonance. It also features a refrain, which lasts for one stanza and is repeated at the end of the song.

Unlike the traditional border corrido that focuses on the heroic or tragic deeds of another person, the song's text elaborates the singer's own emotional involvement and the feelings of anger and frustration of a spurned lover. Ortiz accompanies the vocal line on bajo sexto in a structure similar to that of the guitar accompaniment in Rocha and Martínez's "Gregorio Cortez" example. In the Los Alegres example (transcription in Figure 3.7; lyrics in Figure 3.8), the bajo sexto also emphasizes the alternating movement of the waltz-like bass line

(continued on next page)

FIGURE 3.7 Transcription of "Carta Jugada," mm. 1–85: accordion introduction, first stanza, refrain (B section) and accordion solo playing refrain melody. Written by Jesús Cabral in 1953. Originally performed and recorded in 1953 by Los Alegres de Terán. Featuring vocals, accordion, and bajo sexto.

(From the CD *Cincuenta Años de Historia Musical* [Protel-Uni 6160524, 1999 (reissue)]. "Carta Jugada" by Jesús Cabral. Lyrics copyright © 1953 by Editorial Mexican de Música. Used by permission. All rights reserved.)

(continued on next page)

**FIGURE 3.7** *Continued*

(continued on next page)

**FIGURE 3.7** *Continued*

**FIGURE 3.7** *Continued*

while the offbeat is strummed. Like Rocha and Martínez, Ortiz and Abrego sing in parallel thirds, but with the second voice sung in a high register that produces a vocal strain, thus bringing more emotion to the song and its subject matter. The song also features vocal melismas, which are typical of Mexican popular romantic singing style.

In this composition, Ortiz and Abrego draw the listener more deeply into the story line by organizing each stanza into a complex poetic structure that is framed by the accordion and accompanying instruments. The first two lines, which do not rhyme with each other, act as the stanza's "head," representing an observation of the singer's dilemma or situation:

(1) Hoy no maldigo a mi suerte  Now I no longer curse my luck
(2) hoy no maldigo a tu amor,   now I no longer curse your love,

A short accordion fill follows the second line, which is prolonged on the final syllable. The next two lines (three and four) are the "body" of the stanza and detail a type of action or thought process leading to a resolution or decision to

## Carta Jugada

*A*

Hoy no maldigo a mi suerte,
  1  2   3 4 5   6  7 8
hoy no maldigo a tu amor,
  1  2   3 4 5  6  7/8
sólo maldigo tu vida
1 2  3 4 5 6 7 8
porque me sobra el valor
 1  2  3  4  5  6  7/8
para sacarme una espina
1 2 3 4  5   6  7 8
que me (ha) clavado tu amor.
  1   2     3 4 5 6 7/8

Now I no longer curse my luck,

now I no longer curse your love,

I only curse your life

because it gives me great satisfaction

to remove the thorn

that your love nailed into me.


*A*

Seguir contigo es inútil
tú no me supiste amar.
Me voy por otros senderos
a ver si puedo encontrar
los brazos de otras mujeres
para poderte olvidar.

To continue with you is useless
you did not know how to love me.
I'll travel on other paths
to see if I can find
the arms of other women
so that I can forget you.


*B (refrain)*

Te di mi amor y mi vida
sin que pudiera pensar . . .
que fueras carta jugada
que no se debe apostar,
por eso cuando ganastes
te fuistes sin regresar.

I gave you my love and my life
without realizing that
you were the played card
that should not be wagered,
that's why when you won
you left without coming back.


*A*

Por eso ya que te marchas
no pienses en regresar.
Que no te sigo adorando,
ya me cansé de llorar,
voy a tirarme a los vicios
para poderte olvidar.

That's why you should go
and don't think about coming back.
I don't love you anymore,
I'm tired of crying,
I'll throw myself into vices
so that I can forget.


*B (refrain)*

Te di mi amor y mi vida
sin que pudiera pensar . . .
que fueras carta jugada
que no se debe apostar,
por eso cuando ganastes
te fuistes sin regresar.

I gave you my love and my life
without realizing that
you were the played card
that should not be wagered,
that's why when you won
you left without coming back.


**FIGURE 3.8** "Carta Jugada." Written by Jesús Cabral. Syllabic structure is illustrated in the first stanza, and the AABAB song form is indicated.

(Copyright © 1953 by Editorial Mexican de Música. Used by permission. All rights reserved.)

come (in the final two lines). The fourth line rhymes with the second, though it is not prolonged:

(3) sólo maldigo tu vida      I only curse your life
(4) porque me sobra el valor,      because it gives me great satisfaction,

The fifth and sixth lines represent a "coda" in which the final line is prolonged and indicates a final resolution to the problem hinted in the first two lines. A longer accordion fill places emphasis on this definitive action or decision, linking it back to the first two lines and creating a sense of anticipation for the next stanza:

(5) para sacarme una espina      to remove the thorn
(6) que me ha clavado tu amor.      that your love nailed into me.

The overall stanza form can be described as AABAB (as indicated in the transcription and the song lyrics that follow) and is similar to that of popular ballads and songs heard in North American musicals from the 1930s and 1940s and in Mexican films of the 1940s and 1950s. Like many popular ballads, "Carta Jugada" features a refrain, which is shown in the B section, and is also a six-line stanza in the dominant chord of the key (G major), appearing after the second stanza. The refrain is repeated again as the final stanza of the song. These new poetic and musical features of the canción-corrido are likely the result of demands from recording producers for shorter, more memorable melodies that would help sell recordings. The typical border corrido such as "Gregorio Cortez" lasted for over twenty minutes, while this recording of "Carta Jugada" is two minutes and forty-two seconds long. The overall structure of the song is the following:

Accordion introduction with accompaniment (mm. 1–8)

### A (first stanza):
First line of the stanza is sung with stressed final syllable (mm. 9–11)
The final syllables on the second, fourth, and sixth lines rhyme and are
     prolonged on the second and sixth (mm. 15–16 and 31–32)
Accordion fill with accompaniment (mm. 17–18)
Lines three through six are sung to complete the stanza with rhymed,
     stressed final syllables (mm. 19–32)
Longer accordion fill (mm. 32–36)

### A (second stanza):
Repeat pattern for first stanza

### B refrain (third stanza):
First two lines of refrain are sung with stressed final syllable (mm. 37–44)
Accordion fill (mm. 45–47)

Lines three through six are sung to complete the stanza with rhymed,
   stressed final syllables (mm. 47–60)
Entire melody of refrain played by accordion with accompaniment (mm.
   60–85)
Repeat same pattern for A (fourth stanza)
Repeat same pattern for B (fifth stanza), except refrain melody is not played
   on accordion with accompaniment, only short coda (four measures).

Though Los Alegres attained popularity on both sides of the border, they
were marketed more aggressively by major label distributors such as Discos
Columbia in Mexico City and Orfeo in Monterrey, who marketed the group to
the rest of the country as the first "stars" of norteña music (personal communications with Cavazos, Julián Garza, and García Flores). It is important to note that
Los Alegres is not the first group to sing with the accordion ensemble or other
instruments. Monterrey-based groups—such as Los Rancheros de Topo Chico,
Los Gorriones de Topo Chico, and Los Broncos del Norte—were singing corridos, rancheras, comic songs, and romantic songs, which occasionally paired the
accordion with saxophone. However, these groups did not travel outside the
region much and rarely played for immigrant audiences in the United States. Nor
did they adhere to the dueto singing style and corrido tradition that were so well
established in the border region. Los Alegres' regional audience consisted mostly
of migrants who were traveling back and forth across the border for work, as well
as Norteño migrants living in Mexico City and Monterrey. Since the group
recorded simultaneously in Mexico (with Orfeo and later Discos Columbia and
Del Valle) and for the Texas-based Falcon Records, their music reflected the
nomadic lives of working-class Mexicans, whether they were crossing the border
to work in the fields or uprooting their families from rural parts of Mexico and
moving to cities like Mexico City and Monterrey to look for work.
   Both Ortiz and Abrego were prolific writers of corridos and canción-
corridos; Tomás Ortiz is credited with over five hundred compositions. The
group not only wrote canción-corridos about lost love and the breakup of the
family—"Carta Jugada," "Cuatro Espadas" (Four Swords), and "El Amor de Mi
Madre" (The Love of My Mother)—they also wrote and recorded numerous
corridos documenting border heroes, smuggling, and the myriad of social and
economic hardships that were the result of travel by Mexican workers, such as
"Dos Amigos" (Two Friends), "Los Tequileros" (The Tequila Smugglers), "La
Carga Blanca" (The White Cargo), and "Los Contrabandistas" (The Smugglers).
Los Alegres, however, enjoyed only minor recognition farther north of the border and among Tejanos who credit accordionist Valerio Longoria with introduc-
ing the concept of singing with the accordion to the tejano conjunto repertoire.
Peña describes Longoria's introduction of the Cuban-Mexican bolero (which
was already standard among Monterrey-based groups) to the repertoire as "an
historically significant accomplishment," and Longoria is said to have elevated

the conjunto to a "new level of sophistication" (1999a, 99). Many Texas-Mexicans who had left the border region and migrated to cities like San Antonio, Houston, and Corpus Christi considered popular singing artists from Mexico City and Monterrey to be more "sophisticated." Migrant working-class music groups situated on the border—like Los Alegres and Los Donneños—who either composed new corridos or prominently featured them in their repertoire were not as popular among Tejanos.

However, nearly every norteña musician, historian, producer, radio deejay, or fan I interviewed for this research noted the importance of Los Alegres de Terán as innovators of norteña style and as song writers and recording artists. Even today, almost every young norteña group features songs written by either Ortiz or Abrego or popularized on recordings by Los Alegres de Terán. After the release of "Carta Jugada," the dueto vocal style featuring the accordion and bajo sexto tradition would become standardized in the Rio Grande Valley region of Texas and northern Mexico as well as among new artists establishing themselves in the United States. Popular northern Mexico artists—including Luis y Julián, Carlos y José, El Palomo y el Gorrión, Los Cadetes de Linares, Poncho Villagomez y Los Coyotes del Río Bravo (who paired the accordion with the saxophone), Ramón Ayala y Los Bravos del Norte, and Los Tigres del Norte—would continue the tradition by recording songs based on the canción-corrido song form popularized by Los Alegres and would travel more extensively to immigrant audiences and their families on both sides of the U.S.-Mexico border.

The working-class community in Mexico embraced the accordion-based, norteña ensemble sound of Los Alegres because of the group's ability to merge sophisticated vocal harmonies and arrangements with an updated corrido narrative form that, in addition to love songs, included themes of travel, alienation, and nostalgic images of rural and ranchero life. Roberto Javier, an elderly resident of Santa Inés, a rural village in the state of Puebla, said in a 2003 interview that "Los Alegres de Terán were the fathers of norteña music; from 1948, they were the originals, they were like the Mexican Beatles" (personal communication). When I asked Javier how he first heard norteña music, he said that it was the early recordings of Los Alegres de Terán and their first hit song, "Carta Jugada," in particular, that introduced him, his brothers, and many other migrant workers and farmers from his village and nearby villages to norteña music. Javier also noted that he first heard Los Alegres on the radio and then on the jukebox in a cantina in a working-class neighborhood on the outskirts of Mexico City. The singer and bajo sexto player Poncho Villagomez, who formed his group, Los Coyotes del Río Bravo, in Monterrey in 1955, offered a similar account in an interview. Villagomez is the proprietor of one of the earliest independent record labels based in Monterrey, Del Bravo Records, which is still active and dedicated to the recording and production of norteña music. He also formed the first musicians' union there in 1964 (personal communication). Villagomez recalls being inspired to become a musician at the age of fourteen after seeing Los Alegres de Terán perform in a local village dance: "Yo les vi en un baile y estaba cerquito para verlos bien y para oírlos. Traían guitarra de doce cuerdas, acordeón de dos literas y bajo sexto. Y así pegaran muchísimos, para las voces, la música, y toda su forma de tocar. Porque sus voces eran universales, muy sofisticados por los hechos de que gustaban. En 1948 grabaron en Orfeo y también Falcon y Columbia y fue la 'época de oro' para ellos y su música"[9] (personal communication). As migrant workers and folk musicians, Los Alegres represented Norteño culture and peasant life on many levels. They were viewed as traveling workers, crossing to "the other side" when necessary in an effort to take care of their families. However, their sophisticated arrangements for the accordion, bajo sexto, and tololoche; their expansive repertoire of original epic-like corridos and romantic canción-corridos; and their close harmonies proved a perfect balance between working-class ideology and entrepreneurial spirit. Los Alegres knew how to connect to their local audience but were also aware of their role as representatives of a regional genre that was compelled to compete with the "urban" popular music singers marketed by major labels such as Peerless and Columbia, as well as in Mexican films, during the 1940s and 1950s.

Los Alegres de Terán became a distinctive and long-lived norteña group who, though breaking up temporarily in the 1960s, almost single-handedly introduced norteña music and style to the rest of Mexico during the 1940s and 1950s. Los Alegres, who stopped performing in the late 1970s, continued to base themselves simultaneously in McAllen, Texas, and in Monterrey, Nuevo León, Mexico, and often left the border region for long stays in Mexico City. It was primarily through their recordings for Columbia Records in Mexico that the group became known throughout that country as representatives of what was then a regionally specific music genre. As the music initially associated with migrant laborers in the border region, Los Alegres' narrative corridos and more romantically inclined canción-corridos also struck a chord with the large numbers of rural migrants, many from northern states, who were flooding into Mexico's capital. As the first popular "norteña" ensemble, Los Alegres made an impact that was greatly aided by their ability to tap into the feelings and experiences of the growing Mexican migrant population of the late 1940s and 1950s.

Texas-Mexican conjunto artists, particularly those who have remained close to the border, such as Rubén Vela y su Conjunto, Los Fantasmas, Los Hermanos Cárdenas, and Rubén Naranjo y Los Gamblers, have also continued to sing in

---

[9] "I saw them in a dance, and I was very close, so I could see and hear them very well. They had a guitar with twelve strings, accordion, and bajo sexto. They were a big hit because of their voices, the music, and the whole way that they played. It was because their voices were universal, very sophisticated, and for that the people liked them. In 1948 they recorded on Orfeo, also Falcon and Columbia. It was the 'Golden Age' for them and their music."

the dueto style popularized by Los Alegres, though they primarily sing rancheras and cumbias and still play instrumental polkas, redovas, and huapangos. Contemporary tejano groups (mostly based in and around San Antonio) have completely moved away from the corrido or canción-corrido tradition and, since the late 1950s, have focused more on the brisk, staccato articulations on the accordion that are played continuously behind the voice and not only at the end of stanzas (a legacy of the influence of Tony de la Rosa, Santiago Jiménez Sr., Valerio Longoria, and El Conjunto Bernal). They also perform rancheras, cumbias, and love ballads. Since most Texas-Mexicans had stopped migrating for work by the early 1960s, they lost interest in the corrido, which by this time had begun to focus on the experience of border crossing, migration, work, and marginalization. Later, corridos would address issues of dual identity, Mexican politics and corruption, drug trafficking, changing male-female relationships, and other subjects more specific to the migrating Mexicans and their families.

Rogelio García, a Mexico-based border deejay who has been on the air since the 1960s, said in a personal interview in 1998 that "the accordion is fundamental in norteña music, just as it was in the early development of Texas conjunto. But for Mexicans, and for the undocumented on the other side who wants to remember his history and his family, the corrido is very important. In Texas it is gone and has been so for many years. But every Mexican knows that norteña has to have the corrido, and not just those songs from the past but from today" (personal communication). The late 1940s would prove to be a crucial period both culturally and politically in the border region, particularly as a result of growing numbers of traveling migrant workers. The early stages of the development of Tejano and Chicano identity and the Mexican American middle class created another set of racial and class-based distinctions that were being played out in southern Texas and the border region. The establishment of independent, Mexican American–owned recording studios during this period helped disseminate and establish norteña in response to social experiences. However, the separate and distinct stylistic evolutions and audience responses associated with Ideal and Falcon respectively reveal an ideological split between assimilating, upwardly mobile Texas-Mexicans and nomadic, working-class Mexican nationals.

Until the Bracero Program ended in 1964, most traveling Mexican workers tended not to remain in the United States, making it easier to preserve strong ties to regional Mexican roots as well as to popular music and culture in Mexico. However, the influx of undocumented Mexican workers into the United States, the resulting militarization of the border region by North American politicians, the Mexican government's continued failure to control that country's economic downturn, and the peso devaluation further marginalized the traveling Mexican worker. The perpetual outlaw status of many undocumented workers and ambivalence toward a Mexican nationalist identity has facilitated the development of norteña as a unique northern Mexican and border music phenomenon of a modern Mexican diaspora in the making. As the popular music of Mexican immigrant and migrant workers, norteña has flourished and evolved because it incorporates the celebrated defiance and mythology of the border hero (who was also the first migrant worker) and because the topical nature of the corrido allows for constant dialogue and collaboration between communities on both sides of the border, a back-and-forth that spurred the creation of a dynamic popular music genre and a multibillion-dollar transnational industry.

# 4

# Modern Música Norteña and the Undocumented Immigrant

In his work on Mexican nationalism and the shaping of modern Mexico, Julio Moreno (2003) suggests that, prior to the 1920s, most Mexicans tended to identify with their local region rather than with the nation at large. Because the Mexican Revolution was triggered by upheavals in the country's far North and in states with large indigenous populations such as Oaxaca, Puebla, and Morelos, the Mexican government placed much emphasis on embracing its indigenous and peasant communities. This goal, however, coexisted with the government's commitment to commercial and industrial growth and foreign investment, leading Moreno to conclude that most Mexicans defined national identity as an "all-inclusive concept" (2003, 9). This definition, he asserts, includes indigenous heritage, peasant tradition, entrepreneurship, industrial spirit, and regional diversity of the country as both patriotic symbols and products of the revolution.

The emergence of norteña music, as popularized in the border region and among Mexico's working class by Los Alegres de Terán in the 1940s, is representative of Moreno's notion of Mexican national identity. Not only did the nationwide distribution of recordings by the group transform a regional folk song form—rooted in the Mexican Revolution, social banditry, and rural Norteño life—it also touched the lives of many migrating Mexicans who were leaving their homes for work and, for those crossing the border, coming into contact with a new, more industrialized society. The chronicles of this experience, whether accounts of border crossing or of its impact on family life, make norteña an idiosyncratic fusion of tradition and modernity that helps maintain cohesion within a community that has remained marginalized and is constantly traveling.

## Popularizing Norteña and the Norteño Image in Mexican Cinema

During the 1940s and 1950s, norteña music was also popularized in many Mexican films that idolized rural ranch life in the same vein as Hollywood westerns, especially those featuring singing cowboys like Roy Rogers and the Sons of the Pioneers. Norteña music and Norteño culture were disseminated regionally and nationally not only through radio and the recordings of Los Alegres de Terán and others who followed them (e.g., Los Donneños, Los Broncos de Reynosa, and Luis y Julián) but also through film. The first Mexican-made films, which appeared around the same time that many now-classic revolutionary corridos were written, were documentaries of the Mexican Revolution of 1910 (Paranaguá 1995, 1). The Alva brothers (Salvador, Guillermo, Eduardo, and Carlos) were among the first principal documentary filmmakers of early Mexican cinema. Their exhaustive filmed chronicles of the revolutionary leaders Francisco I. Madero and Pancho Villa celebrated the fearless and defiant nature of the Norteño spirit and culture (Paranaguá 1995, 5–7).

Even after the industry began making feature films instead of documentaries, the Norteño revolutionary hero Pancho Villa (along with Emiliano Zapata) continued to be a favorite topic for filmmakers, particularly after his assassination in 1923. Villa was also a popular hero of border corridos. This topical ballad tradition inspired many films about his exploits, such as *La sombra de Pancho Villa* (The Shadow of Pancho Villa), *El tesoro de Pancho Villa* (Pancho Villa's Treasure), *¡Vámonos con Pancho Villa!* (Let's Go with Pancho Villa), as well as about the exploits of other real and invented border heroes. With large numbers of peasants migrating to Mexico City and across the border after the revolution, it was in the best interest of the industry and filmmakers alike to celebrate rural heroes, ranch life, and the importance of family (Paranaguá 1995, 1). The renowned Mexican novelist and social critic Carlos Monsiváis argues that "the culture industry removes from collective experience a large number of customs drawn from the countryside and rural Hispanic culture, and cinema plays a major part in its pruning" (1995, 120). In particular, the humble though fiercely independent peasant of the North, who instigated the revolution that would eventually change the course of Mexican history, captured the imagination of both national and international audiences and became a favorite source of entertainment for the Mexican people through corrido production and the film industry alike.

The "Golden Era" of Mexican cinema, 1938–1953, saw a marked increase in general film production—to over seventy per year—surpassing that of Argentina and Spain. Though this production level somewhat threatened the domination of North American films in Mexico, it did not erase Hollywood's influence (de la Vega Alfaro 1995, 84). Westerns were hugely popular in Mexico. Like the Southwest for the western, Mexico's northern frontier was the dominant setting for the enormously successful *comedia ranchera* (rural, peasant comedy) film genre (Paranaguá 1995, 3–4). This tradition has its roots in the Spanish *sainete* (one-act farce) and the zarzuela (comedic operetta), which were popularized in the Mexican countryside by traveling tent shows called *carpas* (Medina de la Serna 1995, 163). In his book, *Cinema of Solitude: A Critical Study of Mexican Film, 1967–1983,* Charles Ramírez Berg (1992, 98) explains that the comedia ranchera glorified the prerevolutionary past in which all people—from the powerful *hacendado* (ranch owner) to the tenant farmer to the indigenous Mexican—knew and accepted their positions in society. A central figure was the *charro,* or Mexican cowboy, who often dressed in an opulently decorated riding costume symbolizing his connection to rural aristocracy, and who helped define the macho singing cowboy (particularly in its prototype, Jorge Negrete) in the national consciousness during the 1940s.

Since the nineteenth century, Mexicans have both idolized and fantasized about the valiant and humble "Norteño" peasant cowboy, very much in the way North Americans have imagined the western frontier and the Texas cowboy. However, the late 1930s and early 1940s macho image of the singing charro and the glorification of the northern frontier and ranch life in such films as the 1936 *Allá en el Rancho Grande* (Over on Big Ranch) and the 1937 *Soy charro de Rancho Grande* (I'm the Cowboy of Big Ranch) led some scholars to argue that these films overshadowed the progressive reforms of then president Lázaro Cárdenas, who was shifting land ownership away from the ranch owners (de la Vega Alfaro 1995, 84).

Another genre associated with northern Mexico and the U.S.-Mexico border is films that focus on immigration. From the 1922 silent film *El hombre sin patria* (Man without a Country), Mexican filmmakers historically portrayed Mexican American immigrants as traitors to their country and heritage for having left Mexico and adopted a North American way of life (Martínez 1998, 31). By the early 1960s, the undocumented immigrant became a central character who, though marginalized, developed a distinct identity as defiant and hypermacho, even though it is clear that this is a façade behind which he hides the reality of his existence (Martínez 1998, 32–33). This is because, by the early 1960s, many more individuals had traveled or planned to travel to the United States for work and not just from the country's far North. Mexicans from north-central and central regions were now traveling as well. More families were feeling the loss of having a loved one leave home for the United States, and they were also benefiting from the dollars that were sent back. By the late 1960s and early 1970s, increasing numbers were traveling illegally, making the adventure more dangerous and garnering more sympathy from Mexicans who stayed behind. The undocumented immigrant was portrayed in the films in a sympathetic light as a victim of poverty and governmental neglect. Though, like the Mexican American cowboy, he has left his country, he always carries the hope that he will one day return. Many of these films, such as the 1954 *Espaldas mojadas* (Wetbacks) and the 1958 *Los desarraigados* (The Uprooted) assigned much of the blame for the undocumented immigrant's situation to the Mexican government. Although they deal in sad situations, the border cinema scholar Glenn Martínez describes immigration films, like the comedia ranchera, as largely comedic "oral performance culture" (1998, 32), harking back to the carpa (traveling tent show) tradition. Though there are also dramatic representations of the immigrant experience, most immigration films focus on the loss of a "Mexican" identity and the negative outcomes of such travel to argue against further immigration (Herrera-Sobek 1998, 227–228).

While the corrido tradition has both informed and inspired Mexican cinema, particularly the comedia ranchera and immigration genres, throughout its history, corridos have also been used to frame films, to provide closure, to develop a particular theme, to foreshadow events to come, and to give additional information on a film's plot (Herrera-Sobek 1998, 230). What both the corrido tradition and these film genres have in common is an attempt to extract humor from difficult and oppressive circumstances where the hero's integrity and vulnerability are always challenged.

## El Piporro: Modern Norteño Archetype

The comedia ranchera film genre produced two legendary stars: Jorge Negrete and the comedian Cantinflas (Mario Moreno). These actors, who were also singers, acted out the lives of rural peasants on an idyllic ranch or the lives of migrants navigating their way in urban Mexico City and yearning for the simple ranch life they left behind. Comedia ranchera movies reflected the nostalgia of Mexicans who migrated from their regional homelands to Mexico City beginning in the 1930s. The music generally associated with these films was mariachi, often accompanying leading ranchera singers and film stars. By this time, mariachi had expanded to include brass instruments, and the repertoire merged folkloric *sones* (partially improvised song-poems) from Jalisco and other nearby states with popular ballads and rancheras (pastoral country songs). Comedia ranchera films, and the songs associated with them, became popular not only throughout Mexico but among Spanish-speaking North Americans and throughout Latin America as well.

Beginning in 1950, the singer/songwriter and comedian Eulalio González Ramírez, alias El Piporro, began making movies that might still be classified as comedia ranchera, though they often presented a more realistic view of rural Mexico and the effects of migration. As the decade wore on, and nearly four million Mexicans crossed the border to participate in the Bracero Program, González's films focused more specifically on northern Mexico, the border region, and the experience of border crossing. These films also included original and popular corridos, rancheras, and canciones románticas, often performed by accordion-based norteña ensembles (rather than the typical mariachi), capitalizing on the more modern style popularized in recordings by Los Alegres de Terán. González, who was born in a small border town called Los Herreras in the state of Nuevo León, began his career as a radio personality and later developed into a comic actor, singer, and songwriter. In many of González's films—*Calibre 44* (Colt 44) from 1959, *El terror de la frontera* (The Terror of the Border) and *El rey del tomate* (The Tomato King) from 1962, *El bracero del año* (Laborer of the Year) from 1964, *El pistolero desconocido* (The Unknown Gunman) from 1966, *El pocho* (The Mexican American) from 1969, and others—along with the music, he popularized the Norteño charro look and attitude as both brave and humble, but always with an edge of humor and irony.

González often portrayed comedic heroes who traveled north either as braceros or mojados. Many of his protagonists drew upon stereotyped characteristics of border corrido heroes, such as their macho tendencies and love of tequila, pistols, and women. However, in the end, his character's willingness to sacrifice himself for love of country, family, and an honest and "simple" way of life often prevailed, as it did among scrappy characters in traditional border corridos. González merged stereotyped border characters, such as the tequila smuggler and pistol-packing outlaw, into his witty though often bumbling macho persona. In many ways, González was an imitator of the legendary Cantinflas, known for his almost incomprehensible speaking style filled with puns and wordplay and his *pelado* (poor, urban slum-dweller) characters, who were usually pathetic, misunderstood, and marginalized by society (Medina de la Serna 1995, 167). González also spoke with an identifiable (and often exaggerated) Norteño accent and his song lyrics were riddled with colorful local vernacular. He was a folk hero to Norteños as he struggled to maintain his simple, hard-working life, and this was how he marketed his persona to the Mexican and Mexican immigrant public. González's portrayals of constant run-ins with the border patrol and conflicting Anglo-American social and cultural influences (both in his songs and movies) positioned him—along with his fellow Norteños—on the front lines of a newly expanding and complex Mexican social space that was rapidly developing in the border region and the Southwest during the late 1950s and 1960s.

González is significant because, as did the music of Los Alegres de Terán and other norteña ensembles, his celluloid persona embodied a sense of nostalgia for Norteño machismo, autonomy, and defiance, particularly among Mexican immigrants who were increasingly marginalized by their undocumented status. He expertly merged these traits with the backwardness of an uneducated and unsophisticated rural peasant faced with uprooting himself and his family in order to live a marginalized existence in a foreign culture. For working-class Mexicans who were migrating either to Mexico City, Monterrey, or northward across the border, González represented the schism between harsh reality and collective fantasy and imagination, always portraying an unwavering dedication to his "mexicanidad" and maintaining Mexican pride and patriotism despite the pressure to assimilate. In his films, González (as El Piporro) brings a transnational and transcultural nature to an already fetishized Norteño persona. The merging of the macho, gun-toting Norteño with the border-crossing (and now increasingly illegal) immigrant and the bumbling, unsophisticated peasant represent what Edberg identifies as "shared situations of social stratification" (2004, 123). While few Mexican actors were involved in film production, González wrote, directed, and starred in many of his films, actions that were likely connected to the autonomous nature of Norteño culture and society.

González's initial contributions to the comedia ranchera genre came after its popularity had started to wane among the general public in Mexico. From the late 1960s to the 1980s, he was practically the only actor keeping the genre alive, and, by this period, his audience was largely made up of working-class Mexicans, mostly in the North, and immigrants living in the southwestern United States. Carlos Monsiváis eloquently articulates the impact on Mexican popular culture and society of González's unique persona, one that would be shaped and reshaped by many norteña musicians to come: "Piporro nace y vive en el norte abandonado e ignorado por el centralismo, que protege o inventa su identidad acudiendo a un habla muy asentada todavía en los arcaísmos mexicanos, penetrada por fuerza por los anglicismos y compuesta por refranes, decenas de miles de comprimidos de la sabiduría comunitaria."[1]

Gonzalez was one of the first actors to maintain an audience on both sides of the border, largely through a series of immigrant films he starred in, directed, and produced. He managed to portray either one or a combination of characters from the scrappy border cowboy to the hard-working bracero to the undocumented immigrant. González was a border native who understood and sympathized with the border-crossing experience (see Figures 4.1 and 4.2). He merged his own Norteño identity and experiences with those of undocumented laborers, an increasing number of whom were traveling from regions much farther south in order to cross the border by the late 1960s. González's portrayals not only offered comic relief in the midst of displacement and oppression but also legitimized the existence and transnational importance of this rapidly growing migrant worker community that was burdened by the humbling experience of living outside the law, marginalized by the language barrier and cultural differences, and treated as second-class citizens with no rights to healthcare or wage management.

In his writings about Mexican immigrant films, Martínez asserts that many such films, including those produced by González, functioned as "a device for

---

[1] "Piporro was born and lived in the north (that was) abandoned and ignored by the central government and that protects or invents its identity in a voice that remains deeply entrenched in Mexican archaisms, penetrated by force by Anglicisms, and composed of proverbs and tens of thousands of bits of collected common wisdom." Interview by Arturo García Hernández, "*Piporro, un gran improvisador de la tradición: Monsiváis,*" *La Jornada*, March 25, 1999.

**FIGURE 4.1**  Eulalio "El Piporro" González playing the role of Natalio Reyes Colas (a Nat "King" Cole parody), a Mexican worker who enters a fantasy world where he is celebrated as the "Bracero del Año" (Laborer of the Year) and wins a brand-new convertible and the affections of a beautiful, blonde North American woman.

(From the film *El bracero del año*, directed by Rafael Baledón, First Look Home Entertainment, 1964.)

**FIGURE 4.2**  González (as Natalio Reyes Colas) performing one of the many jobs available to Mexican workers in the United States.

(From the film *El bracero del año*, directed by Rafael Baledón, First Look Home Entertainment, 1964.)

dismantling national borders and the methods used in controlling them" (1998, 45) and thus served to form and strengthen mojado identity. These films might also have been a response to increased restrictions on legal resident visas in the United States after the Bracero Program ended. Undocumented migration rose substantially during this period, and travel was highly circular (Massey, Durand, and Malone 2002, 69–70). Traveling Mexicans often maintained the idea that they would return home, whether this dream was realistic or not. They were unlikely, or unwilling, to identify with the assimilated Mexican American or Chicano who, in many immigrant films, was depicted as a traitor to his own culture and heritage. Martínez observes that the assimilated Mexican American is often viewed in immigrant films (and Mexican society in general) as "lazy and lacking in family values" (1998, 36). The disconnect between the Chicano and his Mexican cultural heritage reduces his identity to a "projection of hegemonic Anglo culture" (Martínez 1998, 37). Moreover, the illegal status of many Mexicans workers and their tendency to hold onto their Mexican and regional identity make it difficult to integrate into a more assimilated Chicano society. The loss of one's legal status once one crosses the border is also connected to the loss of identity and power, particularly among this population. Piporro's focus on the plight of the undocumented Mexican worker offers a new configuration of Mexican identity that is based on the border-crossing experience, the desire to return home and a loyalty to family and one's Mexican (and regional) heritage. Piporro's use of the accordion-based norteña ensemble and the corrido song form to express these things positioned the music and the industry to focus more directly on migrating Mexican workers and the mojado experience.

González's high visibility and commercial success as El Piporro in films and recordings among Mexican audiences both north and south of the border signaled the beginning of the transnational reach of norteña music and culture. His popularity came at a time when upwardly mobile Texas-Mexicans and Mexican Americans claiming Spanish (but not Mexican) heritage in the Southwest were demanding equal rights as North American citizens in an emerging Mexican American civil rights movement (known as the Chicano Movement or El Movimiento). The movement began in 1966 with the demand for restoration of land grants to descendants of Spanish and Mexican settlers in New Mexico. By the early 1970s, the movement took up the cause of farm workers' rights in California and demanded better schools in largely Mexican American neighborhoods and fair access to colleges and universities.

The Bracero Program's demise in 1964 meant that legal Mexican immigration was more heavily restricted, and it led, in part, to a massive influx of illegal immigrants. In 1965, the United States passed the landmark Hart-Celler Act, the basis of immigration law in the United States, which abolished nation-of-origin restrictions. It prohibited the denial of immigration and naturalization on the basis of race, sex, or nationality. This law established a new criterion for immigration that was based on kinship ties, refugee status, and "needed skills" (Graham 1995).

It was viewed as an extension of the civil rights movement, shifting the focus to non-European, or "third world," countries. It also gave higher preference to relatives of U.S. citizens and resident aliens, rather than to applicants with special skills, who had been the priority in the past. While the act abolished discriminatory and racially exclusive national origin quotas, it also had negative impacts. The law also established immigration ceilings for the Western Hemisphere, making it almost impossible for poorer immigrants to enter legally. These ceilings prompted massive increases in illegal immigration from the most impoverished places, such as Mexico, Central America, and the Caribbean. In the case of Mexico, travel to the United States for work had become a way of life for many (and for their American employers) since the turn of the twentieth century and had later been institutionalized by the Bracero Program, so it was difficult to control.

While organizations that emerged from the Mexican American civil rights movement (*El Movimiento*) lobbied federal and state officials on behalf of undocumented immigrants, they still experienced growing anti-Mexican sentiment among North Americans and tighter restrictions at the border (Gómez-Quiñones and Maciel 1998, 42–43). Although many of the more politically active Mexican Americans, now calling themselves Chicanos, took the undocumented immigrant's cause to heart, they also sought recognition as U.S. citizens. David G. Gutiérrez notes that many Mexican migrant and immigrant workers who traveled to the United States, particularly the Southwest, after World War II would have been able to improve their economic status by moving from entry-level, low-skilled jobs to skilled blue-collar positions with better pay and social status. Their children, who had the added advantage of greater fluency in English and access to higher levels of education, enjoyed even better chances of assimilating and finding higher-paying jobs. However, says Gutiérrez, by the early 1970s, spurred in part by the massive movement of undocumented immigrants, the prospects of better-paying jobs and a higher economic status began to flatten. By the 1990s, they were in serious decline (Gutiérrez 1999, 507–508).

Illegal status, economic disadvantage, the language barrier, lack of education, and increasing anti-Mexican and anti-immigrant sentiment among the general North American population created a schism within the ethnic Mexican population in the United States. By the early 1970s, class distinctions among the Mexican American population became more clearly defined. Along with these economic and class differences, the stylistic and compositional elements of the two accordion-based Spanish-language popular music genres that existed in the border region and the Southwest evolved to appeal to the two distinct Mexican American communities. As noted in Chapter 3, while Texas-Mexican conjunto, orquesta tejana, and later *música tejana* became more closely aligned with Chicanos and Tejanos living in southwestern states (e.g., California, Texas, Arizona, New Mexico, and southern Colorado), norteña musicians and their promoters concentrated on the newer (and increasingly undocumented) population that was spreading throughout the United States.

González, as El Piporro, was one of the first film actors to address the plight of the bracero (who, as a seasonal migrant laborer, returned often to Mexico) and later the undocumented immigrant. He was the first to record songs that, through sardonic humor and wit, transcended the dangers and trauma of border crossing to express a more modern and transnational notion of mexicanidad. It is a mexicanidad that reflects an identity that is not bound by Mexican and North American social, political, or geographic boundaries. González's songs, written in the narrative corrido form and backed by the typical norteña ensemble, created a space for both the Norteño and the mojado in the now politically volatile and increasingly hostile border region as well as in locations farther north in the expanding Mexican diaspora. This merging of the well-established and widely popularized image of the macho Norteño as cowboy, rebel, bandit hero, and outlaw with the border-crossing mojado—whose illegal status makes him an enemy of the (U.S.) state and naturally an outlaw—was personified by El Piporro on-screen and in his songs. This image would be copied and refined by many modern norteña groups, such as Ramón Ayala y Los Bravos del Norte, Los Tigres del Norte, Luis y Julián, Los Terribles del Norte, and more recently Los Tucanes de Tijuana. Similarly, the emerging transnational norteña music industry would continue to track the movement of Mexicans throughout the United States and systematically network with local Mexican promoters to establish Spanish-language radio stations, clubs, and an exhaustive touring circuit.

González wrote "Chulas Fronteras del Norte" (Beautiful Northern Borders) in 1963, and it inspired his film, *El bracero del año* (1964). The song was recorded by González as El Piporro, along with the norteña ensemble Los Madrugadores del Valle. In the song, written in Los Alegres-style canción-corrido form, El Piporro portrays the bracero who has just returned to Mexico and recounts how he managed to escape a border patrol officer by getting him drunk on tequila. The song's anarchistic humor plays against the vulnerable state of the mojado and the constant fear of being caught (and deported) by the border patrol, "reducing" this threat by defying authority and laughing in the face of the fear that dogs every undocumented worker in the United States (Martínez 1998, 34–35). El Piporro's invitation to his fellow workers and mojados to come to the "beautiful borders" where you will have a good time ("donde se van a gozar") serves to subvert the real-life danger of crossing and the constraining authority that the border has come to represent for Mexicans.

Prior to this recording, most songs about illegal border crossing focused on the hardship of the experience and its fearful consequences, such as jail, deportation, and even death. And though many songs by norteña composers have continued in this tradition, promoting what Martínez (1998, 34) describes as a "psychology of fear" among undocumented Mexicans, "Chulas Fronteras" (see Figure 4.3) and other mojado-themed songs written by González introduced a new sense of pride and commitment to a more defiant definition of "mexicanidad,"

## Chulas Fronteras

**_Hablado:_**
Ajúa! Ajúa!
"Chulas fronteras del norte,
como las extraño, no las diviso
desde hace un año." Ajúa!

**_Cantado:_**
Andándome yo pasiando [paseando]
por las Fronteras del Norte
¡Ay qué cosa tan hermosa!
De Tijuana a Ciudad Juárez,
de Ciudad Juárez a Laredo,
Laredo a Matamoros
sin olvidar la Reynosa.

Una muchacha en el puente,
blanca flor de primavera
me miraba me miraba.
Le pedí me resolviera,
si acaso yo le gustaba.
Pero ella quería otra cosa
¡le ayudara en la pasada!

**_Hablado:_**
Me vio fuerte de brazo,
amplio de espalda, ancho de pecho.
Pos me cargó de bultos.
ah qué mujer vieja tan chivera,
y yo haciéndole tercera.
Al llegar a la aduana me dice el
de la cachucha. "¿Qué llevas ahí?"
"Pos pura cosa permitida,
llevo comida."
"Mentira, llevas géneros."
Ah, qué sopor y qué bochorno
empecé a pasar aceite, raza,
sudé y sudé
de pura vergüenza.

**_Spoken:_**
Ajúa! Ajúa!
"Beautiful northern borders,
how I've missed you, I've not seen you
for a year." Ajúa!

**_Sung:_**
I was traveling
around the northern borders.
Oh what a beautiful thing!
From Tijuana to Ciudad Juárez,
from Ciudad Juárez to Laredo,
Laredo to Matamoros,
don't forget Reynosa.

A young woman at the bridge,
a beautiful spring flower,
was looking at me, looking at me.
I asked her to tell me, please,
if she liked me.
But she wanted something else,
for me to help her cross the bridge!

**_Spoken:_**
She saw my strong arm,
broad back, and wide chest.
She made me carry her stuff.
What a bossy woman.
When I reached the
customs office, the officer with the cap
asked, "What are you carrying there?"
"Only permitted things,
I bring food."
"Liar, you have other things."
Oh, what a stupor and what shame,
then came the heat, people,
I sweated and sweated
from embarrassment.

*(continued on next page)*

FIGURE 4.3   "Chulas Fronteras." Written by Eulalio "El Piporro" González Ramírez in 1964. The word *güey* (see page 111) sounds like "wai(t)." It is a popular Mexican explicative that is derived from *buey,* which means "ox" or "bull." *Güey* has many translations, such as "asshole," "jerk," and "idiot."
(From the CD *Lo Mejor de El Piporro,* a collection of songs by Lalo "El Piporro" [Musart CDN-034, 1987]).

## Chulas Fronteras *(continued)*

**Cantado:**

Antes iba al otro lado
escondido de la gente
pues pasaba de mojado.
Ahora tengo mis papeles
ya estoy dentro de la ley.
Tomo wiskey o la tequila
¡hasta en medio del highway!

**Hablado:**

"Ey tú, mecsicano. ¿Tú eres mojado?"
"Guara moment, güero, guara moment,
I am working here,
I working en di pizcas,
en the betabel an en di los arroces
I gara peipers, I gara peipers,
dis is mai picture, un poco bigotón
pero is mai picture."
"Bueno, sí, pero tú estas tomando."
"Bicos I jev money, and wit di money
dancing di dog.
Con dinero baila el perro.
Criatura, échate un trago,
no te vayas dioquis." "Oh, no!"
"I jev whiskey and tequila!"
"Oh, my, my tecaila!"
"No digas 'tecaila' porque
ándale, échate un trago."
"Este tecaila mucho caliente,
mucho picoso."
"Don't bi so flamer, don't be so flamer,
no seas flamero. Échate otro."
"No, otra vez será,
otra vez será."
"Bueno, I wait for you,
or you wait for me.
¡Mejor you güey!"

**Cantado:**

Yo les digo a mis amigos
cuando vayan a las pizcas
no se dejen engañar.
Con los güeros ganen lana
pero no la han de gastar.
Vénganse pa' la frontera
¡donde sí van a gozar!

**Sung:**

I used to cross over,
hiding from people,
because I crossed as a wetback.
Now I have my papers,
and I'm within the law.
I drink my whiskey or tequila
even in the middle of the highway!

**Spoken:**

"Hey, you, Mexican. Are you a wetback?"
"Wait a moment, whitey, wait a moment,
I am working here,
I am working in the 'pickings,'
in the beets and in the rice fields,
I got my papers, I got my papers,
this is my picture, I've got a moustache,
but this is my picture."
"Well, yes, but you are drinking."
"Because I have money and with money
'dancing the dog.'
With money the dog dances,
they say. Have a drink,
don't leave." "Oh, no!"
"I have whiskey and tequila!"
"Oh, my, my tecaila!"
"Don't say 'tecaila,' because . . .
go ahead, have another drink."
"This tecaila is very hot,
very spicy."
"Don't be so picky, don't be so picky,
no reason to be picky. Have another."
"No, another time I will,
another time I will."
"Okay, I wait for you,
or you wait for me
Better you güey!"

**Sung:**

I tell my friends
that when they go "picking,"
not to be deceived.
Make your money with the white men,
but don't spend it there.
Come to the border instead,
where you will have fun!

FIGURE 4.3  *Continued*

thus refashioning the rebellious attitude of the Norteño into a conscious resistance to acculturation and political socialization by North American society.[2]

El Piporro had a significant role in expanding the reach of norteña music through his unique and multifaceted personality and his close reading and representation of Norteño life, border culture, and border crossing. I met González in 1999, the year his autobiography ("autobiogr . . . ajúa!" as he called it) was published. He was performing at the impressive Auditorio Nacional in Mexico City as the headliner of a variety show featuring lesser-known musicians, comic actors, and dancers who harkened back to the 1950s and 1960s. Wearing his signature charro outfit with the ever-present pistol attached to his belt, the Norteño legend stood larger than life. At seventy-eight, he performed with mariachis, son ensembles, and norteña groups, but, as always, accompanied by his fellow Norteño Juan Silva, his accordionist since the 1960s. As he autographed a copy of his book for me, he spoke of why he wrote songs about braceros, mojados, Norteños, and *pochos* (Mexicans born or raised in the United States). "To me, it's not important that they live here or there," he said. "But they are Mexicans with the same skin color and the same blood running through their veins. My songs are for them and for me . . . so that we can laugh together" (personal communication). Because the artist's success depends on his or her fans, it is fitting to conclude this discussion of El Piporro with a quote from a fan in Monterrey, Nuevo León. This fan celebrates the comic actor/musician's humble, but proud, representation and reinvention of Norteño culture and identity through his mastery of the local idiom and comedic prowess. He also recognizes El Piporro's ability to redefine Norteño identity to include the migrating population from outside the region and, in particular, the illegal immigrant. This quote was posted on a Web site for El Piporro fans shortly after his death in September 2003:

Murió una parte del noreste. El ingenio del campo, de nuestra región, lo que éramos, hacer reír sin groserías, ser irónico con el machismo. Murió parte de lo bueno de nosotros, de nuestra identidad regional, lo mismo representaba al hombre Bronco del Norte. Pero con un gran corazón, como también representaba al norteño que se va de ilegal, que no es lo mismo un ilegal del norte, que los paisanos del centro y del sur de la república, todo encarnado en un personaje. Murió Don Eulalio González Ramírez, y con el se llevó [e]l crisol de nuestra identidad. "Piporro" qué vergüenza que ahora nuestros representantes sea el del otro rollo, que hace su comicidad a base de burlarse de su público, con groserías, a falta de ingenio. Murió el ingenio y ahora da paso a la generación del insulto y del lenguaje limitado. En fin, así es la vida.

---

[2] María Herrera-Sobek, who translated a different version of this song (1993, 168), also identifies "Chulas Fronteras" as part of a tradition of traveling songs because it mentions several border towns and cities (Ciudad Juárez, Laredo, Matamoros, Reynosa).

A part of the Northeast died. The genius of the countryside, of our region, of how we were able to laugh without vulgarity, to be ironic with machismo. The best part of ourselves died, our regional identity, which was represented by this man, "The Untamed of the North." With a big heart, he also represented the Norteño who traveled illegally—but not only the illegal [migrant] of the North but also countrymen from the central and southern states, all embodied in this one person. Sir Eulalio González Ramírez died, and he carried with him the crucible of our identity. "Piporro," how sad that our representatives will be of another type, who create their comedy by mocking their public, with vulgarity, and without talent. The genius died, and now comes the generation of insult and limited language. In the end, that's life.[3]

The music and popular persona created by El Piporro in the 1960s set the stage for norteña's future commercialization and transformation as the popular music of migrating and working-class Mexicans on both sides of the border. As I continued my research, I would be reminded of this time and again in conversations with numerous border-based norteña artists, fans, and scholars.

## Bringing Norteña to the People

Another important aspect of El Piporro's career was his many appearances in Mexico and the border region as part of traveling variety shows and concerts. These shows were rooted in the tradition of the carpa, which was popular in Mexico during the nineteenth and early twentieth centuries. Carpas were typically run by a family of entertainers and featured a mix of bawdy comedy, music, dancing, acrobatics, and clowns (Kanellos 1984, 43–45). Carpas became popular in the Texas-Mexican border region in the 1920s, eventually extending their reach across the Southwest. By mid-century, Mexican carpas had evolved into sophisticated floor shows or *caravanas* (caravans), which were organized by promoters and also featured Mexican folkloric dancing, mariachis with popular singers, comedians, movie personalities, and charros (rodeo cowboys who performed rope tricks and other horseback riding stunts). Eventually, these variety shows became too expensive to tour outside Mexico and played only occasionally in large urban centers like Los Angeles, Chicago, Houston, and San Antonio (Kanellos 1984, 14–16). As a result, El Piporro's popularity remained in Mexico. He explained to me that at that time it was difficult for Mexican artists to penetrate the migrant circuit dominated by Texas-based conjunto artists. However, through his songs and movies, El Piporro became the voice of not only Norteños but also migrating Mexicans to a national Mexican audience, both rural and urban and

[3] Sergio Javier García Zapata, "Correos pa'l neto relacionados con El Piporro," September 3, 2003, http://www.mxl.cetys.mx/neto/piporrp/popocor3.htm (accessed April 23, 2004).

### Los Mandados

| | |
|---|---|
| Crucé el Río Grande nadando, | I swam across the Rio Grande, |
| sin importarme dos reales, | without making a fuss, |
| me echó la migra pa' fuera | the border patrol threw me back out |
| y fui a caer a Nogales, | and I landed in Nogales, |
| entré por otra frontera, | I entered by another border crossing, |
| y que me avientan pa' Juárez. | and then I was thrown out to Juárez. |
| | |
| De ahí me fui a Tamaulipas | Here I headed to Tamaulipas |
| y me colé por Laredo, | and sneaked through Laredo, |
| me disfracé de gabacho | I disguised myself as a white boy |
| y me pinté el pelo güero, | and dyed my hair blond, |
| y como no hablaba inglés, | but since I didn't speak English, |
| que me retacharon de nuevo. | once again I was thrown out. |
| | |
| *(Chorus)* | |
| La migra a mí me agarró, | The border patrol has caught me, |
| 300 veces digamos, | say three hundred times, |
| pero jamás me domó, | but they haven't tamed me, |
| A mí me hizo los mandados, | they can't get the best of me, |
| los golpes que a mí me dio, | the beatings I took |
| se los cobré a sus paisanos. | were later paid for by their countrymen. |

FIGURE 4.4  "Los Mandados." Written by Jorge Lerma.

(Copyright © 1978 by Peer International Corp. Used by permission. All rights reserved.)

of all classes. His songs also inspired other well-known artists to reach out to the migrating Mexican audience, recognizing, among other things, their growing numbers, increasing spending power, and desire to remain connected to Mexico. One obvious example is the song "Los Mandados,"[4] written by Jorge Lerma and first recorded in 1965 by the legendary ranchera singer Vicente Fernández. The song, which makes clear references to El Piporro's "Chulas Fronteras," emerged as an anthem for border crossers (and relatives and friends in Mexico). According to many of my informants in Mexico, "Los Mandados" also served as a means for family members to support and share in the migrant experience. It has been recorded by numerous norteña and cumbia (also, *onda grupera*) artists through the years—including Monterrey's Los Bukis and Sinaloa's Banda el Recodo—and remains relevant today. The excerpt shown in Figure 4.4 reveals the song's defiant message.

---

[4]Literally translated, *los mandados* refers to those sent to do chores or errands. However, in the context of this song, the title refers to the Mexican slang phrase *Me hacen los mandados,* which can be translated as something like "They can't get the best of me" or "They can't keep me down."

## The Taco Circuit

By the late 1950s and early 1960s, as many Mexican immigrants and migrants were relocating to states farther north in small agricultural communities such as the Yakima Valley in Washington and in cities and towns in Illinois, Ohio, and Michigan, the demand for Spanish-language music became more widespread (Ragland 1994, 14–16). The Seattle-based musician/songwriter and former migrant worker Juan Barco told me in an interview that Texas-Mexican conjunto groups (initially those on Ideal and later popular tejano artists like Little Joe y la Familia) traveled outside the Southwest to perform for migrant worker communities (personal communication). By the late 1960s, fewer Texas-Mexicans and U.S.-born Mexicans traveled outside Texas and the Southwest for work and were subsequently replaced primarily by Mexican-born laborers, increasingly from regions farther south of the U.S.-Mexico border. Similarly, fewer tejano and orquesta groups traveled outside Texas and California. By the mid-1960s, the touring circuit for Spanish-language music (nicknamed the "taco circuit"), which had been mapped out in the first half of the twentieth century first by Tejano conjunto and later by orquesta groups, was increasingly dominated by norteña groups who were based on both sides of the border in the Texas-Mexico border region (Barco, personal communication). These groups expanded the reach of the touring circuit in response to the demand for Spanish-language music in new immigrant locales across the United States.

The extended reach of the Mexican immigrant population, driven largely by undocumented laborers, and norteña groups' subsequent expansion of the touring circuit, paralleled the commercialization of norteña music in the border region. The Texas-based independent recording labels were shifting their focus to orquesta and tejano music and the emergence of a regional recording industry and a network of Spanish-language radio stations. Subsequently, many bilingual, upwardly mobile Texas-Mexicans were leaving the border region and finding jobs in urban centers like San Antonio, Corpus Christi, Houston, and Dallas, which prompted similar moves by many border-based labels. In San Antonio and Corpus Christi in particular, Spanish-language and bilingual radio stations were rapidly dominating the airwaves, and local recording studios and labels, such as Zarape, Hacienda, and Dina, were responding to the demand for Tejano music.

In a similar fashion, the recording and promotional aspects of norteña music had shifted to the sprawling metropolis of Monterrey, Nuevo León (Raúl García Flores, personal communication). Rural-to-urban migration and the growth of breweries and large factories producing cement, glass, and automobiles helped to make Monterrey the third-largest city in Mexico and one of the most important manufacturing and trade centers. As the birthplace of Mexican radio, Monterrey was already established as a center for music recording activity. Since the early 1920s, México Music Copartícipe had administered commercial music recording and distribution, and by the later part of the decade, many other music recording houses, such as Orfeo, Disa, DLV, and Del Bravo Records, were established in the city (Ayala Duarte 1995, 27). While these labels initially focused on classical, jazz, municipal brass bands, and popular music genres, they eventually began to turn to norteña, particularly as the rapidly growing Mexican diaspora in the United States presented a new market for music production and touring (personal communications with Rogelio García and Ramiro Cavazos).

## Ramón Ayala

Servando Cano was one of the first Monterrey-based promoters to recognize the transnational popularity of norteña music. Today, Cano (who now runs the business with his nephew, Joel) is recognized within the norteña music industry as a pioneer who methodically mapped out an intricate touring circuit for artists, first in the United States and later in Mexico. Joel Cano said that, while the songs and films of El Piporro helped popularize norteña music outside the border region, particularly among undocumented immigrants, his uncle saw the importance of sending norteña artists across the United States to perform in cities with large Mexican populations as well as small rural towns where new immigrants were traveling (personal communication). Though Servando Cano worked initially in the region promoting artists such as Los Alegres de Terán and Los Donneños, by the late 1960s, these groups were considered too folksy for record producers in Monterrey. Additionally, these musicians were older and unable, or unwilling, to travel extensively outside the region. Cano was hoping to identify a young group with a contemporary norteña sound that he could market to commercial labels and radio stations in Monterrey and that would also be amenable to an exhaustive touring schedule. He found such a group in 1963 (Joel Cano, personal communication).

Los Relámpagos del Norte (The Lightning Bolts of the North) was formed as a duo in 1959 by two teenagers: Ramón Ayala on accordion and Cornelio Reyna on bajo sexto and lead vocals (see Figure 4.5). By the time Cano came across the group, which was based in Reynosa, Tamaulipas (just across the border from McAllen, Texas), they had added an electric bass and drums in the style of the popular Tejano conjunto dance hall sensation Tony de la Rosa (Ayala, personal communication). Ayala recalled that Los Relámpagos were originally "discovered" on the streets of Reynosa by Paulino Bernal, the cofounder (along with his brother Eloy) of El Conjunto Bernal, a popular Texas-Mexican conjunto group based in Kingsville, Texas. The Bernals had become known in Texas and California for their "experimentations" with the conjunto sound by performing with two accordions, singing in close three-part harmonies in a style similar to that of Trio Los Panchos (instead of the typical pinched, nasal, dueto vocal style of the border), incorporating string and brass instruments with "mariachi-style" arrangements, and adding original and popular Mexican romantic ballads and boleros to their repertoire (Peña 1985, 90–91). The Bernals realized that their

**FIGURE 4.5** Los Relámpagos del Norte: Ramón Ayala (*seated*) and Cornelio Reyna from the late 1960s or early 1970s. (Photo courtesy of Arhoolie Records.)

enormous success was due, in part, to their appeal to the newer Mexican immigrant population. In fact, they were unique among Texas-Mexican artists in their interest in actively pursuing this audience.

When the brothers decided to establish their own label, Bego Records, they sought out other new artists who might have a similar crossover appeal. What drew Paulino Bernal to Los Relámpagos was Reyna's voice, which, though clearly influenced by the popular ballad singer José Alfredo Jiménez, also featured elements of the rustic nasal sound of border dueto ensembles. As a songwriter, Reyna was a master of tragic love ballads, and while neither of these features was "typical" of norteña music of the time, Bernal envisioned a perfect blending of modern Mexican love ballads and the norteña ensemble sound forged by Los Alegres de

Terán (Ayala, personal communication). At this time the Mexican popular music industry, with its nationalist notions, had recruited romantic and ranchera singing stars from the different Mexican regions (Lola Beltrán from Sinaloa, Vicente Fernández from Jalisco, José Alfredo Jiménez from Guanajuato, Agustín Lara from Mexico City). But in northeastern Mexico the dueto singing tradition was still strong, and no one singer/songwriter had emerged. Reyna could be the one.

The first recording of the group released on Bego featured a collection of traditional rancheras and an original ballad by Reyna titled "Ya No Llores" (Don't Cry Anymore). The Bernals had hoped to market the music on both sides of the border, particularly in Monterrey, where they rightly believed a more sophisticated and widespread industry existed. However, the group's sound initially did not spark interest from Monterrey radio jockeys. Los Relámpagos did, however, pique the interest of Mexican immigrants in Texas. This development was enough to prompt Bernal to obtain work visas for the group and send them out on the taco circuit to great success (Ballí 2004). By the time Cano discovered the group, he felt they were ready to take on commercial radio in Monterrey and travel well beyond the Southwest-dominated taco circuit. Eventually, Cano did what the Bernals were unable to do: He connected the group with DLV Records, which began to distribute their recordings throughout northern Mexico. Los Relámpagos made eighteen records by the end of the 1960s, and by 1970 they were traveling to cities and rural villages throughout the United States and, eventually, Mexico (Ballí 2004).

What endeared Los Relámpagos to Mexican immigrant audiences in the United States initially was a combination of three primary factors: (1) musical and stylistic elements that updated the sound initially forged by Los Alegres; (2) the group's willingness to perform several concerts a week and in a wide range of makeshift venues, particularly in rural locations, often for much less money than they would make where they were better known in the Southwest and northern Mexico; (3) Reyna's Norteño image (the charro look), his loyalty to his northern Mexican heritage, and his interest in cultivating an audience in Mexico as well as the United States, all of which stood in contrast to tejano groups who created a distinctly U.S. regional music genre and identity based loosely on an older, almost fetishized imagination of Mexico.

Many of the musical and stylistic elements that Los Relámpagos added were similar to those introduced by Tony de la Rosa and other Tejano conjunto artists (i.e., electric bass and drums). However, Los Relámpagos revolutionized norteña style and established a standard for a modern commercial norteña sound. One important innovation was to play at least two full verses of the song's melody on the accordion and bajo sexto in the introduction, rather than playing no accordion introduction or a short introductory phrase. Another was the addition of extended melodic phrases and rhythms after each verse along with decorative runs on the bajo sexto. Finally, though the group maintained the pinched, nasal dueto harmonies, they were now sung with more precision and reserved primarily for the chorus, while the verses were dominated by Reyna's soulful voice. It is these stylistic elements that norteña groups continue to imitate today.

While several of my informants, whether they were musicians, promoters, or fans, identified one or all of these stylistic features, the majority also mentioned that Los Relámpagos were enormously popular because they were willing to travel the migrant route extensively and perform several concerts weekly. As a result, their popularity grew among audiences on both sides of the U.S.-Mexico border, something no other norteña or tejano group had accomplished before. The group's popularity, at first greatest among the largely undocumented migrant and immigrant traveling laborer community, soon soared among families and friends of migrants and immigrants who remained in Mexico, thus extending the popularity of modern norteña music farther south and across that country as well.

The concept of traveling for work is very much ingrained in rural and working-class Mexican society and culture, particularly in rural areas. Los Relámpagos' willingness to travel extensively on both sides of the border proved to be crucial not only to their own success but also later to Ayala's when he became the leader of his own norteña ensemble, Los Bravos del Norte. Ayala's own experience as a migrating, working-class musician deeply connected him and his music to the Mexican immigrant community in the United States. Joel Cano, who now handles most of the touring arrangements for Ayala and several other norteña groups, told me that what made Los Relámpagos and, ultimately, norteña music, so popular is that they would play anywhere, no matter what the location or how small the fee (personal communication). Tejano groups, in contrast, restricted themselves and their music to Texas, California, and a handful of other cities in the Southwest. Norteña groups, Cano says, would perform anywhere—plazas, clubs, dance halls, bingo halls, shopping malls—and in any village, town, or city on either side of the border. "The norteña groups opened up all of the markets that they could and the tejano [groups], no," he said. Ayala himself recognized Cano's vision of bringing the music directly to the people very early on when he would book the group to play at the bank where he had been working as a cashier: "I feel that he [Cano] was very important for our coming out. He brought the music to the people—initially in the banks, because he was a bank cashier, and he brought the employees together at the end of every month and created dances that were paid for by the employees of the bank in Mexico [Monterrey] and he contracted us. We went to Mexico and registered our group and he became our manager" (personal communication).

Los Relámpagos del Norte, featuring Reyna and Ayala, ceased to exist in 1981 when Reyna's star as a songwriter and singer began to rise in Mexico after his classic hit "Me Caí de la Nube" ("I Fell from the Clouds"). Reyna wanted to make a name for himself in Mexico City as a solo singing star and actor in Mexican musicals (Ballí 2004). During his lifetime, Reyna never reached the level of success he had hoped for, even though posthumously he became one of Mexico's most respected songwriters, alongside José Alfredo Jiménez, Agustín Lara, Fernando Solís, and others. Moreno Rivas states that Reyna is also the only norteña singing star to gain national attention, though she specifies that his "acclaim is from the Mexican immigrant public" (1979, 223). Reyna and Ayala eventually reunited in the mid-1990s (in actuality, Ayala allowed Reyna to join his already successful group) and performed a series of reunion tours, one concert of which I attended in Corpus Christi, Texas, in 1996. Reyna and Ayala played to a packed house in a large dance hall, and it was as though the Beatles had reunited; women and girls were screaming, and a sea of cowboy hats bobbed to the classic corridos, romantic ballads, and rancheras Los Relámpagos had made so famous. The group was dressed in the flashy charro outfits first popularized by El Piporro and now standard among norteña groups. In comparison to El Piporro and Los Alegres, Los Relámpagos had a more serious, deeply expressive tone that reflected the real-life experiences of the community for whom they performed. In 1997 Cornelio Reyna died of liver damage from years of drinking too much (Ballí 2004). Reyna truly lived the hard life he sang about: Heartbreak and estranged family life were often primary themes in his songs, such as "Aunque Tengas Otros Amores" (Although You Have Other Lovers), "Tengo Miedo" (I'm Afraid), "Rompiendo el Retrato" (Tearing Up the Picture), and "Me Caíste del Cielo" (You Threw Me from the Sky).

On his own, after Reyna's initial departure, and continuing today, Ayala and his extremely popular and important group, Los Bravos del Norte (see Figure 4.6), maintained the Los Relámpagos style and the gutsy emotion that is expressly directed to the traveling migrant laborer. However, Ayala made one important change after Reyna's departure that not only significantly increased his own popularity but also impacted the music of future norteña groups. While Ayala found a series of singers and bajo sexto players over the years to replace Reyna, he did not seek out a professional songwriter. Instead, he relied on a stable of respected amateur songwriters, usually fans, to supply him with songs, particularly rancheras and corridos, from both sides of the U.S.-Mexico border. Ayala's repertoire is not as strictly based on corridos as were those of groups before him; while he has recorded many corridos, he is also known for love ballads and rancheras based on true-life stories. In an interview in McAllen, Texas, Ayala explained that, though he had a handful of songwriters, many of his songs were collected on the road: "I've received songs and corridos from women and men on both sides [of the border]. They are simple and humble songs, but are about real life . . . from those who travel for work" (personal communication).

There is a feeling among many U.S.-based fans of Ayala, and also among many norteña groups whom he has influenced, that he is one of them. He understands their struggle, their pain and tragedies. In an interview, Raúl García Flores explained how Ayala's unique connection to the immigrant community and to the formation of a collective identity that still maintains a present-day Mexican framework in the United States helped to create today's transnational norteña

**FIGURE 4.6** Ramón Ayala (*seated*) with his new group, Los Bravos del Norte, in a publicity photo taken just after the group signed with the Mexican label Discos DLV in the mid-1970s. (Photo courtesy of Arhoolic Records.)

industry. "His [Ayala's] songs are simple and modest, but they are about the reality of life . . . especially those about the people who travel for work," García Flores said. "For the people who search for their identity, often the songs are about the experience of crossing or being in the United States. These songs are only listened to by these people who have more of a Mexican identity. This is how the Ramón Ayala phenomenon came about. The people have given him their experiences and then he gained popularity on the other side [Mexico] away from the border" (personal communication).

While casually talking to many immigrant fans of Ayala in Texas, Washington, Chicago, and New York, I often heard people call Ayala a hard worker, someone who "works as hard we do." It is widely known that Ayala and his group play no fewer than three shows a week, year-round (Ballí 2004). Though many Mexican workers in the United States are undocumented, they often participate in unions that fight for workers' rights (Gómez-Quiñones and Maciel 1998, 49). Pride in work and attention to a strong work ethic is part of Mexican rural and working-class culture, a value both respected and often exploited by many North

American employers. Traditionally the "job" of musician and, in particular, the conservation of musical practice is the domain of "músicos campesinos que la ejecutaban en sus ranchos" (peasant musicians who perform on their ranches; Medina Montelongo 1995, 97). The association of norteña with Mexican laborers, particularly fieldworkers who worked in the slave-like peonage system in sprawling haciendas, is deeply rooted in northern Mexican history and culture. María Herrera-Sobek notes that some of the earliest recruitment of Mexican workers was for the building and maintenance of railroads throughout the United States beginning in the mid-1850s. Campesinos, primarily from the northern states, who were tired of the oppressive peonage system, gladly accepted work on the railroads in the hope of bettering their station in life. They brought their music tradition with them, and Herrera-Sobek collected numerous songs dating back to this period that detail their grueling labor (1993, 34–35). Most corridos and rancheras in the norteña tradition have continued to focus primarily on experiences associated with work, whether it involves traveling, crossing the border, obtaining a green card, having conflicts with bosses and the border patrol, or struggling through an economic crisis. Work (particularly physical labor) is central to the construction of identity and collective consciousness among Mexican laborers who cross the border, even though there is a feeling among them that it is valued less in North American culture (personal communications with García Flores and Ayala). In my conversation with Ayala, he showed an acute awareness of norteña's deep association with work experiences and the great respect afforded to those who do not shy away from hard work. Ayala said that he felt compelled to "trabajar tan duro como mis paisanos" (work as hard as my countrymen), performing all year long in small villages, towns, and cities, anywhere migrant and immigrant workers are located, throughout the Mexican diaspora (personal communication). Ayala's sentiment was echoed time and again by many of the musicians whom I interviewed, whether they are local musicians known only to their community or, like Ayala, part of a transnational network of recording and touring artists. To their fans, these musicians' work ethic is just as important as their music itself.

After Los Relámpagos dissolved, Ayala formed his own group and became known to the Mexican immigrant public and working-class people in Mexico by many grand and endearing names: "El Rey de la Acordeón" (The King of the Accordion), "El Más Grande de la Música Norteña" (The Greatest in Norteña Music), and "El Triunfador de Siempre" (The Victor, as Always) (Ballí 2004). And though he is not known for his technical prowess as an accordion player, his status as a pioneer of the genre is deeply associated with his accessibility to his fans and his willingness to act as a true voice of the people by singing their songs. As Ayala's popularity grew among Mexican immigrants in the United States and their families and friends in Mexico, he never ceased traveling and always maintained a humble, working-class image and strong family life (having four children and being married to the same woman for thirty-five years), all of which his fans know well. Furthermore, Ayala is seen as a true border artist, born in Reynosa on the Mexican side and living most of his adult life just two miles from the border on the Texas side. His physical presence in the border region, his dual status as both Mexican and North American, and his position as the first truly transnational recording and touring artist make him an authentic Norteño as well as a norteña musician. The following is an excerpt from an article on Ayala written by the journalist Celia Ballí in 2004 for the monthly English-language glossy magazine, *Texas Monthly*. Though Ayala has sold more records than most other Texas-based popular music artists, this is the first full-length article on him to appear in an English-language publication. This excerpt eloquently describes the working-class appeal of Ayala and his music, which, in a sense, is what unites Mexicans living on both sides of the border:

> The city awakes. It is dark still in the Rio Grande Valley, but the bus drivers, the construction workers, the college students, the office secretaries switch on their radios, and it's Ayala who begins their day, with a tragic corrido or a jumpy cumbia that makes the feet dance. In Monterrey, Mexico, the sun pokes its head; the dump-truck operators, taxicab drivers, nannies, and housewives turn on their radios, and there too, it's Ayala. This stretch running north through Mexico, crossing the border and spilling east, west, and north into Texas, is a land of song, a place where music wakes up before most and goes to sleep after all, providing a constant backdrop for everyday life. Take a drive, listen. It is creeping out of everywhere, seeping through crevices, breathing: alive. And in this region, despite efforts in the music industry to distinguish between tejano and norteño—between Texan and Mexican music—Ayala is universally king. (Ballí 2004, 140)

## Tejano versus Norteña: Dueling Accordions in the Border Region

Ayala's popularity as a true border artist depended at first on his ability to compete with Texas-Mexican conjunto artists and the local tejano recording industry while maintaining a connection with new immigrating Mexicans who continued to cross the border in ever greater numbers. Later the emergence of a commercial genre called cumbia norteña (or *onda grupera*) promoted by major Mexican labels in Monterrey—beginning in the late 1970s and continuing through the early 1990s—prompted Ayala to record more love ballads and commercial rancheras, many of which were sung to a "danceable" cumbia rhythm. However, Ayala knew his audience, and his dedication to the corrido and to employing composers of topical corridos was also crucial to his survival among local audiences. The emergence of the narcocorrido during the early 1970s—spearheaded by the California-based Los Tigres del Norte—led Ayala to focus on songs that only slightly updated the pistol-packing border bandit hero. While drug trafficking was a way of life for some Texas-Mexican border residents, modern corridos composed by songwriters in this region rarely celebrated it as such. It was up to the listeners to scrutinize the song and decide for themselves the nature of the clandestine activities of many of the outlaw characters in Ayala's corridos, as well as those by many other northeastern Mexican composers. As it was for working-class border heroes such as Gregorio Cortez and Mariano Reséndez, the new outlaws' fight for the right to make a living and to preserve the dignity and honor of one's family is made difficult by border patrol agents, poverty, racism, and attempts by both the Mexican and American governments to "tame" the last frontier.

Ayala's growing popularity among the Mexican immigrant population in the United States and a growing population settling in the Texas-Mexico border region did not go unnoticed by *música tejana* groups, particularly in the lower Rio Grande Valley region (Ragland 1994, 91). While musicians in San Antonio and cities and towns farther away from the border region focused their attention on an upwardly mobile and bilingual Tejano population, many groups located in border towns on the Texas side—such as Brownsville, Mission, Harlingen, Edinburg, McAllen, and Laredo—were forced into direct competition with Ayala and other rising norteña groups from the other side of the border, such as Los Invasores del Norte, Los Cachorros de Juan Villarreal, and Los Cadetes de Linares; these groups were crossing over more often to play at the norteña dance clubs sprouting up throughout Texas. Many Tejano conjunto groups in the lower Rio Grande Valley region began including more corridos in their dance hall repertoire, particularly very early "classic" revolutionary and social bandit corridos and a handful of those made popular by Ayala (personal communications with Cavazos and Guillermo Berrones).

"El Corrido de Gerardo González" was written by one of the most colorful border personalities and well-known Mexican corrido composers in the region, Narciso "Chito" Cano. Though Ayala recorded many of Cano's songs, this corrido is one of Ayala's most popular and it has since been recorded by numerous norteña groups (e.g., Los Amigos, Luis y Julián, and Los Cadetes de Linares). The exact date of its composition is unknown, but it was probably written in the early 1970s and was sung for years by local groups in and around Reynosa, Tamaulipas, before Ayala recorded it on Freddie Records in 1976. One of the few Texas-Mexican groups to record this song was the Edinburg-based Los Dos Gilbertos in 1993.

The popularity and longevity of "El Corrido de Gerardo González" and the fact that it was recorded by both norteña and Texas-Mexican conjunto groups (though only a handful of those located closer to the border) offer the opportunity to examine briefly some of the stylistic distinctions between norteña and conjunto style. Though corridos are rare in conjunto repertoire, they are still included for purposes of nostalgia and often as the primary reference to Mexican culture and history, albeit a Norteño history. Beginning with the accordion introduction in both versions (see Figures 4.7 and 4.8), we see that the instrument's role is stylistically distinct in each genre (Ragland 1994, 88–89). It is primarily an accompanying instrument in norteña music, and Ayala plays an almost straight rendering of the melody during the first eight measures of the final two lines of text in the song's opening stanza, which tell the hero's tragic fate:

> Por eso las leyes ni tiempo le dieron
> el día que a mansalva y cobardemente le dieron la muerte.
>
> That's why the authorities didn't give him a chance
> the day that without taking any risk they cowardly killed him.

The next six measures represent an extended improvisation on this melody, which is an influence from conjunto, though the scalar runs are simple and repetitive. The final two measures (mm. 15–16), just before the vocals enter, represent a typical pattern employed by many norteña groups to introduce the beginning of a stanza and the sung text. (See also transcriptions of "Carta Jugada," Figure 3.7; "Contrabando y Traición," Figures 5.1 and 5.2; and "Vivan los Mojados," Figures 5.8 and 5.9.)

In the version by Los Dos Gilbertos (Figure 4.8), the accordion introduction begins with part of the melody of the corrido's first line but quickly veers off into a much more elaborate improvisation, complete with grace notes, accidentals, and more complex and expressive scalar runs. Additionally, this introduction is accompanied by a sustained *grito* (high-pitched yell) that is distinctly emblematic of Tejano identity and is used to create a celebratory, dance hall atmosphere (and to call dancers to the dance floor). Norteña groups, on the other hand, never interrupt the music or text with their *gritos*. Transcriptions of the accordion introduction for each group are shown in Figures 4.7 and 4.8.

In the Ayala version (Figure 4.7), the typical 3/8 corrido tempo is maintained as groupings of three in the melody line and is also expressed in the song text. However, in the Los Dos Gilbertos version (Figure 4.8), the song is played in 2/4, which allows for more notes per measure, though the three stressed syllables in each measure are distinctly felt, thus making it sound as if it were in three. While Los Dos Gilbertos have rewritten the song so that it better complies with the faster two-step dance hall pattern that Tejanos are more accustomed to, they maintain the corrido's triple meter feel by stressing the three strong syllables in every line. (See also my discussion of the "Contrabando y Traición" transcription, Figures 5.1 and 5.2, on pages 146–152.)

Norteña and tejano conjunto artists, particularly in the border region, are often critical of each others' playing styles. While conjunto groups tend to criticize norteña groups' approach to rhythm—which is often unsteadied by erratic drum rolls and offbeat improvisations on the electric bass—norteña artists criticize the conjunto musician's virtuosic instrumental display on the accordion and its dominance of the song's melody, which they claim takes away from the text and its meaning. Ramón Ayala's following comment to me about the role of the

**FIGURE 4.7** Transcription of the accordion introduction to "El Corrido de Gerardo González," mm. 1–16. Performed by the norteño group Ramón Ayala y Los Bravos del Norte and recorded in 1976. Featuring accordion, bajo sexto, electric bass guitar, and drum set: (c) cymbal; (h) hi-hat; (s) snare; (b) bass drum.

(From the 1991 CD *Corridos del '91* by Ramón Ayala y Los Bravos del Norte, Freddie Records FMC-1572. Also available on *Borderlands: From Conjunto to Chicken Scratch. Music from the Rio Grande Valley of Texas and Southern Arizona*, various artists, Smithsonian/Folkways CD 40418, 1993. "Corrido de Gerardo González" words and music by Aciano C. Acuña. Copyright © 1978 by Grever Music Publishing S.A. de C.V. All rights in the United States and Canada administered by Universal Music–Z Songs. International copyright secured. All rights reserved.)

**FIGURE 4.8** Transcription of the accordion introduction to "El Corrido de Gerardo González," mm. 1–16. Performed by the tejano group Los Dos Gilbertos and recorded in 1993. Featuring accordion, bajo sexto, electric bass guitar, drum set: (c) cymbal; (s) snare; (b) bass drum.

(From the cassette *Bajo Sexto y Acordeón,* Capitol/EMI Latin 42803 4 1. "Corrido de Gerardo González" words and music by Aciano C. Acuña. Copyright © 1978 by Grever Music Publishing S.A. de C.V. All rights in the United States and Canada administered by Universal Music–Z Songs. International copyright secured. All rights reserved.)

accordion in Tejano conjunto addresses a very important distinction between tejano and norteña styles: "The Tejano puts a lot more accordion in his songs, and for those of us who play norteña music, we only use it where it is necessary, like connecting the phrases of the song. Tejano accordionists also like to make a show with the accordion, you know, show off their playing. They even dance while they are playing. We don't do that because then, you lose the song, you know, the corrido, and that's what Mexicans want to hear" (personal communication). In other words, for the norteña musician, the accordion's primary role is to introduce the song and each verse. It provides a musical framework for the telling of the story. In tejano conjunto, the accordion takes a more central role: It guides dancers and serves as a means for the accordionist (generally the bandleader) to show off his playing technique and personal style (which is very often the way Tejano listeners identify the group). In this recording, the accordionist Gilberto García of Los Dos Gilbertos is respectful of the corrido as he confines his elaborate improvisations to the song's introduction and the instrumental bridge after the third stanza. This approach is rare because most Tejano accordionists, particularly those in San Antonio, would continue to play the accordion behind the text and throughout the entire corrido, as they would if they were playing a cumbia or ranchera. Norteña groups, however, would never do so for the very reason Ayala gave earlier: to maintain the integrity of the Spanish-language text and to allow for the telling of the story.

Another very telling distinction is that Tejanos know conjunto groups by the names of their accordionists (e.g., Flaco Jiménez, Santiago Jiménez, and Mingo Saldívar) or, in the more contemporary *música tejana* genre, by the vocalists' names (e.g., Selena Quintanilla, Emilio Navaira, Roberto Pulido, and Michael Salgado). However, with the unusual exception of Ayala—often called the "father of modern norteña" more for his interpretation of corridos than for his accordion playing—the majority of norteña groups are recognized for how successfully they interpret the songs that have generally been written by professional and amateur songwriters and the corrido in particular. For this reason, one corrido might be recorded over and over by several different groups. In norteña music, no one group "owns" a corrido.

Bobby Salinas is the bajo sexto player in Los Dos Gilbertos, and in an interview he addressed how the way he plays the instrument differs from that of players in norteña groups. He noted that norteña players strummed fewer strings on the instrument (anywhere from three to four) whereas he and most other Tejano players strum at least ten strings: "The idea among tejano conjunto players is to get a fuller, more penetrating sound that is more clearly balanced with the accordion. The bajo sexto marks the rhythm on the upbeat and is what people listen to for dancing. It helps them glide across the dance floor. Norteña players sound 'kinky,' you know, they just don't emphasize the rhythm as strongly as they should" (personal communication). Salinas also noted that the drums in conjunto should also play on the upbeat, just behind the bajo sexto, to enhance the fullness of the rhythm. Norteña groups tend to play around the beat, which seems to throw the rhythm off at times. However, when one listens more closely, it is clear that, while the norteña bajo sexto plays the second and third beat (which are both stressed), the bass plays on the first beat (though it is not stressed) and often plays around the second and third beats. The rhythm, though, is not as smooth and steady as in the typical tejano conjunto. Salinas noted also that the drum rolls "seem to be erratic," a feature that has become a trademark of the norteña sound. The San Antonio–based tejano conjunto accordionist and bandleader Mingo Saldívar agreed with Salinas's comments and added the following observation: "They [norteña drummers] improvise more on the drums, more rolls and hi-hat as opposed to a set beat like conjunto. Norteño players do a lot of rolls on the snare drum, and so do we. I like that, but they seem to make them longer and at different places, not right on the beat all the time" (personal communication). The transcriptions of the first verse of "El Corrido de Gerardo González" as performed by Ramón Ayala y Los Bravos del Norte (Figure 4.9) and Los Dos Gilbertos (Figure 4.10) exemplify this difference in drumming.

While the Los Dos Gilbertos conjunto example (Figure 4.10) also has drum rolls, they do not break up the rhythm as they do in Ayala's norteña example (Figure 4.9). It seems that these drum rolls appear at the drummer's discretion; however, in the norteña example (as in many others) they appear just before the beginning of the sung text as an introduction and to emphasize crucial words like *prisionero* (prisoner) and *ni tiempo* (from the phrase *por eso las leyes ni tiempo le dieron*; it points out that González was "not" given the "chance" to fight back). Drum rolls also appear on the words *mansalva* (without taking risk) and *muerte* (death). Therefore, as the story of González's fate unfolds, the listener's attention is repeatedly drawn to the real crime, the cowardly murder of a helpless prisoner. In the Ayala example, the instruments clearly not only maintain the rhythm for dancing but also provide an interactive framework for the song text that is a hallmark of norteña style.

### Ramón Ayala: Norteña's First Border-Crossing Star

As early as 1973, Los Relámpagos held recording contracts with companies on both sides of the border. In the United States, Los Relámpagos and Ayala's own group, Los Bravos del Norte, recorded for Freddie Records in Corpus Christi, Texas. In Monterrey, Mexico, they signed with DLV, which was eventually purchased by Capitol EMI Latin (Ayala, personal communication). In an interview, Freddie Martínez Jr. of the Corpus Christi-based Freddie Records explained to me that his label never signed contracts with artists but rather recorded artists for a negotiated price, which depended on the artist's popularity, and then later sold the recordings to the artists and local distributors. (Freddie Records and similar independent labels such as Falcon, Hacienda, and Zarape often sold records primarily to flea-market vendors and small record shops, at least until

*(continued on next page)*

**FIGURE 4.9** Transcription of "El Corrido de Gerardo González," mm. 14–43 (first stanza). Probably written in the 1970s. Performed by Ramón Ayala y Los Bravos del Norte. Featuring vocals, accordion, bajo sexto, electric bass guitar, drum set: (c) cymbal; (h) hi-hat; (s) snare; (b) bass drum.

(From *Corridos del '91*, Freddie Records FMC-1572. "Corrido de Gerardo González" words and music by Aciano C. Acuña. Copyright © 1978 by Grever Music Publishing S.A. de C.V. All rights in the United States and Canada administered by Universal Music–Z Songs. International copyright secured. All rights reserved.)

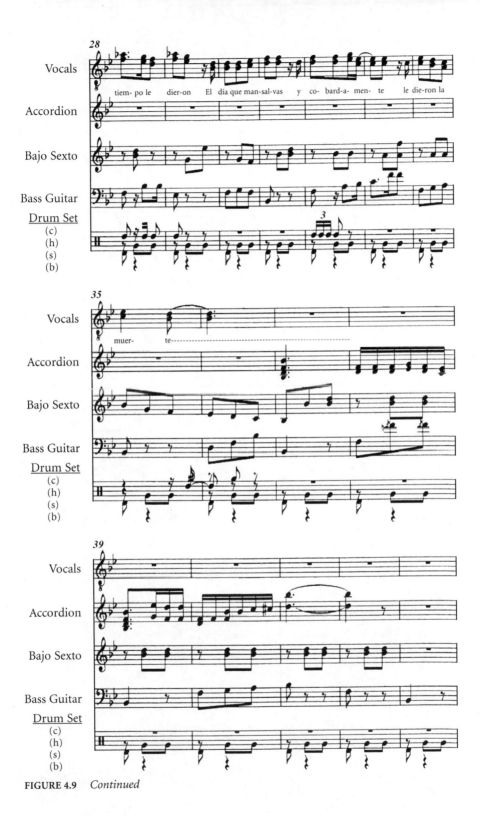

FIGURE 4.9    *Continued*

*(continued on next page)*

**FIGURE 4.10**   Transcription of "El Corrido de Gerardo González," mm. 17–40 (first stanza). Performed by Los Dos Gilbertos. Featuring vocals, accordion, bajo sexto, electric bass guitar, drum set: (c) cymbal; (h) hi-hat; (s) snare drum.

(From *Bajo Sexto y Acordeón,* Capitol/EMI Latin 42803 4 1. "Corrido de Gerardo González" words and music by Aciano C. Acuña. Copyright © 1978 by Grever Music Publishing S.A. de C.V. All rights in the United States and Canada administered by Universal Music–Z Songs. International copyright secured. All rights reserved.)

**FIGURE 4.10** *Continued*

the1990s, when distribution to department stores like K-Mart and Wal-Mart became available.) Artists typically bought recordings at a greatly reduced price to sell on their own. This arrangement was common in the days when most recordings of norteña groups were sold at dances and concerts by the artists themselves (personal communication).

For Ramón Ayala, Freddie Records made an exception. Martínez said that they signed their first exclusive artist contract with Ayala and, at least through the 1970s and 1980s, he "kept the label afloat as the top-selling artist" (personal communication). Today Freddie Records has a large roster of predominantly norteña—and some banda, cumbia, and tejano—artists, but Ramón Ayala y Los Bravos del Norte continues to be one of their most prolific and popular acts. Through most of his career with Freddie Records, Ayala would often record the same album and songs for both Freddie Records and DLV simultaneously, though the album would be released in each country under a different title and with different cover art. "Very often he would make a recording with us and take the master across the border to DLV, and then at other times, he would bring a recording he made in Mexico, and we would release it here," Martínez said. "Sometimes we'd have three or four albums a year from Ayala. We didn't see any competition either because we couldn't sell our records over there [in Mexico], and they really didn't have the distribution set up to sell theirs here" (personal communication). Throughout the 1970s and 1980s, Ayala (see Figure 4.11) would continue to be the most popular and visible norteña artist, always expanding his reach. He rarely took any time off once he began traveling and touring in the late 1960s (Rogelio García, personal communication). "It is important that we keep traveling and working," Ayala said. "That is what the people expect of us. This is a group that is disciplined; we travel though we are sick, and we go wherever the people want us and like us" (personal communication).

Other artists based in Monterrey and the border region capitalized on Ayala's success and set out on the taco circuit with the support of either Cano or a Monterrey-based rival tour promoter and manager, Óscar Flores. The two entrepreneurs sent several norteña artists traveling throughout the United States, most sporting the "del Norte" moniker to distinguish them from Texas-Mexican artists and to "show that they were authentic and from the North of Mexico, the heart of norteña." These groups included Los Broncos del Norte (also a pioneering group), Los Invasores del Norte, Los Huracanes del Norte, and Los Cadetes de Linares (Rogelio García, personal communication). Other groups who toured in the United States included Luis y Julián, Carlos y José, and El Palomo y el Gorrión; all still active, they compose and arrange their own songs, as do most dueto groups. These artists are well-known throughout northern Mexico as composers and performers of original corridos, canción-corridos, rancheras, and romantic ballads.

I mention these men because Ayala and Reyna (as Los Relámpagos del Norte) began their career in the same fashion, though Reyna mostly wrote tragic love

**FIGURE 4.11**  The cover of Ramón Ayala's 2002 CD "El Número 100" (The Number 100) celebrating his hundredth recording for the Texas-based label Freddie Records. Notice that Ayala (*front left*) stands with his group, Los Bravos del Norte, on a map of the Texas-Mexico border, where Ayala's name is emblazoned.
(Reprinted, with permission, from Freddie Records/MARFRE Music [JMCD 1845], 2002.)

ballads rather than corridos. However, Ayala did not continue this tradition with his own group. Ayala viewed himself as an "interpreter" of corridos and other songs, and it was he who established the idea of collecting songs, particularly corridos, from the Mexican immigrant public and from independent songwriters (García Flores, personal communication). Ayala's popularity spread from the border region to immigrant communities across the United States, not only because he meticulously followed the migrant circuit but also because he collected and recorded corridos and rancheras about the hardship of travel and displacement experienced by this community. Ayala mixed these corridos with those about legendary border heroes like Pancho Villa and Gregorio Cortez and with popular corridos written and recorded by Tomás Ortiz of Los Alegres de Terán, Julián Garza of Luis y Julián, Miguel Luna of El Palomo y el Gorrión, El Piporro, and others. Not only did Ayala give a voice to the authors of the new corridos he collected and to their community; he also allowed them to share in a border history that is conflicted because of racial, political, and social tension. In many of his songs, these obstacles are overcome by the ordinary, working-class hero who becomes a champion for his persistence, bravery, hard work, and ability to subvert the power of U.S. immigration restrictions and their enforcers. Ayala's popularity is grounded in the fact that his music gave the nomadic migrant an opportunity to participate in a Mexican identity that is rooted in autonomy, racial and social conflict, economic struggle, travel, and duality. It offered a necessary redefinition of nationhood, a new sense of mexicanidad, and the impetus for a new Mexican global nation.

## Cumbia Norteña

By the late 1970s, norteña artists in the Texas-Mexican border region like Ramón Ayala y Los Bravos del Norte, Luis y Julián, and Los Invasores del Norte were products of an increasingly commercialized music industry that was emerging in Monterrey (Carrizosa 1997, 4–5). Having experienced enormous growth as a result of migration, the city had been transformed from a Spanish colony to a European outpost for entrepreneurs to an industrialized city with thousands of immigrants from mostly rural villages throughout Mexico. By the 1970s, the city's close proximity to the border meant that it was absorbing North American culture at a much faster pace than Mexico City and Guadalajara and was a crucial passageway for migrants traveling to and from the United States. Transborder commerce, migration, and economic opportunity linked Monterrey to San Antonio, Houston, Chicago, and other points throughout the southern and midwestern United States. Monterrey was also experiencing migration from Central American and other Latin American countries, particularly Colombia; many migrants came looking for work in the city's cement, glass, and brewery businesses, and others moved closer to the border to work in U.S.-owned factories. However, the migrants greatly outnumbered the jobs. Unemployment and poverty were the results of such rapid growth, and slums sprang up on Monterrey's outskirts, reaching up into the city's surrounding mountain ranges (Olvera 1992, 2–5).

It was in these slums and barrios that young men calling themselves *sonideros,* or deejays, began playing cumbia (also known as *colombiana,* or *tropical*) music in local clubs and at dance parties. Folkloric genres in Colombia's Caribbean coastal region, cumbia *sabanera* and its cousin, cumbia *vallenata,* were forged from a fusion of the accordion, the indigenous *guacharaca* (a bamboo scraper), and African rhythms played on the *caja,* a small single-headed drum (Olvera 1992, 5). While salsa took the rest of Mexico by storm in the 1960s and 1970s, cumbia *colombiana* found fertile ground in Monterrey. Also popular in impoverished slums outside Mexico City, cumbia came to be associated throughout Mexico (as well as in other parts of Latin America) with young people in marginalized communities (Olvera 1992, 11). In Monterrey, *sonideros* mixed and re-recorded mostly pirated cumbia songs and sold them at local flea markets. Soon, the local recording industry, realizing that it must compete with Texas-Mexican orquesta and *música tejana* just across the border, began recording and promoting what was now called cumbia norteña, also known as *onda grupera* (Carrizosa 1997, 4; Rogelio García, personal communication). This cumbia sound was simple but infectious and easy to dance to, being primarily based on a repetitive four-beat rhythm with heavy emphasis on beat one and secondary accents on three and four.

In the late 1970s, the Monterrey-based promoter and manager Óscar Flores said he began to record and tour artists who dressed in glittery charro outfits and paired the accordion and bajo sexto with keyboards, *guacharaca,* and other percussion taken from salsa and merengue (personal communication). Groups like Los Bukis, Bronco, and later Límite were heavily promoted to the sons and daughters not only of Mexican immigrants but also of other Latino immigrants throughout the United States. Unlike the norteña groups, these artists were featured on television and radio, and some appeared as actors in popular Mexican telenovelas (limited-run soap operas), most notably the Bronco members who appeared in the hugely popular *Dos mujeres, un camino* (Two women, one road), a telenovela produced by Televisa and aired in both the United States and Mexico, which starred Erik Estrada, known to North American audiences for his portrayal of a hunky highway patrol officer in the popular 1970s television series *CHiPs.* Estrada played a Mexican truck driver who transports goods from Mexico to the United States and debates between staying with his wife and children or running off with a younger woman he met on the road. The members of Bronco occasionally appeared in the series (norteña groups like Los Tigres del Norte and Luis y Julián often appeared in movies, but this telenovela appearance was a first for norteña musicians), reminding Estrada's character of the importance of keeping his family together and encouraging him to do the right thing. While cumbia norteña groups like Bronco represented a more "modern" norteña sound, making a play for upwardly mobile Mexican, Chicano, and pan-Latino audiences on both sides of the border, this role as the conscience of Estrada's character is not unlike that of the traditional Norteño corridista, who composes songs that represent the collective opinion of the community (see McDowell 1981 and Limón 1999). While cumbia norteña groups like Bronco rarely recorded corridos, in interviews and at concerts they often connected themselves to Norteño culture and to the legacy of its music tradition. Likewise, they often dressed in Norteño charro (cowboy) attire and featured the accordion and bajo sexto, along with keyboards and synthesizers.

Ramón Ayala, Los Invasores, Los Huracanes, and other norteña artists responded to the success of cumbia norteña by adding cumbias as well as popular love ballads to their repertoires and began recording fewer corridos in order to compete with these groups. Even the California-based Los Tigres del Norte, Ayala's closest rival in the 1970s and 1980s, jumped on the bandwagon with the marginally successful *Con Sentimiento y Sabor* (With Feeling and Taste), a 1992 album of cumbias. Ironically, while the cumbia norteña groups were desperately trying to maintain a connection to norteña as a means to attract the working-class, immigrant audience, this recording was a blatant attempt to reach out to a pan-Latino audience. Los Tigres abandoned the morally and politically charged corridos for which they were known in favor of love ballads and pop songs set to the cumbia rhythm. On the album cover, the band members sport stylish boating and sailor-inspired outfits instead of their trademark charro suits. But Los Tigres' association with the corrido and a more "traditional" norteña sound proved too strong and this recording did not sell. The group soon went back to the charro look—this time influenced by the "Rhinestone Cowboy" outfits of popular Nashville artists—and to corridos and rancheras whose themes were poignant, political, and more relevant to the immigrant community's experiences.

The well-known *música tejana* singer Selena Quintanilla tapped into the cumbia norteña sound in the early 1980s, achieving commercial success—first in the border region; then Corpus Christi and San Antonio; and later throughout the rest of Texas, California, New Mexico, Colorado, and Chicago (Patoski 1996). She was the first Texas-Mexican artist to attain popularity in Mexico, a feat that no other Texas-Mexican or Chicano artist has accomplished since. During the 1980s, several norteña groups, Ramón Ayala y Los Bravos del Norte and Los Tigres in particular, released all-cumbia norteña recordings in an effort to compete, but these recordings, like the one by Los Tigres, were not received well by the public. In the mid-1990s, the popularity of banda and *technobanda* in California and, in the latter half of the decade, a second resurgence in the popularity of narcocorridos—coinciding with further militarization of the border and a new wave of anti-immigrant (i.e., anti-Mexican) sentiment among the North American public—have since ended the decade-long domination of cumbia norteña groups among immigrant communities in the United States and Mexico.

## The Mojado and Modern Norteña Music

The image of the mojado in norteña music is just as important as the concept of the border itself. One cannot exist without the other, whether in songs, films, or in writings about the history of Mexican immigration in the United States. The border is both a gateway and a barrier to the hundreds of thousands who have crossed or attempted to cross it illegally. Every year there are stories in local newspapers about undocumented Mexicans and, more recently, Central Americans, who die from heat exhaustion or lack of oxygen in storage containers in the backs of trucks, in railroad cars, or in the trunks of cars as they cross the border into Texas or Arizona. Today, fewer individuals are actually being caught wading across the Rio Grande (which was the inspiration for the term *wetback* over forty years ago). Paredes's definition of the "border man," likely inspired by border heroes like Gregorio Cortez, Juan Cortina, and Pancho Villa, also fits the mojado (and in some cases the narcotraficante): "The border man . . . was origi-nally a peaceful man goaded into violence by outsiders while defending his rights with a 'pistol in his hand.' The border man's idea of 'right' was related to feelings of separation and personal independence" (1958, 109).

Through the years, *wetback* has taken on a variety of derogatory meanings in North American society and has been used as a form of insult to all Mexicans. Ironically, the U.S. government is largely responsible for the widespread use of this word. In 1954, it instituted a military operation known as "Operation Wet-back."[5] A task force of over eight hundred border patrol officers was assembled to rid southern California, Texas, and western Arizona of "wetbacks" (Samora 1971, 51–54). The operation expanded throughout the Southwest and officers swarmed into neighborhoods and randomly identified people on the street. Though the government said it was targeting all "illegal aliens," the overwhelming majority of people under attack and deported were Mexicans (Samora 1971, 53).

Opponents in both the United States and Mexico complained of the pro-gram's "police-state" tactics, and eventually it was abandoned, but only after more than one million people (many with U.S.-born children) were deported. For the Mexican immigrant population as a whole, the damage had already been done. The publicity surrounding Operation Wetback only fueled the fire of rac-ism in America, and *wetback* became a popular slang term that was used to identify all Mexicans and people of Hispanic descent. Today, the word appears in dictionaries like the *American Heritage Dictionary*, which defines *wetback* as "a disparaging term for a Mexican, especially a laborer who crosses the U.S. bor-der illegally."

The National Association of Hispanic Journalists considers the term to be among the "worst of racial epithets."[6] Over the past twenty-five years, the literal Spanish-language translation of "wet"—*mojado*—has been used as a loose trans-lation of *wetback*. *Mojado* is now used widely within the Mexican population, particularly among young Mexican-national immigrants living in the United States. This community's use of *mojado* resembles the use of the word *nigger* in counterhegemonic discourse by young African Americans, particularly musi-cians and comedians. However, like the African American community, Mexican Americans in the United States are divided along lines of class, economic status, and political positioning when it comes to the use of this word.

---

[5] Operation Wetback was inspired by a national reaction against illegal immigration. The then com-missioner of the INS, Joseph Swing, oversaw the border patrol and organized state and local officials along with police to carry out the operation. The target of border enforcement was "illegal aliens" in general, but Operation Wetback became strictly focused on Mexicans, even extending its reach into Mexican American neighborhoods throughout the southwestern United States (see Gonzales 1999, 175–178).

[6] See "Latinos in the United States, Words and Facts to Know: A Glossary of Terms and Historic Events," National Association of Hispanic Journalists, http://www.nahj.org/resourceguide/chapter_1.html (accessed September 8, 2004).

The more politically powerful Chicano or Mexican American population, primarily in the Southwest, has shunned the word *mojado,* while marginalized, still traveling, working-class Mexican nationals use the word to describe themselves and others within the community as an act of solidarity and resistance to assimilation. As a symbolic triumph over an unwelcoming North American society, Martínez writes that the strengthening of the mojado identity in the Mexican diaspora since the mid-1970s "functions as a device for dismantling national borders and the methods used in controlling them" (1998, 45). The liberal use of *mojado* in songs and in casual conversation among immigrants who are aware of the general population's ignorance of the term (unless as the English "wetback") and the Chicano's disdain for it ascribes a Mexicanness or mexicanidad to the mojado and the undocumented experience in the United States (Martínez 1998, 45–46). The undocumented as protagonist in traditional Norteño corridos of the mid-nineteenth and early twentieth centuries appeared at a time when the border was not as clearly defined or regulated as it is today. Corridos about revolutionary leaders, tequila smugglers, pistol-packing bandits, and border heroes portrayed fearless and defiant men who managed to hold off Anglo-American encroachment, at least for a while. Corridos about mojados (and some about narcotraficantes) continue the tradition of underclass heroes fighting to better living conditions for themselves and their community, though many of the stories now take place on the U.S. side of the border.

During the late 1950s and early 1960s, *espaldas mojadas,* the literal translation of "wetback," began to appear in songs, likely inspired by the 1954 film *Espaldas mojadas.* By the early 1960s, the nameless mojado emerged as a protagonist in newly composed Norteño corridos. These early portrayals present the undocumented laborer as a tragic individual who, in addition to being poor, alone, and separated from family and friends, was mistreated by North American authority figures (i.e., border patrols, INS agents, and so on) and employers and lived in fear of being deported, arrested, or killed while trying to cross over or while living in the United States. By the early 1970s, as the numbers of undocumented Mexicans began to swell in the Southwest, the mojado began to appear more often in corridos as the protagonist involved in a range of activities from border crossing to searching for work to avoiding capture to raising a family.

The mojado theme emerged most strongly around the time when corridos about the exploits of narcotraficantes began to appear in popular norteña repertoire in the 1970s. However, when narcocorridos went out of fashion for a time during the 1980s, mojado-themed songs continued to be composed and recorded, as they do today (personal communications with Rogelio García and Ramón Ayala). In some songs, the mojado and the narcotraficante are one and the same: These characters share the stereotypical traits of Norteños as proud, macho Mexicans who live life outside the authority and the power of the state, in this case the U.S. government, giving them heroic status among traveling Mexicans on both sides of the border.

Historically, through their exploits the mojado and the narcotraficante merge real life and fantasy amid the fight for economic survival, the struggle against border patrol and authority figures, and the negation of social space, however marginal, all of which bond the immigrant community—first in the border region and now in rural towns and urban centers across the United States and Mexico—even more strongly. Like the revolutionary bandit hero of northern Mexico and the narcotraficante who amasses his fortune by avoiding capture, the mojado can live and work in the United States because he has also managed to "outsmart" the border patrol and the INS and is, therefore, a hero to others who are ready to make the same sacrifice.

In a neoliberal and late capitalist society where the value of human life is measured only by its ability to produce wealth for the elite culture, the mojado in many contemporary norteña songs and corridos has discovered his own power within the system. Though he lives a clandestine life in order to improve that of his family, he has also negotiated an existence outside the grip of the dominant North American culture and society. For him, the United States is merely a more prosperous extension of Mexico, and his undocumented status allows for freedom of movement within a larger social system. This powerful definition was established initially by Los Tigres del Norte. Inspired by the music and films of El Piporro, they recorded, in 1976, one of the first "mojado-themed" songs to gain popularity on both sides of the U.S.-Mexico border—"Vivan los Mojados" (Long Live the Wetbacks).

This song was the first in a series of highly successful "mojado corridos" recorded by the group, among them "Tres Veces Mojado" (Three Times a Wetback), "La Tumba del Mojado" (The Wetback's Tomb), and "El Mojado Acaudalado" (The Wealthy Wetback). "Vivan los Mojados" also inspired countless other songs by norteña groups from the 1970s to the present. While Maria Herrera-Sobek (1993) and other collectors of corridos (Paredes 1958, 1976; Nicolopulos 1997; Hernández 1999) have identified numerous historical and modern themes, the two themes that have dominated modern norteña music over the past two and a half decades are mojados and narcotraficantes. However, much of the contemporary research by sociologists, anthropologists, and journalists (including Wald 2001) on both sides of the border has focused almost solely on the more evocative and commercial narcocorridos and the artists who sing them. However, mojado songs are more widespread, more likely to be sung by community-based groups as well as popular recording artists, and more reflective of the real-life experiences of both the singers and the audience.

# 5

# Los Tigres del Norte and the Transnationalization of Música Norteña in the Working-Class Mexican Diaspora

## El Corrido de los "Little Tigers"

The story of the "Little Tigers" has been told so many times now that it is part of Mexican immigrant folklore and still gives hope to all who cross the border seeking work and a better life. It is the story of four teenage brothers who left the small town of Rosa Morada in the western state of Sinaloa, Mexico, crossing the border into California to make a few dollars playing music. They managed to get themselves booked as part of a musical revue for a Mexican Independence Day celebration in San José and for prison inmates at Soledad. The oldest brother, Jorge, was only fourteen, and just before crossing the border, he had persuaded a couple to pretend to be the boys' parents. They entered in 1968 with a ninety-day visa. A border patrol agent who was impressed with their musical talents nicknamed the brothers the "Little Tigers." Like many other immigrants, they remained in the United States, where they built their musical career. Over the next thirty-five years, the Hernández brothers, along with a cousin, would become a musical dynasty popularly known as Los Tigres del Norte (The Tigers of the North). To date, they have sold more than thirty-two million albums and CDs in both the United States and Mexico. They helped launch a highly lucrative and expansive norteña music industry that relies almost solely on the tastes and interests of Mexican laborers living in the United States and their families back in Mexico.

Settling in San José, California, where they soon began recording for the independent Fama Records (later known as Fonovisa), Los Tigres were instrumental in moving norteña music, and a large part of the industry, away from the Texas-Mexican border region. They also introduced innovative stylistic and compositional elements that would further change the music's sound. The group merged the emotion and working-class ideology of Los Relámpagos del Norte with the sardonic wit, humor, and Norteño-style machismo of El Piporro. They also fused their own regional musical and cultural influences with a direct way of speaking (and singing in) the language of working-class Mexicans.

By the early 1970s, Los Tigres would distinguish themselves from Ramón Ayala and, by extension, the Texas-Mexican sound of border groups such as Los Invasores del Norte and Los Huracanes del Norte. As products of the Monterrey recording industry in the late 1970s and 1980s, these groups were moving away from the corrido, as many Tejano conjunto and orquesta groups had done years before and were recording love ballads and cumbias in an attempt to compete with popular groups in Mexico City and Texas. In contrast, Los Tigres brought the focus back to the corrido and added stylistic nuances to the ensemble sound. Though the Hernández brothers do not come from the border region, they represent the impact of norteña music and culture on working-class communities in Mexico. Rather than playing music in the brass band (banda) tradition of their native Sinaloa, the brothers featured accordion, bajo sexto, electric bass, drums, and the occasional saxophone. The group was aware that the audience they wanted to connect with was not all from Sinaloa. They also knew that border-based groups, like Los Relámpagos, who had popularized norteña music among Mexicans in the United States, did so by following the migrant route, which was now extending across the country. Los Tigres would follow their lead.

## The Narcocorrido and Norteña Music

For the next few years, Los Tigres played Mexican rancheras, polkas, corridos, and even some contemporary cumbias (which were becoming popular among working-class communities throughout Mexico) at Sunday afternoon gatherings in local parks, in furniture stores, and at private parties for the Bay Area's growing Mexican immigrant community. The group's popularity remained predominantly regional. Even though they had recorded three albums, they rarely penetrated the transnational "taco circuit" that was dominated by the manager/promoter Servando Cano and his Texas-Mexican border-based groups. But that would soon change. In 1973, Los Tigres recorded a song that they had originally heard a woman singing in a local bar. It was an unusual corrido that told the story of a woman, a Tejana named Camelia, who, along with her Mexican partner, Emilio Varela, smuggles marijuana from Mexico to Los Angeles. When it comes time to sort out the trip's earnings, Emilio announces his intention to take his half and be reunited with "la dueña de mi vida" (the love of my life), a woman living in San Francisco. A jealous Camelia responds by shooting him to death and taking off with all the money, leaving the car and the pistol behind for the police to sort out. The song "Contrabando y Traición" (Smuggling and Betrayal) became a huge hit for Los Tigres and introduced the controversial and hugely popular "narcocorrido" genre to norteña music.

"Contrabando y Traición" was not the first corrido about smuggling and drug trafficking. Smuggling across the border began in the late nineteenth century, when import duties were exceptionally high and North Americans illegally transported textiles into Mexico (Wald 2001). For their part, Mexicans crossed over with contraband candle wax when it became a pricey commodity in the United States. Prohibition prompted the highly profitable smuggling of tequila and other alcohol into the United States, particularly along the West Coast. With the end of Prohibition in 1933, smugglers turned their attention to drugs. The first corrido about drug smuggling may have been written in San Antonio, Texas, by Juan Gaytán of the singing duo Gaytán y Cantú in 1934. "El Contrabandista" tells the story of a smuggler who is captured by the Texas Rangers for smuggling heroin (Hernández 1999). Though a few other drug-smuggling songs were written during the years that followed, none attained commercial success.

"Contrabando y Traición" was different. It was like a real-life news item and tragic love story all rolled into one song. It captured the imagination of Mexican immigrants and warned of the dangers of life in the United States. Though one of the smugglers meets his death—the fate of many smugglers in earlier corridos—his accomplice, a woman no less, gets away with the fruits of their labor. During the early 1970s, drug trafficking was a way of life on the border, particularly between Tijuana and San Diego, though there were also popular routes between Ciudad Juárez, Nuevo León, and El Paso, Texas. Los Tigres' lead singer and musical director Jorge Hernández described the impact of "Contrabando y Traición" in the following quote from an interview with the journalist Sam Quiñones: "It was like a film in the mind's eye. And it was the truth of what was happening in those years. It came out at exactly the right moment. It spoke of the total chaos that is drug trafficking. Perhaps, also, people had never heard these things said so clearly in a song" (Quiñones 1998). To be sure, they had not. The language of the song was less poetic than the typical corrido's and less emotional than the typical love ballad's, but it was the language of the working-class Mexican.

"Contrabando y Traición" also contained the perfect balance of imagination and reality to make it the kind of modern-day outlaw corrido to appeal to hundreds of thousands of undocumented Mexican immigrants whose illegal status places them outside authority and constantly on the run. Like many traditional border corridos, "Contrabando y Traición" fits into Edberg's "zone of [the] imaginary," where border crossing, Norteño history and folklore, economic hardship, and a newly formed "mexicanidad" reside (2004, 206). This song, like many narcocorridos that would follow it, is inspired by the constant flow of labor and global capital and the struggle for identity, money, and power (Edberg 2004, 107). Also, it is important to consider that, when this recording was released, the U.S. government had launched what seemed like an all-out war against undocumented Mexican workers and drug trafficking. In 1972, Congressman Peter Rodino introduced a bill to amend existing legislation. This bill sought to make the employment of undocumented workers a crime and to penalize employers who knowingly hired them. The bill passed the House of Representatives but failed in the Senate. It eventually was passed as the Immigration Reform and Control Act in 1986. The original Rodino measure became a well-publicized symbol of anti-immigrant sentiment and outraged immigrant rights activists (Goméz-Quiñones and Maciel 1998, 42). In 1973, by executive order, President Richard Nixon consolidated several drug enforcement programs and agencies to create an elite drug fighting agency, the Drug Enforcement Administration (DEA).

The DEA's mandate was to suppress domestic and foreign production of narcotics intended for sale in the United States, particularly at a time when drug use was viewed by the general population as out of control (Epstein 1977). For undocumented Mexican immigrants, the DEA meant an increase in border patrol agents (collectively known as *la migra*) in the U.S.-Mexico border region and the tendency to link illegal border crossing with drug trafficking. Beginning with President Nixon and escalating through President George W. Bush, the "War on Drugs" has been highly publicized as a response to a national crisis and has also led to further militarization of the border (Lytle 2003, 4). The subsequent confounding of illegal border crossing and drug trafficking also resulted in an increase in the incarceration of Mexican immigrants in the United States and the implicit criminalization of Mexican immigration (Lytle 2003, 6). The transformation of the border space into a perceived "criminal zone" fueled the panic about race and immigration that was already simmering among the U.S. public. "Contrabando y Traición" was only the beginning of an explosion of narcocorridos that became popular among the Mexican immigrant population in response to the oppression and alienation it experienced in the United States. Involved with drug trafficking on not, an individual who crossed the border illegally was a criminal in the eyes of the public and the U.S. government. Ramírez-Pimienta (2004, 27) claims the arrival of "Contrabando y Traición" and the ensuing surge of narcocorridos came at a time when Mexico's social, political, and economic fabric ruptured, never to be repaired again. In either case, the migrant had no hope in his own country, and while he could come to the United States for work, he had to come illegally and live the life of an outlaw.

## "Contrabando y Traición"

For many, "Contrabando y Traición" signaled a return to the border corrido form and bandit hero tradition, though the lyrics addressed such contemporary issues as illegal border crossing, drug smuggling, and the independence of women.

While the song's form resembles the canción-corrido (six-line stanzas with refrain) pioneered by Los Alegres de Terán, it also had many features that harkened back to traditional border ballads. One example is that there is no accordion introduction, a feature introduced by Los Alegres and imitated by Los Relámpagos and nearly all popular norteña groups. By omitting this element, Los Tigres refocus on the corrido and the story being told. There is no repetition of lyrics in each stanza, as is typical of the border corrido as well. The song form, AABAAB1 (B1 indicates a modified B), is a modification of the AABAB canción-corrido form discussed earlier (see "Carta Jugada," Chapter 3, pages 93–95).

In the transcription of the first stanza of "Contrabando y Traición" shown in Figure 5.1, the protagonist (Camelia) and the antagonist (Emilio) are introduced, though the date and time of the event are omitted. The couple's location is given, though not until the fourth stanza. There is even a farewell at the end of the song (omitted in most canción-corridos); however, it is from the antagonist to the protagonist rather than from the corrido singer to the audience. Also, as in the traditional border corrido, the singer is removed from the action and is merely a storyteller—he is not emotionally involved in the event (the typical role of the border corridista)—which was not the case of the canción-corridos of Los Alegres and other commercially popular norteña groups who followed them.

Los Tigres have also modified and expanded upon some of the musical nuances introduced by Los Alegres in relation to the traditional corrido's basic song structure and rhyme scheme. While there are eight syllables in each line and assonant rhyming on even-numbered lines (two, four, and six), the lengthening of poetic lines (*diéresis*) is reserved for the fifth and sixth lines of each stanza. There are also short fills after each of these stanzas' last two lines (mm. 18–22 and mm. 28–31)—instead of after lines two and six as in the "Carta Jugada" example—thus giving more emphasis to the "coda," where an important action or resolution takes place, adding a sense of anticipation for the next stanza.

Additionally, lines five and six of this first stanza introduce the listener to the main characters, Emilio Varela and Camelia la Tejana. In the second stanza (Figure 5.2), the fifth and sixth lines inform the listener that Camelia is from San Antonio and that she is "una hembra de corazón" (a woman with a lot of heart). This last line is crucial, as it foreshadows what the listener will later find out: If her heart is broken, she will take revenge. Prolonging the final syllables on lines five and six and placing the accordion fills between these lines add energy and emotion to the events as they unfold and propel the song to the next stanza, and then the next, until the final climax is reached in the last stanza. It is also important to note that in a departure from the typical corrido and canción-corrido, the first four lines of each stanza are sung by a solo voice, which breaks from the dueto tradition; however, the final two lines of each stanza are sung by two voices with the second voice straining very high in the range (typical of border dueto singing style).

The addition of electric bass and drums provides a steady dance rhythm, but occasionally they are used to punctuate the end of certain verse lines or to emphasize some action or important bit of information that keeps the story interesting and moving forward. For example, in most border corridos and canción-corridos, the first syllable generally enters on the final beat of the first measure as a "pickup," and the instrumentation enters on the second syllable and in the second measure. In this song, the first five syllables are sung for the first three measures with the first syllable as the "pickup" and the second syllable prolonged with no instrumentation: *Sa-lier-on de San* . . . (They left San . . .). This feature could be read as a means of propelling the listener into the journey across the border.

The instrumentation begins with a drum roll on the snare that occurs on the final beat of the third measure and is followed by three strokes on the hi-hat (which is never heard in this song again); then the drums fall into a steady rhythmic pace with accents on the upbeat along with the bajo sexto. The bass guitar plays the downbeat. Drum rolls also appear at the end of certain lines of poetic verse (often—but not always—the second, third, fourth, or fifth lines), providing emphasis to the text and the storyline. In the first stanza, there is a drum roll after the fourth line (m. 13)—the first mention of marijuana (*yerba mala*)—and on the sixth line, corresponding with the first syllable of *Camelia* (m. 23); it is followed by two eighth-notes played on the electric bass (m. 24) after the last syllable of *Camelia*. The final two syllables of this line, *jan-a*, are prolonged for three measures (mm. 26–28) and lead into the accordion fill.

In the second stanza, there is a drum roll on the second syllable in the first line (*Pa-sar-on,* m. 33) as Emilio and Camelia pass through San Clemente, which connects the sense of "leaving" (*salieron*) from the first line of the first stanza to "passing" (or crossing) in the first line of the second stanza. In the third line, when the two encounter the immigration officer who asks for their papers—"Les pidió sus documentos" (He asked for their documents/papers)—there is a drum roll on the first syllable of that line (m. 38), followed by the two eighth notes played again on the electric bass (m. 42) in the fourth line following *les dijo* (he asked them), and then a drum roll is played in measure 44 after the line *¿De dónde son?* (Where are you from?).

Finally, though the song maintains the three-stress rhythmic pattern of the text, the meter is in duple rhythm, not the triple meter typical of corridos and canción-corridos. This change in meter is probably influenced by the Texas-Mexican conjuntos and orquestas that were traveling the Southwest during this time. Typically, in Texas-Mexican conjuntos the bajo sexto and drums place stronger emphasis on the weaker upbeat (two and four) while the electric bass plays the downbeat (one and three). This rhythmic feature slows down the pace in order to accommodate a two-step dance rhythm—an influence from the honky-tonk country and Texas swing regularly heard in local dance halls. However, in keeping with the corrido and canción-corrido song form, though the

*(continued on next page)*

**FIGURE 5.1** Transcription of "Contrabando y Traición," mm. 1–29 (first stanza). Written by Ángel González, possibly in 1972. As performed and recorded by Los Tigres del Norte in 1973. Featuring vocals, accordion, bajo sexto, electric bass guitar, and drums: hi-hat and snare (bass drum not included in transcription).

(From Los Tigres del Norte's *Contrabando, Traición y Robo* [Smuggling, Betrayal and Robbery], Fonovisa FLK-COR-TIGR-032 [reissue], 2000. "Contrabando y Traición" by Ángel González. Lyrics copyright © 1973/76 by Peer International Corp. Used by permission. All rights reserved.)

**FIGURE 5.1** *Continued*

**FIGURE 5.2** Transcription of "Contrabando y Traición," mm. 32–62 (second stanza). (From the Los Tigres del Norte CD *Contrabando, Traición y Robo*, Fonovisa FLK-COR-TIGR-032 [reissue], 2000. "Contrabando y Traición" by Ángel González. Lyrics copyright © 1973/76 by Peer International Corp. Used by permission. All rights reserved.)

*(continued on next page)*

**FIGURE 5.2** *Continued*

### Contrabando y Traición

**A**

| | |
|---|---|
| Salieron de San Isidro | They left San Isidro |
| 1 2 3   4   5 6 7 8 | |
| procedentes de Tijuana. | traveling from Tijuana. |
| 1  2  3  4  5  6 7 8 | |
| Traían las llantas del carro | They had their car tires |
| 1  2  3  4  5   6  7 8 | |
| repletas de yerba mala. | full of bad grass [marijuana]. |
| 1 2 3  4  5 6  7 8 | |
| Eran Emilio Varela | They were Emilio Varela |
| 1 2  3 4 5   6 7 8 | |
| y Camelia La Tejana. | and Camelia la Tejana. |
| 1 2  3 4  5  6 7 8 | |

**A**

| | |
|---|---|
| Pasaron por San Clemente, | They passed through San Clemente |
| los paró la migración. | and were stopped by an immigration officer. |
| Les pidió sus documentos, | He asked for their documents. |
| les dijo "¿De dónde son?" | He asked them, "Where are you from?" |
| Ella era de San Antonio, | She was from San Antonio, |
| una hembra de corazón. | a woman with a lot of heart. |

**B**

| | |
|---|---|
| Una hembra así quiere a un hombre. | A woman who loves a man so much |
| Por él puede dar la vida. | that she would give her life for him. |
| Pero hay que tener cuidado, | But you must be careful, |
| si esa hembra se siente herida. | if this woman gets hurt. |
| La traición y el contrabando | Betrayal and smuggling |
| son cosas incompartidas. | are not a good mix. |

*(continued on next page)*

FIGURE 5.3   "Contrabando y Traición." Written by Ángel González.
(Copyright © 1973/76 by Peer International Corp. Used by permission. All rights reserved.)

meter is duple and the emphasis is on the upbeats, the three strong syllables in every line of text are stressed: *Salieron de San Isidro / procedentes de Tijuana / Traían las llantas del carro.* "Contrabando y Traición" (lyrics shown in Figure 5.3) has features of the "traveling corrido" (like El Piporro's "Chulas Fronteras") in outlining the couple's route along the border and then northward to Los Angeles. Similarly, elements of outlaw corridos are invoked, as in Camelia's quick use of her pistol to avenge herself on Emilio. Norteño outlaws are known for taking the law into their own hands, which is why many a corrido describes the protagonist

---

### Contrabando y Traición *(continued)*

**A**

| | |
|---|---|
| A Los Ángeles llegaron, | They arrived in Los Angeles |
| A Hollywood se pasaron. | and went through Hollywood. |
| En un callejón oscuro, | In a dark street, |
| las cuatro llantas cambiaron. | they changed the four tires. |
| Ahí entregaron la yerba | There they delivered the grass |
| y ahí también les pagaron. | and they were paid. |

**A**

| | |
|---|---|
| Emilio dice a Camelia: | Emilio said to Camelia: |
| "Hoy te das por despedida. | "Today I bid you farewell. |
| Con la parte que te toca | With your share |
| tu puedes rehacer tu vida. | you can make a good life. |
| Yo me voy pa' San Francisco | I'm going to San Francisco |
| con la dueña de mi vida." | to be with the love of my life." |

**B1**

| | |
|---|---|
| Sonaron siete balazos, | Seven shots rang out. |
| Camelia a Emilio mataba. | Camelia killed Emilio. |
| La policía solo halló | All that the police found |
| una pistola tirada. | was a discarded pistol. |
| Del dinero y de Camelia, | Of the money and Camelia, |
| nunca más se supo nada. | nothing more was known. |
| *(Coda)* | |

---

FIGURE 5.3  *Continued*

"with a pistol in his hand" (see Herrera-Sobek 1993, 3–16). In corridos, outlaws are not simply bandits but are often rebels and heroes fighting for their basic rights to be free and prosper.

In an update, as drug smugglers, the modern-day outlaws of "Contrabando y Traición" drive cars rather than cross by foot or on horseback as in the typical corrido. And though they are stopped at the border (the implicit understanding is that Emilio is undocumented), they manage to pass through easily. Here the song differs from "Chulas Fronteras," whose protagonist has a hard time bringing whiskey into Mexico or tequila into the United States, even though he shows his legal documentation to the immigration officer who detains him. The encounters with immigration officers and border patrol described in the typical corrido are rarely without incident, and the undocumented Mexican crossing the border is always vulnerable. By allowing its characters to cross easily, "Contrabando y Traición" renders the border and border patrol almost insignificant. Their authority is openly mocked by the smugglers and, by extension, the largely undocumented listening public (Martínez 1998, 34–35). The fact that Camelia and Emilio cross without incident suggests that the actual power of the border patrol and, by extension, the U.S. government is diminished by the mojado and the drug trafficker, who subvert authority merely by their existence.

One of the most identifiable elements Los Tigres introduced on their recordings, and in this song in particular, is the gunshots that erupt in the last stanza (B1) after the word *balazos* (gunshots). Beginning with this song, many of Los Tigres' corridos, particularly the narcocorridos, contained sound effects to emphasize events in the storyline: for example, human voices in conversation, shouting (*gritos*), a crowing rooster, a car or truck motor, an airplane flying overhead. These features, both musical and nonmusical, all attempt to place the listener at the heart of the action and to imitate reality as much as possible. "We present what is real for the public," Jorge Hernández insisted in a 2005 interview with Mario Kreutzberger, or Don Francisco, on his television program *Don Francisco Presenta*.[1] These nonmusical effects derive, in part, from El Piporro, whose songs were often partially spoken in characteristic voices that the singer/composer himself created. It is probable that, as a movie actor and radio personality, El Piporro was simply bringing together the various forms of media in which he functioned and that made him a highly popular figure in Mexican popular culture.

The success of many immigrant films may also have prompted Los Tigres to make the connection between music, noise, and entertainment value for marketing purposes. However, it is also important to consider that these nonmusical effects can be viewed as a means of disrupting the structure and order of the traditional corrido, which since the 1930s, has been rigorously studied by music researchers and intellectuals in Mexico and the United States (Hernández 1999, 71). Many scholars of the corrido (Limón, Peña, and others) continued to reinforce Paredes's (1963, 1976) contention that after the 1930s the "heroic" corrido entered a decline from which it never recovered (Nicolopolus 1997). The years between the 1950s and early 1970s were particularly slow for corrido production, especially in the border region, where the canción-corrido and its songs about love and border life prevailed.

With this and other songs, Los Tigres gave the genre new protagonists—the narcotraficante and the mojado. In addition, they introduced to the once rather rigid song form exciting new musical nuances and a new interpretation of corrido poetic meter. The group revived the genre as a living tradition associated with the working-class migrant. They also situated the corrido in a new era and, through this song, located its characters farther north of the border and inside the United States.

Moreover, like El Piporro, Los Tigres created new performance settings for the corrido beyond those identified by Américo Paredes (1976) and further described by the folklorist and corrido scholar John McDowell (1981, 71):

---

[1] The quote is from *Don Francisco Presenta* (Univision, May 18, 2005).

(1) the solitary setting, in which the singer and audience may be one; (2) the family setting, in which the (usually) male singer performs for family members or close friends (men and women of all ages); and (3) the cantina or *parranda*, an all-male setting. Each of these settings would determine how subdued or lively the corrido performance would be, and in the last performance context, the corrido would be punctuated by *gritos* (colorful shouts from the audience or the singer himself) and audible audience commentary. The *grito* (for example, El Piporro's ¡*ajúa!*) is a constant companion to the corrido performance, carefully timed, contoured, and inserted (often by audience members) into the musical fabric of the song. El Piporro inserted *gritos* into his songs as an indicator of his Norteño identity; they helped him to create an identifiable expressive personality that became his calling card. McDowell describes the aesthetic of traditional border corrido performance as "expressive ecology," which he says is present in the "everyday articulation of sound, space, time and motion but comes into focus through the genres of artistic expression recognized within the community" (1981, 71). For El Piporro and Los Tigres, the setting might be any one of those Paredes identified or in one's car or at a dance or anywhere a recording could be played and heard. By expanding the corrido performance context, El Piporro and Los Tigres added features of sound that represent a larger, more expanded Mexican immigrant community (beyond the border region and Norteño culture) and bring the corrido to life for these new listeners, allowing them to take part in the "expressive ecology" of the Mexican diaspora. It is not surprising, then, that modern corridos inspired numerous films.

While this song evokes many characters of traditional border conflict corridos (outlaws, bandit heroes, smugglers, gunslingers, pesky border patrol agents), new personalities emerge. In the first stanza, Camelia is described as a woman who loves hard and should never be crossed, a description that gives her more personality and power than women are typically given in traditional corridos. Maria Herrera-Sobek's "feminist analysis" of the Mexican corrido identifies five principal female archetypes in the corrido: "the good mother," "the terrible mother," "the mother goddess," "the lover," and "the (revolutionary) soldier" (1990). Camelia, however, does not fit into any of these categories, and—other than her heightened emotional nature—she seems to exhibit more of the typical traits of male corrido characters (e.g., self-reliant, macho, averse to betrayal, and drug smuggling). Edberg notes that both Paredes (1976) and Herrera-Sobek (1979) claim that "narcocorridos reflect the community's strong moral stance against drug smuggling, along with a certain sadness about the almost inevitable consequences of a life in that world" (2004, 43).

Camelia's show of power and independence demonstrates the changing role of women in modern U.S. society and indicates that Mexican immigrant males should take heed. A Mexican American citizen (specifically a "Tejana"), Camelia may "look" Mexican, but her actions show that she has assimilated and therefore possesses qualities of the more dominant (albeit, dangerous) North American female. As the narcotraficante who "got away," Camelia makes another strong statement through her actions: She did not let this man get away with two-timing her. During a research interview in Mexico in the summer of 2003, a woman who was married to a local musician told me that "when men get married, they continue to have relationships with other women [*aventuras*, as she called them] and the women are expected to tolerate them." Camelia, however, makes it clear that she is *not* tolerating this behavior from a man any longer. I would suggest that the strong, independent personality of "Camelia la Tejana" captured the imagination of a newly forming Mexican immigrant society in the United States. This song might be interpreted as a reflection of the disruption of the migrating Mexican community's "strong moral stance" against drug smuggling, its view of male/female relationships, and other cultural conventions: a result of people's leaving the family nest and the social and cultural foundations that shaped life back in Mexico.

In addition, it is easier for Mexicans to accept that Camelia is both a woman and a drug smuggler because she is an outsider, a non-Mexican, and by all accounts not really a woman in the traditional "Mexican" sense because of her actions. However, her status as a Tejana supports the belief among many Mexican immigrants—particularly the undocumented—that the U.S.-born Mexican American has turned against Mexico and its heritage and, ultimately, cannot be trusted. As I mentioned previously, numerous Mexican films about immigrants, including many by El Piporro, featured the Mexican American as an antagonist or as a character who had "sold out" to U.S. culture, attitude, and lifestyle. (It is a widely known fact, and confirmed by many of my own informants who are undocumented immigrants, that the Mexican American or Chicano border patrol agents are much tougher than their Anglo counterparts on Mexicans who cross the border illegally.) Martínez writes that these films often show how "illegal immigrants and Mexican Americans are configured in a position of cultural conflict with one another" (1998, 42). One interesting sidebar is that these films began to surge in popularity and production in the late 1960s and early 1970s, coinciding with the Chicano civil rights movement and with the writing and recording of this corrido.

The Chicano movement addressed issues of education, urban labor rights, agricultural unionization, and increased political ties with Mexico, all of which directly affected the majority of Mexican immigrants coming into the United States at that time (Gómez-Quiñones and Maciel 1998, 41–42). However, these new immigrants were not included in nor did they fully align themselves with what most viewed as a sociopolitical movement of Mexican Americans who wanted to be defined as something other than Mexican (Limón 1981, 201–203). For the undocumented, maintaining a Mexican identity is important because rejection of North American assimilation and acculturation allows them to reject authority and, by extension, the border (Martínez 1998, 38). This attitude is particularly evident among the undocumented immigrants who are looked

**FIGURE 5.4** The album cover for *Contrabando, Traición y Robo,* a 1976 collection of corridos by Los Tigres that inspired such films as *Contrabando y traición* and *Vivan los mojados.* (Reprinted, with permission, from Fonovisa, 1976 [reissue, 053308-90282-8, 2000].)

down upon by both Anglos and assimilated Mexican Americans. By transcending the border and all of the limitations and powerlessness it represents, "Contrabando y Traición" documents the experience of this community of travelers by first embracing the past (through the traditional border corrido) and then reconfiguring it as a means of creating a new history and new social space.

After "Contrabando y Traición" made Los Tigres stars on both sides of the border, a Mexican-made film by the same name followed in 1976, also featuring the band members (see Figure 5.4). In the next years, the drug-smuggling Camelia became a household name among Mexican immigrants in the United States, so much so that "Contrabando y Traición" is more popularly known by another title, "Camelia la Tejana." Camelia's saga also spawned a number of corridos such as "Ya Agarraron a Camelia" (They've Caught Camelia) and "Ya Encontraron a

Camelia" (They've Found Camelia), which were recorded by Los Tigres and other norteña groups. Even more impressive is the number of sequel films inspired by Camelia: the 1976 *Mataron a Camelia la Tejana* (They killed Camelia the Texan), the 1977 *La hija de Camelia* (The daughter of Camelia), *Emilio Varela vs. Camelia la Tejana* (1980) and *Emilio Varela vs. Camelia la Tejana* (a 1987 remake by a different director), and the 1988 *El hijo de Camelia la Tejana* (The son of Camelia the Texan). The continued interest in Camelia—the woman, Tejana, and drug smuggler—among the Mexican immigrant population was likely spurred, in part, by the fact that, as a woman, she is marginalized by her gender (Connell and Gibson 2003, 209). Her status resembles that of the marginalized mojado, a status that allows the community to bring her into a "Mexican" framework where they can identify with her (and closely monitor her exploits) as she struggles to avoid capture by authority figures on both sides of the border.

Corridos have been connected to Mexican film since the 1920s (Herrera-Sobek 1998). One of the earliest Mexican immigrant films, *Espaldas mojadas,* featured several regional folk songs that were carefully situated throughout the film to convey its primary message to immigrants: that crossing illegally is dangerous and that undocumented immigrants should return home (Herrera-Sobek 1998, 237). However, the films and corridos that were inspired by "Contrabando y Traición" piqued the imagination of Mexican immigrants as well as that of their compatriots in Mexico. Not only did this corrido link the immigrant community through its real-life account of illegal border crossing, smuggling, and the revenge of a scorned lover; among the working class in Mexico, many of whom have relatives in the United States, the song also reignited an already fetishized image of life on the lawless border.

This corrido's imagining of border life, contraband, and marginalization piqued the interest of the renowned Spanish novelist Arturo Pérez-Reverte, who heard "Contrabando y Traición" while drinking tequila in a famous bar, Tanapas, in Mexico City's Garibaldi Square. With murals of Cornelio Reyna and Fernando Solís and famous ranchera singers looking down at him, Pérez-Reverte was apparently struck by the moment and inspired to write a five hundred–page novel entitled *La reina del sur* (The queen of the South) published in 2002. In an interview with Ángeles García published that same year in the Spanish newspaper *El País,* Pérez-Reverte said that he wrote the book "like a corrido"—the title of each chapter is also the title of a narcocorrido. The novelist said that he was moved by the hardship, danger, and power experienced by the narcotrafficker and the degree to which drugs are part of everyday life, folklore, and music among Mexicans in Sinaloa, the state most often associated with drug trafficking. Los Tigres recorded many more narcocorridos that have become norteña classics, such as "La Banda del Carro Rojo" (The Red Car Gang), "La Camioneta Gris" (The Gray Pickup), "Pacas de a Kilo" (One-Kilo Packets), "El General" (The General), and "Jefe de Jefes" (Boss of Bosses). The group did not stick solely to narcocorridos; they also explored other themes that would enhance their position as stars of the norteña genre and inspire further literature and the scholarly study of "corrido culture." In 2002, the group responded to Pérez-Reverte's novel by releasing a CD with the same title. It is fourteen tracks of modern-day narratives that speak about family issues, for example, "Mi Sangre Prisionera" (My Prisoner Blood); political issues, for example, "El Artista" (The Artist) and "El Soldado" (The Soldier); and themes of love and hope, with one narcocorrido, "La Reina del Sur." Currently in production is a film based on Pérez-Reverte's *La reina del sur,* which will star Eva Mendez and Ben Kingsley. Los Tigres had originally signed with Universal Pictures to coproduce and star in the movie, but the film is now being produced by Warner Independent Pictures and the group is expected to have a cameo appearance. These and other events over the past ten years have launched Los Tigres and, by extension, norteña music onto the global music scene.

## A New Age of Decadence and Danger for the Narcocorrido

There is no doubt that the life of the drug trafficker is intriguing and exciting, providing endless stories for corridos and films. Journalists, novelists, and scholars have been equally motivated by narcocorridos, and most of the writing about corridos and norteña music in recent years has focused on this theme in particular, if not solely. Elijah Wald explains that "what critics often ignore is that narcocorridos, as part of a tradition, are only tangentially about drugs. As with the old ballads of Jesse James and Billy the Kid, the songs are less a celebration of crime than of ordinary guys who strike out against authority" (1998). This interpretation is confirmed by James Nicolopulos, a scholar of the Mexican corrido, who adds that these songs are also the result of a "long-running theme in Mexican culture. Because the United States is so intrusive into Mexico in terms of drug policy, if you beat the system, you're also beating the cultural antagonist" (quoted in Wald 1998). However, the genre's popularity is also partly due to the Mexican government's efforts to censor narcocorridos on the radio and in the press. Ramírez-Pimienta writes that the first censorship campaign came in 1987 when the Sinaloan governor labeled the songs "violent" and "strongly suggested" that local radio stations not play them (2004, 32). However, both Ramírez-Pimienta (2004) and the narcocorrido researcher Luis Astorga (1996a) suggest that, because the popularity and sale of narcocorrido recordings never depended on radio or television, the Mexican government merely increased the narcocorrido's reach among young people by labeling it "dangerous" and "violent." Interestingly, one of the most popular narcocorrido recordings was Los Tigres' 1989 release. During the 1980s, the commercial popularity of cumbia norteña groups like Los Bukis and Bronco began to eclipse that of more "traditional" norteña groups like Ramón Ayala, Luis y Julián, and Los Tigres, who themselves released a collection of cumbias that did not do well among their fans (Carrizosa 1997, 11). In 1989, Los Tigres returned to their narcocorrido roots with *Corridos Prohibidos* (Prohibited Corridos); the cassette recording's title was likely in response to the

**FIGURE 5.5** *Corridos Prohibidos*, the 1989 collection of controversial corridos by Los Tigres del Norte. (Reprinted, with permission, from Fonovisa, 1989 [reissue, 053308-88152-9, 2000].)

Sinaloan government's calls for narcocorrido censorship and to the California governor Pete Wilson's support of Proposition 187. These actions by both governments were viewed as attempts to disenfranchise and marginalize the Mexican traveling laborer population, who appeared to be creating a distinct Mexican identity that rejected the laws and authority of both nation-states. The album cover of *Corridos Prohibidos* (Figure 5.5) proved as controversial as the songs it contained. It pictured the group on the front page of a newspaper standing in a police lineup. The headline under the photo read: "Los famosos corridos de Los Tigres del Norte fueron prohibidos porque" (The famous corridos of Los Tigres del Norte were prohibited because), leaving the answer to the listener. The cassette, later released on CD, became one of the group's best-selling recordings to date and sparked a resurgence of narcocorrido production by this group and a stable of newcomers (Ramírez-Pimienta 2004, 33).

Narcocorrido producers and groups soon discovered that if their songs were targeted by Mexican government officials and were banned from radio airplay, it meant big money and increased popularity. And while there are Monterrey-based groups who have written numerous narcocorridos and have starred in movies inspired by their songs from the 1970s through today (in particular Luis y Julián, Carlos y José, and Los Huracanes del Norte), the narcocorrido genre and the bulk of its audience became most firmly established by the early 1990s in California and Sinaloa, the two states that participate in the majority of drug production and trading activity. California-based groups such as Los Tucanes de Tijuana, Grupo Exterminador (Exterminator Band), Chalino Sánchez, and Los Dorados (The Gilded Ones) emerged in the mid-1990s as a new generation of norteña artists whose songs grew increasingly violent, often praising the drug-smuggling lifestyle and celebrating death (all features recalling gangsta rap). Narcocorridos composed for widely distributed commercial recordings are often written by songwriters hired by a popular group such as Los Tigres del Norte or Los Tucanes de Tijuana. However, the genre also includes songs commissioned by local drug smugglers and made available on CDs that are sold locally and in small record shops (Simonett 2001a, 229–230).

The phenomenon of banda (or *technobanda,* referring to groups who pair brass instruments with keyboards) emerged among the Mexican population in Los Angeles in the 1990s. This genre is rooted in the village brass band tradition that was at the time more specifically connected to states with the largest emigrant populations, such as Sinaloa, Nayarit, and Oaxaca. Narcocorridos became part of banda repertoire in the early 1990s and were partially responsible for the revival of and renewed interest in norteña music among the California immigrant population (Simonett 2001a, 227). One banda artist, in particular, brought the genre to a whole new level of danger and decadence, blurring the lines between real life and fantasy and influencing the second wave of norteña groups (e.g., Los Tucanes and Grupo Exterminador) who have been topping the Mexican popular music charts in the United States and Mexico since the late 1990s. The singer Rosalino "Chalino" Sánchez Félix began his career in jail and went on to be recognized by fans and journalists as a first-rate "star" of the narcocorrido. Sánchez came from Sinaloa, which is known for producing high-quality marijuana and is the home of many well-known drug lords. What made Sánchez unique as a singer and songwriter of narcocorridos was that he actually lived the narcotraficante life. At fifteen, he had already shot and killed a man who had raped his sister. He avoided jail by emigrating illegally to California, where he eventually went to jail for smuggling illegal immigrants and drugs across the border. While in prison Sánchez began writing songs, initially corridos for fellow inmates; once on the outside, he was commissioned to write songs for drug smugglers, drug lords, and other wealthy immigrants for around $2,000 each (Quiñones 2001).

Sánchez assembled his own group and began making recordings, and while he sang out of tune and his voice was rougher than that of the average corridista or Mexican crooner, his lyrics were filled with graphic details of the drug world, including torture and execution. As his career progressed, he also performed with accordion-based norteña groups. Sánchez positioned himself as a true macho male who lived a hard life. He shunned the flashy charro dress of norteña groups like Los Tigres and Los Huracanes del Norte, dressing simply in solid cotton shirts and jeans. However, on the cover of his recordings, he always posed with a handgun, which he often tucked into his belt instead of in a holster as El Piporro or Julián Garza often had. Like many of the drug lords and smugglers Sánchez wrote about, he was murdered. In 1992 he was brutally killed at the age of thirty-one in Sinaloa after a performance in a local club. The story goes that Sánchez and two acquaintances had left the club in a Suburban and were stopped along the road by what appeared to be police cars. The next day, local farmworkers found Sánchez's severed head, along with those of the two men who were with him, in nearby fields (Ramírez-Pimienta 2004, 33–34). Though no one has ever been charged in Sánchez's death, many Sinaloans speculate that he had gotten in too deep with the local drug mob and, as a result, had overstepped the boundary as a corridista and singer of narcocorridos. Sánchez, the man and his personal stories and exploits, had become more popular than his subjects, and that may have been his gravest mistake.

That Sánchez often flirted with death in his corridos as well as in his life is representative of the "heroic world view" in traditional border corridos as described by McDowell (1981, 53). In classic corridos such as "Gregorio Cortez," "Jacinto Treviño," and the many songs about Pancho Villa, dying is an honorable act and is confronted without fear (McDowell 1981, 53). The Mexican poet and essayist Octavio Paz explains that, unlike his North American or European counterpart, the "Mexican" does not fear or avoid death, but rather "looks at it face to face, with impatience, distain or irony." Paz writes, "Our songs, proverbs, fiestas and popular beliefs show very clearly that the reason death cannot frighten us is that life has cured us of fear. It is natural, even desirable, to die and the sooner the better" (1985, 58).

It is understandable, then, that after his death, Sánchez's popularity soared throughout California and Sinaloa, and more recordings were released posthumously than while he was alive. While his recordings did make their way across the Texas-Mexico border and as far north as Chicago, his popularity was primarily a regional phenomenon. Like many border corrido artists (Luis y Julián, El Palomo y el Gorrión, and Carlos y José), Sánchez fashioned an image that was drawn from a combination of the norteña bandit hero, mojado "power" identity, regional Sinaloan folklore, and his own real-life (or supposed real-life) experiences. While Sánchez's fame was geographically limited, his dramatic personal story and commercial success opened the contemporary narcocorrido floodgates once again for a whole new generation of composers and artists who would become known throughout the Mexican diaspora.

While the popularity of banda (which never traveled far from the West Coast) has since waned, norteña music has enjoyed a new influx of fans and groups. Even Los Tigres have "toughened up" their narcocorridos in order to keep up with the new competition. Early narcocorridos by Los Tigres often warned of the danger and destruction of the drug-trafficking life; however, thanks to Sánchez's popularity, particularly after his death, newer groups have focused their songs on the fame and economic benefits of the narcotraficante lifestyle, with some also meeting the wrath of drug lords. In newer songs by Los Tucanes, Grupo Exterminador, Explosión Norteña (whose singer/songwriter was nearly killed in an assault in Tijuana in August 2006), Valentín Elizalde (who was murdered in the border town of Reynosa in November 2006), and others, drug traffickers are celebrated for their innovative methods of smuggling and killing; their womanizing; their extravagant purchases of fancy clothes, boots, hats, and cars; and their ability to avoid capture. Most of these artists claim they are not connected to drug cartels and are not privy to their activities, though the details in their songs suggest otherwise. "The groups write what people want to hear," claims Alberto Cervantes Nieto, the wounded singer of Explosión Norteña, in an interview that appeared in the *San Diego Union-Tribune* on January 2, 2007, in which he speculated that he might have been attacked because "someone didn't like how I sing, or . . . because someone just didn't like me" (Clearley 2007). This article mentions that the search for the killer (or killers) by local authorities has been hindered by the fact that Nieto refuses to press charges and has been uncooperative with the investigation.

In my own experience interviewing musicians and songwriters who write about drug trafficking, I have received similar and equally dismissive answers. Back in 1998 I asked the pioneering norteña musician and celebrated writer of narcocorridos Julián Garza about his seemingly detailed knowledge of narcotraffickers and their exploits, which appears in numerous songs and in movies based on his corridos in which he has starred, and he asserted that his songs were based purely on fantasy. He then went on to describe an extravagant, weekend-long party (many attendees were "probably drug dealers") near Reynosa, where he and his group (which includes his brother Luis) performed. "De repente, sonaron unos cuantos balazos. No supimos de donde vinieron, pero caímos al piso y nos quedamos allí hasta que no vimos a nadie. ¿Quizá fue la canción? Quién sabe. Volvimos a tocar y lo fue el fin de semana más chingón que tuvimos jamás."[2] When I pressed for more detail about the weekend, Garza added only that the compensation was well worth the scare and shrugged it off as part of life as a musician on the border.

---

[2] "Suddenly, some shots were fired. We didn't know where they came from, but we hit the floor and stayed there until we didn't see anyone. Could it have been the song? Who knows. We went back to playing, and it went on to be one of the most 'badass' weekends ever."

However, unlike Sánchez, Garza (in keeping with his role as corridista) is careful to note the presence of his group as mere performers and observers who are not intimately connected to these individuals or their activities, though many of their local fans seem to think otherwise. Garza is aware of such suspicions, but does not speak out publicly to defend himself or his group. In fact, his group's popularity thrives on such suspect and potentially dangerous associations. But Garza is from a different time, when norteña musicians generally occupied a rather privileged place: closer to the action than most, but never as at risk of meeting a tragic fate as many of their more fascinating subjects. When Sánchez became the subject of his songs, that respected privilege of the corridista (and by extension the norteña musician) began to erode, making the lives of these individuals just as expendable as those of the drug traffickers themselves.

Since 2006, there has been a bizarre rash of murders of popular Mexican singers—not only those of norteña groups but also those of groups performing another popular genre called *música duranguense* (also, *pasito duranguense*), which blends elements of norteña and banda (see the Glossary). Reports from both the Mexican press and fans themselves indicate that many of these artists had aligned themselves with powerful drug cartels as part of an elaborate patronage system and that the deaths are the result of violent turf wars. Murdering a popular musician with known connections to a particular cartel sends a strong message not only to that cartel but also to the community at large. In the case of the singer Jesús Rey David Alfaro Pulido's death (along with that of his manager and assistant) in Tijuana in February of 2008, authorities were investigating his alleged connections to the notorious Arellano Félix cartel. They were perplexed by a note pinned to Alfaro Pulido's tortured body that read, "you are next." There is speculation that this message was directed at the newly elected Mexican president, Felipe Calderón, who sent thousands of federal police and troops into Tijuana and cities with known cartels and corrupt police forces[3] (see McKinley 2008). It appears not only that these musicians have lost privileged immunity but also that their heightened popularity and blurring of the line between the corridista and the protagonist have made them superstars in their own tragic corrido.

Drug trafficking songs, however questionable the activities of their protagonists, appeal to the general Mexican immigrant population because they speak about the possibility of social mobility from poverty to wealth and power over U.S. authority (Edberg 2004, 56). The narcotraficante overcomes the very obstacles that most undocumented Mexican immigrant workers must confront on a daily basis. Ironically (though not surprisingly), the beginning of the resurgence in the popularity of narcocorridos such as "Mis Tres Animales" (My Three Animals)—the phenomenally popular early recording by Los Tucanes de Tijuana—coincided with

---

[3] See the international Web site Freemuse for a January 26, 2008, article about Alfaro Pulido and for links to other articles about Mexican singers murdered since 2006, http://www.huliq.com/51217/mexican-singer-jesus-rey-david-alfaro-killed (accessed October 17, 2008).

### Mis Tres Animales

| | |
|---|---|
| Aprendí a vivir la vida | I learned to live life |
| hasta que tuve dinero. | until I had money. |
| Y no niego que fui pobre | I don't deny that I was poor, |
| tampoco que fui burrero. | or that I was a mule-skinner. |
| Ahora soy un gran señor, | Now I am a great gentleman; |
| mis mascotas codician los güeros. | the gringos covet my pets. |
| | |
| Traigo cerquito la muerte | Death is always near me, |
| pero no me sé rajar. | but I don't know how to give in. |
| Sé que me busca el gobierno | I know the government is looking for me, |
| hasta debajo del mar. | even under the sea. |
| Pero para todo hay maña, | But there's a way around everything, |
| mi escóndite no han podido hallar. | and my hideout hasn't been found. |
| | |
| El dinero en abundancia | Too much money |
| también es muy peligroso. | is also very dangerous. |
| Por eso yo me lo gasto | That's why I spend it |
| con mis amigos gustosos | with my willing friends. |
| Y las mujeres, la neta | And with women, the bottom line is |
| con dinero y nos ven más hermosos. | we look more handsome with money. |

FIGURE 5.6 "Mis Tres Animales" (excerpt). Written by Mario Quintero Lara in 1995. Performed by Los Tucanes de Tijuana.

(From the CD *14 Tucanazos Bien Pesados* recorded by Los Tucanes de Tijuana [Universal Music Latino 017 672 (reissue), 2002]. Lyrics by Mario Quintero Lara courtesy of Flamingo Music, Inc.)

the passage of a comprehensive immigration bill proposed by President Bill Clinton in 1996. Among many things, the law doubled the border patrol to ten thousand agents over five years, allowed for the construction of a triple fence along the San Diego–Tijuana border, made it easier to deport undocumented workers, toughened sanctions for smuggling, made it more difficult for legal immigrants to bring relatives to the United States, and made it almost impossible for immigrants to prove discrimination by employers (Gómez-Quiñones and Maciel 1998, 44).[4]

In fact, "Mis Tres Animales" also blames drug-dependent North Americans for increased drug trafficking, a notion that is not too far removed from the notion of U.S. dependence on the physical labor of Mexican immigrants. These elements are illustrated in the excerpt of the lyrics from "Mis Tres Animales" shown in Figure 5.6. In the song, the three animals represent three types of drugs: parakeet (cocaine), rooster (marijuana), and goat (heroin). The song also contains

---

[4]The Illegal Immigration Reform and Immigrant Responsibility Act (IIRIRA), Pub. L. No. 104-208, 110 Stat. 309, was enacted as Division C of the Omnibus Appropriations Act of 1996.

thematic elements of the border corrido such as the constant nearness of death, machismo, and dominance over women. Throughout, there is a constant play on words that recall the Norteño *pelado* characterization and humorous double-speak of many songs by El Piporro. Finally, by allowing the listener, particularly the undocumented, into the narcotraficante world, the song recalls the loss of identity that is experienced after crossing the border. This element also gives the narcotraficante "everyman" qualities that hark back to the social bandit hero of traditional border corridos (Martínez 1998, 37).

While few musicians and community members will actually admit to supporting the narcotraficante lifestyle and means of earning a living, it is well-known that many successful drug smugglers and kingpins send money back to villages in Mexico to support churches and to build hospitals and schools (Ramírez-Pimienta 2004, 23). In this sense, the narcotraficante is honored and respected because he "helps the poor" (Ramírez-Pimienta 2004, 34). This sense of obligation to one's hometown and region is shared by the primarily undocumented immigrants, many of whom have founded grassroots organizations in the United States in order to send money back to help their communities at home (Smith 2003, 298–300). Many Mexican immigrants (and nonmigrant Mexicans) admire the bravery, power, and fearlessness of the drug dealer who reminds them of celebrated social bandits of the border (Villa, Cortez, Quintero, et al.)—valiant men and outlaws who offered hope in the midst of economic despair.

## Los Tigres as the Sociopolitical Voice of the People

As the group who first popularized the narcocorrido in norteña music, Los Tigres have enjoyed a long and increasingly successful career. Without a doubt, they are the most popular and sought-after group in the history of modern norteña music (Quiñones 1998; Wald 2001; Edberg 2004; personal communications with Rogelio García, Ramiro Cavazos, et al.). After the success of "Contrabando y Traición," their popularity spread throughout the United States and then into Mexico, largely as a result of their narcocorrido films. The explosion of cassette recording and video production greatly expanded their reach, particularly as immigrants returned home with their music and manufacturers of pirated recordings and videos sold them in scores of outdoor markets, record and video shops, furniture stores, restaurants, and bars. The group also traveled the taco circuit weekly, playing small towns and cities throughout the Mexican diaspora, taking little time to rest.

### "Vivan los Mojados"

In 1976, the group recorded a song given to them by a local songwriter named Jesús Armenta. The song, also written in the canción-corrido form, was titled

"Vivan los Mojados" (Long Live the Wetbacks). It proved to be a turning point in the group's still-blossoming career and was the first of many highly successful "mojado corridos" that would surpass the group's numerous narcotraficante songs in popularity. "Vivan los Mojados" draws attention to the U.S. public's growing dependence on the Mexican laborer and speculates on the disastrous consequences for society if the mojados were suddenly to be ejected from the fields and sent home. In a 1999 interview posted on the music journalist Elijah Wald's Web site, Jorge Hernández said, "We wanted to sing about immigration, about the life of the mojado, because that is how we came over—a lot of Mexicans were coming over illegally. But we had to be careful not to offend anyone with the use of that word, *mojado*, we had to find intelligently written songs . . . a whole new level of writing."[5]

Intelligent, but not intellectual. "Vivan los Mojados" uses street lingo, particularly that of immigrants, such as *mojado* and *la mica* (green card), and in a very direct, almost obstinate, tone. It dismisses anti-immigration laws and aggressive tightening of the border as futile because the modern-day mojado knows his new power and worth on "el otro lado" (the other side). It warns that the mojado is more persistent in his or her efforts to cross the border and has sorted through the social terrains of the host country (United States) and is now beginning to create a distinctly Mexican immigrant space and an identity that is no longer helpless, fragile, or susceptible to the forces that kept the community marginalized. The counterhegemonic discourse that unfolds in this song is contrary to that of earlier songs about the immigrant who silently endures racial slurs, mistreatment by employers, and the constant fear of deportation, such as "Los Alambrados" (The Wire Jumpers), "Por el Puente" (Over the Bridge), and "El Deportado" (The Deported). The last was initially recorded by the vocal/guitar duo Los Hermanos Bañuelos (The Bañuelos Brothers) in 1929 and later adapted as "El Emigrado" (The Emigrant) by Eugenio Abrego of Los Alegres de Terán (Herrera-Sobek 1993, 128–129). The excerpt shown in Figure 5.7 is the last three stanzas from "El Deportado" by an unknown writer. It is an example of the shame and vulnerability experienced by the humble immigrant who crosses the border to work. This song was typical of illegal border-crossing songs from that period.

In contrast to this song, "Vivan los Mojados," and many contemporary corridos by Los Tigres and other norteña groups that followed in the late 1970s and 1980s, openly mocked the authority of the border patrol and the immigration laws implemented by the United States. The mojados' persistence and ability to cross in large numbers, despite the U.S. government's efforts to keep them out, dismantles the border and the hegemonic interests that maintain it (Martínez 1998). Mojado identity is then strengthened as the barriers that once made the

---

[5] See http://www.elijahwald.com/jhernan.html (accessed April 16, 2004).

## El Deportado

| | |
|---|---|
| Llegamos por fin a Juárez (2×)<br>allí fue mi apuración.<br>"¿Que dónde vas, que de dónde<br>vienes?"<br>"¿que cuánto dinero tienes<br>para entrar a esta nación?" | We finally arrived in Juárez; (2×)<br>there my worries began.<br>"Where are you going, where do you<br>come from?"<br>"How much money have you<br>to enter this nation?" |
| "Señores traigo dinero (2×)<br>Para poder emigrar."<br>"Tu dinero nada vale;<br>te tenemos que bañar." (2×) | "Gentlemen, I have money, (2×)<br>so that I can enter."<br>"Your money is not worth anything;<br>we have to bathe you." (2×) |
| Ay, mis paisanos queridos, (2×)<br>yo les platico nomás.<br>Que me estaban dando ganas (2×)<br>de volverme para atrás. | Oh, my beloved countrymen, (2×)<br>I won't talk about it anymore.<br>They were making me feel (2×)<br>like going right back. |

FIGURE 5.7 "El Deportado" (excerpt of lyrics from Part 2). Author unknown (probably written in the early 1920s). Performed by Los Hermanos Bañuelos, vocal duet with guitar. (Recorded in Los Angeles, California, circa 1929 for Vocalion [8287]. Available on *Mexican American Border Music, Vols. 6 and 7: Corridos y Tragedias de la Frontera* [Arhoolie/Folklyric CD 7019/7020]. Lyrics courtesy of Freddie Records/MARFRE Music. English translation courtesy of Arhoolie Records.)

illegal immigrant vulnerable (i.e., the border patrol, illegal status, the green card, poverty, and racism) are deconstructed. Another element of this and other immigrant corridos is humor, which El Piporro demonstrated in the "Chulas Fronteras." Humor and joking are very much a part of Mexican border culture; they were common features of the carpa tradition and later transferred to Mexican films. Corridos, in particular, have always contained macho boasts, insults, and clever wordplay and are filled with figurative speech associated with the oral tradition of the community (McDowell 1981, 61–63).

Rather than reporting about an individual or a particular event in the third person (as in the traditional border corrido) or in the first person (as in many canción-corridos by Los Alegres de Terán, Los Relámpagos del Norte, and Ramón Ayala y Los Bravos del Norte, which are about love or a personal story), this song ·is written in the first person plural ("we"), thereby including the group members themselves (referring to their own original crossing as mojados) as part of a large community of mojado immigrants. In this manner, Los Tigres situate themselves as spokespersons for the community and address, simultaneously, the U.S. government:

El problema de nosotros
fácil se puede arreglar
que nos den una gringuita
para podernos casar
y ya que nos den la mica
volvernos a divorciar.

Our problem
is easy to solve
let them give us a white woman
to marry,
and when they give us the green card,
we'll get divorced.

the border patrol:

Si uno sacan por Laredo
por Mexicali entran diez.
si otro sacan por Tijuana
por Nogales entran seis.
Ahí nomás saquen la cuenta
cuántos entramos al mes.

If one of us is kicked out in Laredo,
ten more enter through Mexicali.
If another is kicked out in Tijuana,
six enter through Nogales.
It's better to stop counting
how many of us enter each month.

and the U.S. public at large:

Cuando el mojado haga huelga
de no volver otra vez.
¿Quién va a tapiar la cebolla,
lechuga y el betabel,
el limón y la toronja?
Se echarán toda a perder.

When the wetback goes on strike
and decides not to return again.
Who is going to pick the onions,
lettuce and beet,
the lemon and the grapefruit?
All of them will spoil.

In each of these situations, the nameless and illegal mojado defines an identity for himself or herself through the ability to outsmart authority and move freely across the border and through dedication and pride in his or her ability to work hard. Speaking in the collective "we" gives strength and solidarity to this new, more powerful mojado identity. It is also important to note that mexicanidad is very much attached to this identity because it separates the mojado from the Anglo-American and the assimilated Mexican American. In this song, mexicanidad is expressed through macho boasting, a distinctly Norteño and Mexican trait (Martínez 1998, 45), which is manifested in this song by the mojado's assumed ability to seduce, conquer, and marry a white woman. The next line is a further play on these stereotypes, which have been transferred to the mojado: "Porque si se va el mojado, ¿quiénes van a ir a bailar? Y a más de cuatro del vuelo no las podrán consolar" (Because if the wetback leaves, who is going to dance? And when these women want more, they will not be satisfied).

"Vivan los Mojados" displays musical, rhythmic, and poetic virtuosity similar to that of "Contrabando y Traición." The accordion is used in novel ways, though always at the end of a verse line or stanza, never interrupting the flow of the song. In the transcription shown in Figure 5.8, note that the accordion never enters the poetic space of the corrido, which remains one of the most significant differences between Texas-Mexican conjunto (where the accordion dominates the melody throughout, whether sung or not) and norteña. Mexican immigrants, both fans of norteña music and musicians, often comment that giving the words more prominence in a song is what makes norteña more "Mexican." In the traditional border corrido, like "Gregorio Cortez" (see Figure 3.4), the final words in the even-numbered lines are typically controlled for rhyme or assonance (McDowell 1981, 57). In other words, the last word is either shortened or prolonged, depending on the number of syllables present (generally eight per line), and it also rhymes. In the Los Alegres' "Carta Jugada" example (see Figure 3.7), the accordion fills come after the prolonged final syllable of the second line and the sixth, which is also true in "Vivan los Mojados," though not in the previous Los Tigres example, "Contrabando y Traición" (see Figure 5.1).

In this song, as in the last Los Tigres example, there are rests after each line, except those that are followed by an accordion fill. These rests add an almost "spoken" quality to the corrido, emphasizing the telling of a story. Again, the insertion of a drum roll or additional notes on the bass seems to depend on the poetic discourse and on the emphasis the musicians choose to place on a certain word, or to punctuate an action or thought in the story line. Such stylistic innovation allows, then, for a deeper level of communication between the singer and audience, enabling the singer to comment on the text. In the musical transcription

*(continued on next page)*

FIGURE 5.8 Transcription of "Vivan los Mojados," mm. 1–24 (first stanza). Words and music by Jesús Armenta Minjarez. As performed and recorded by Los Tigres del Norte in 1976. Vocals, accordion, bajo sexto, electric bass guitar, snare drum (hi-hat and bass drum not included in transcription).

(From the CD *¡Vivan los Mojados!* Fonovisa [reissue], 2002. "Vivan los Mojados" words and music by Jesús Armenta Minjarez. Copyright © 1996 by Grever Music Publishing S.A. de C.V. All rights administered in the United States and Canada by Universal Music–Z Songs. International copyright secured. All rights reserved.)

**FIGURE 5.8** *Continued*

excerpt from "Vivan los Mojados" shown in Figure 5.9, notice that in the second line the word *ley* (law) is counted as two syllables in the first measure and sustained for the next two measures (mm. 6–8).

The accordion enters in measure 7 and plays a short pattern that ascends and descends, completing the short phrase in measure 9. In line 4, the accordion plays an open sixth chord and is followed by a drum roll on the third beat in measure 15, following the word *inglés* (English). Additionally, *inglés* is sung with a melisma on its final syllable. This fourth line of the stanza has only seven syllables, and rather than count the final syllable as two, the accordion unexpectedly provides the eighth syllable. The group clearly uses these musical devices to comment upon or indicate a double meaning for this line. The full text of this line reads *y no hablamos en inglés* (and we don't speak English). Reading this line in the context of the song, that the mojado does not speak English seems to be one of the many obstacles that keep him marginalized in North American society. However, by inserting the melismatic slur followed by the open sixth chord and drum roll (as a "punch line"), the group clearly refers to the mojado's resistance to assimilate into North American society by *choosing* not to speak English.

In this way, the mojado maintains his or her loyalty to Mexico and, by extension, mexicanidad, the source of power through which the mojado constructs his Mexican identity in the United States (Martínez 1998, 39). While it may

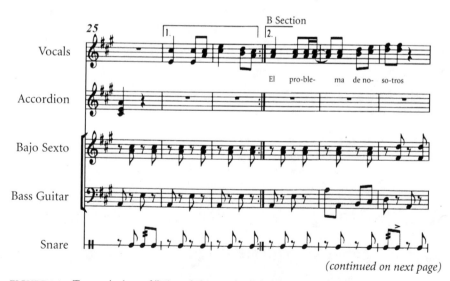

*(continued on next page)*

**FIGURE 5.9** Transcription of "Vivan los Mojados," third stanza (B section—chorus), mm. 28–48. Words and music by Jesús Armenta Minjarez. As performed and recorded by Los Tigres del Norte in 1976. Vocals, accordion, bajo sexto, electric bass guitar, snare drum (hi-hat and bass drum not included in transcription).

(From the CD ¡*Vivan los Mojados!* Fonovisa [reissue], 2002. "Vivan los Mojados" words and music by Jesús Armenta Minjarez. Copyright © 1996 by Grever Music Publishing S.A. de C.V. All rights administered in the United States and Canada by Universal Music–Z Songs. International copyright secured. All rights reserved.)

**FIGURE 5.9** *Continued*

appear on the surface that the mojado's inability to speak English and his loyalty to Mexico is what keeps him marginalized, the mojado reinterprets these obstacles as a means to construct a new identity that is separate from that of the assimilated Mexican American (*malinchista*) and the U.S. outsider. To a marginalized community, this song (as well as the double meanings that can be found throughout) represents the opening of a new space for a community that is beginning to come into its own.

In the first chorus, or B section, of this song (third stanza), the accordion does not follow the same rules that applied in the first two stanzas. Rather than playing fills after the second and sixth lines, it executes short rhythmic "punctuations" after the third line (chromatic triplet in m. 36) following the word *gringuita* (white woman) and after the fourth line (open chord in m. 39) following the word *casar* (to marry). The bass also ascends, along with the accordion, after *gringuita* and before *casar*. There are other musical devices employed to draw special attention to these lines, leading up to these two words. In measure 33, before the third line begins, the bass moves in a downward motion (A, F#, E) while a three-stroke drum roll lands on the final beat. The third line reads: "que nos den una gringuita" (let them give us a white woman). The open-chord, single-note accordion fill after *casar* is followed by a drum roll in the same measure. The fourth line reads: "para podernos casar" (so that we can get married). These two lines not only outline an option for the mojado—as the following two lines in the stanza state, "y ya que nos den la mica / volvernos a divorciar" (so that we can get a green card / and then get divorced)—but also emphasize the immigrant's ability to subvert the law (very much in the way the narcotraficante buys off the border patrol and U.S. and Mexican authority figures and politicians).

It also engages a long-standing tradition of the virile, macho bandit hero as womanizer; however, this trait is refashioned by the mojado as a means of ascribing power to himself in overcoming the obstacles of his low racial and class-based status. Beginning in the 1970s, women crossed the border in larger numbers—many with their husbands but some as single women and mothers—to look for work as well. Some immigrant films and songs that have come out since that time depict Mexican women leaving their husbands for gringos or crossing the border in search of North American husbands who could better support them financially. In the last three lines in this stanza, it is the male mojado who seduces a white woman to get what he wants (a green card). However, unlike many Mexican women who marry white men, the mojado asserts his mexicanidad by discarding his gringa wife when she is no longer useful. He asserts his loyalty to Mexico (and Mexican women) by choosing not to stay married to a white woman and eventually assimilating. In fact, in a sequel to this song, "Ya Nos Dieron Permiso" (They Finally Gave Us Permission), a green card is obtained through marriage (Martínez 1995, 333).

Within the growing Mexican immigrant community, not just in California, but throughout the United States, the reaction to "Vivan los Mojados" was unprecedented, and for the first time, it placed the marginalized Mexican laborer in the foreground of an expanding Mexican diaspora. "Vivan los Mojados" (lyrics shown in Figure 5.10)—along with numerous "mojado" songs that continue to be written and performed today—represents a living history of immigrant life that balances experiences of separation, lost love, displacement, and economic struggle with a solidarity that is formed through the shared experience of living life on the margin. Mojado-themed songs also provide an alternative definition of self that moves the Mexican immigrant worker further away from cultural assimilation and political socialization. Whether depicted as fearless narcotraficantes or nameless mojados, through these songs, the Mexican immigrant laborer places himself or herself outside the authority and the power of the state, where the struggle for survival and respect only makes this community—now located in rural towns and urban centers throughout the United States—even more strongly bonded and unified (Gutiérrez 1999).

Songs about immigration and mojados turned out to be what Mexican immigrants living not only in California but also throughout the United States responded to most. Like Ramón Ayala, Los Tigres began working with a handful of songwriters, most of them Mexican immigrants living in the United States. Los Tigres also received songs from many of their fans. The group also enlisted Ayala's promoter, Monterrey-based Servando Cano, who organized concerts, dances, and performances in cities and villages on both sides of the border. Though many of the songs that followed "Vivan los Mojados" continued to focus on issues of migration and mojado identity, as Mexican immigrants continued to travel to the United States and established permanent communities, Los Tigres' songs began to reflect the psychological impact of building a life in a foreign country. Some of these songs include "Jaula de Oro" (Golden Cage), "Camisa Mojada" (Wet Shirt), "Los Tres Amigos" (The Three Friends), "El Otro México" (The Other Mexico), "Tres Veces Mojado" (Three Times a Wetback), and "Ni Aquí ni Allá" (Neither Here nor There). These songs were widely popular and served to unite the community in the "third space" of marginality and in the formation of a new identity constructed through the collective experience, both real and imagined, of the immigrant (Soja 1996; Bhabha 1994). The border became less significant as more contemporary issues emerged. Hernán Hernández, a member of Los Tigres, explained the evolution of the themes of the group's songs to the reporter Claudia S. Meléndez in an interview that appeared in the August 29, 2003, issue of *Nuevo Mundo*: "Nosotros empezamos a cantar corridos en 1968, cuando sacamos el primer disco, y desde entonces hemos cantado lo que sucedía: en los años setenta cantamos historias de los ilegales, en los años ochenta cantamos lo de la amnistía y así hemos cantado lo que va sucediendo."[6] Part of what

---

[6]"We began to sing corridos in 1968, when we released our first record, and since then we have sung about what has happened. In the seventies, we sang stories about illegal (immigrants), and in the eighties, we sang about amnesty, and we have sung about what has continued to happen."

### Vivan los Mojados

**A**

| | |
|---|---|
| Porque somos los mojados | Because we are wetbacks, |
| siempre nos busca la ley | the law is always looking for us. |
| porque estamos ilegales | Because we are illegal |
| y no hablamos en inglés | and we do not speak English, |
| el gringo terco a sacarnos | the obstinate gringo throws us out, |
| y nosotros a volver. | and we return. |

**A**

| | |
|---|---|
| Si uno sacan por Laredo | If one of us is kicked out in Laredo, |
| por Mexicali entran diez. | ten more enter through Mexicali. |
| si otro sacan por Tijuana | If another is kicked out in Tijuana, |
| por Nogales entran seis. | six enter through Nogales. |
| Ahí nomás saquen la cuenta | It's better to stop counting |
| cuántos entramos al mes. | how many of us enter each month. |

**B**

| | |
|---|---|
| El problema de nosotros | Our problem |
| fácil se puede arreglar | is easy to solve |
| que nos den una gringuita | let them give us a white woman |
| para podernos casar | to marry, |
| y ya que nos den la mica | and when they give us the green card, |
| volvernos a divorciar. | we'll get divorced. |

*(continued on next page)*

FIGURE 5.10 "Vivan los Mojados." Words and music by Jesús Armenta Minjarez. Performed by Los Tigres del Norte.

(Copyright © 1996 by Grever Music Publishing S.A. de C.V. All rights administered in the United States and Canada by Universal Music–Z Songs. International copyright secured. All rights reserved.)

has allowed Los Tigres to continue to reinvent the corrido is their ability to find composers who give them corridos that not only speak to the immigrant community but also reflect a collective imagination of self and the shared experiences of those who were newly arrived as well as those who were establishing roots and creating their lives in the United States. Some of the most memorable songwriters in the Los Tigres stable are Paulino Vargas (whose career goes back to 1955 and the group Los Broncos de Reynosa), Enrique Franco, Teodoro Bello, and Jesús Armenta. Like the group, many of these writers came illegally to the United States and wrote about their experiences or those of others in the community.

In 1984, Enrique Franco, having worked five years as a musical director at the now-defunct Fama Records in San Jose, found himself unemployed and without immigration papers. In an interview with the political science scholar

---

### Vivan los Mojados (continued)

**A**

| | |
|---|---|
| Cuando el mojado haga huelga | When the wetback goes on strike |
| de no volver otra vez. | and decides not to return again. |
| ¿Quién va a tapiar la cebolla, | Who is going to pick the onions, |
| lechuga y el betabel, | lettuce and beet, |
| el limón y la toronja? | the lemon and the grapefruit? |
| Se echarán toda a perder. | All of them will spoil. |

**A**

| | |
|---|---|
| Esos salones de baile | All the dance halls |
| todos los van a cerrar | will close down. |
| Porque si se va el mojado, | Because if the wetback leaves, |
| ¿quiénes van a ir a bailar? | who is going to dance? |
| Y a más de cuatro del vuelo | And when these women want more, |
| no las podrán consolar. | they will not be satisfied. |

**B1**

| | |
|---|---|
| Vivan todos los mojados | Long live the wetbacks, |
| los que ya van a emigrar, | those who are about to emigrate, |
| los que van de vacaciones, | those that come on vacations, |
| y los que van a pasar, | and those that are going to cross over, |
| los que van a casarse | those that are going to marry |
| para poder arreglar. | so that they can get their papers. |

---

FIGURE 5.10 *Continued*

Jesús Martínez, Franco recalls hearing a fellow undocumented immigrant describe the United States as a "gold cage," referring to the perception of wealth and a better life here that draws many people and to the reality that exists for the disenfranchised undocumented immigrant (quoted in Martínez 1995, 330). Today, having legalized his status under the Immigration Reform and Control Act of 1986, Franco continues to write songs for other norteña groups, though many of the songs that he gave Los Tigres were some of their most evocative and socially conscious. Franco's "Jaula de Oro" (lyrics shown in Figure 5.11) is sung from the perspective of an immigrant who has become successful in the United States but still feels trapped by his illegal status. He also laments that his children have become assimilated, speak little Spanish, and know little about their Mexican heritage. This song struck a chord with so many immigrants that a Mexican movie titled *Jaula de oro* and based on the song's premise was released in 1987. The song employs the sung and spoken text dynamic that El Piporro used in "Chulas Fronteras" (see Chapter 4, pages 110–111), among other songs. Franco

# Jaula de Oro

*Cantado:*
Aquí estoy establecido en
los Estados Unidos.
Diez años pasaron ya,
en que crucé de mojado.
Papeles no he arreglado,
sigo siendo un ilegal.
Tengo mi esposa y mis hijos
que me los traje muy chicos.

Y se han olvidado
ya de mi México querido,
del que yo nunca me olvido
y no puedo regresar.
¿De qué me sirve el dinero
si estoy como prisionero,
dentro de esta gran nación?
Cuando me acuerdo hasta lloro,
y aunque la jaula sea de oro
no deja de ser prisión.

*Hablado:*
"Escúchame hijo, te gustaría que
regresáramos a vivir a México?"
"What're you talking about Dad,
I don't want to go back to Mexico.
No way, Dad."

*Cantado:*
Mis hijos no hablan conmigo.
Otro idioma han aprendido;
y olvidado el español.
Piensan como americanos
niegan que son mexicanos,
aunque tengan mi color.

De mi trabajo a mi casa
yo no sé lo que me pasa.
Que aunque soy hombre de hogar.
Casi no salgo a la calle,
pues tengo miedo que me hallen
y me puedan deportar.

*Sung:*
I am established here in
the United States.
Now, ten years have passed,
since I crossed illegally.
I have not gotten my papers,
so I continue to be illegal.
I have my wife and my kids,
that I brought with me when they were young.

And they have forgotten
my dear Mexico,
that I will never forget
but cannot return to.
What is this money for
if I live like a prisoner,
in this great nation?
Sometimes I think about it until I cry,
and about the cage of gold,
I don't forget that it is a prison.

*Spoken:*
"Listen to me, son, would you like it if
we went back to live in Mexico?"
"What're you talking about Dad,
I don't want to go back to Mexico.
No way, Dad."

*Sung:*
My children don't talk to me.
They have learned another language;
they have forgotten Spanish.
They think like Americans;
they refuse to admit that they are Mexicans,
though they have my skin color.

From my work to my house
I don't know what will happen.
So now I'm a man of the house.
I rarely go out into the street,
but I'm afraid that they will catch me,
and they could deport me.

**FIGURE 5.11** "Jaula de Oro." Lyrics by Enrique Franco (1984). Performed by Los Tigres del Norte. (Courtesy of TN Ediciones Musicales.)

wrote other songs based on his own experience as well as those of other immigrants, such as "Tres Veces Mojado" and "El Otro México." The latter, Martínez notes, "portrays immigrants as nationalists ... and as heroes and progressive social actors who make important contributions to the homeland" (1995, 333). These corridos, focusing on the undocumented experience, continued to move beyond the border and to more personal issues and conflicts experienced daily by the Mexican worker living in the United States. Spurred on by Franco's gifted songwriting and the overwhelming response to these songs, Los Tigres emerged as the undisputed voice of the undocumented, the mojado. While groups such as Los Humildes (The Humble Ones), Los Terribles del Norte (The Bad Guys of the North), Los Cadetes de Linares (The Cadets of Linares), and others record mojado corridos from time to time, Los Tigres consistently dedicated either entire albums to the theme or at least one or two songs on each recording. Their fans have come to not only expect such songs but also assume that the songs will make strong social and political statements (whether directed at the U.S. or the Mexican government). This was so important that once the group stopped working exclusively with Franco in the early 1990s, they found other writers like Teodoro Bello and Jesús Armenta, who would continue to focus on issues relevant to mojados. The group's dedication to this segment of the Mexican immigrant population has earned it the moniker "Los Ídolos del Pueblo" (The Idols of the People).

While many of Los Tigres' songs celebrated the courage, defiance, pride, and power of the mojado and the Mexican immigrant in the United States, the group's popularity also soared in Mexico. In the late 1970s, with the advent of cassette recordings, migrants and immigrants who traveled back to Mexico to visit family members often brought recordings of the group's music with them, further broadening their popularity in that country. By the 1980s, cassettes of norteña music were readily available in a wide variety of locations, such as flea markets, grocery stores, cafes, restaurants, and street corner kiosks, thanks to the low cost of manufacturing and distributing. Additionally, cassette recording technology opened the door to pirating, which goes unconstrained in Mexico and which has helped norteña surpass Tejano music in popularity and develop a broader audience (see Manuel 1993). Since there were only a handful of labels dedicated to the recording, manufacturing, and distributing of norteña music, such as Fonovisa, Freddie Records, DLV (now Disa), and Rio Bravo Records, thousands of local entrepreneurs on both sides of the border (particularly in Mexico) went into the less expensive business of pirating. Though the recordings of Los Tigres and Ramón Ayala are probably the most pirated, their exhaustive touring schedules keep the groups and their record labels financially solvent.

By the late 1980s, the popularity of norteña decreased somewhat as other Spanish-language popular music genres such as salsa, cumbia, *música tejana,* and *rock en español* were heavily marketed to second- and third-generation youth by Latin divisions of major label distributors such as Capital EMI, Sony, and BMG.

Similarly, recording companies in Monterrey began to turn their attention to such cumbia norteña artists as Los Bukis and Bronco, who modeled themselves after norteña groups but sang predominantly love ballads and cumbias rather than contemporary corridos. Like their Tejano counterparts, these groups played large concert halls, rather than dance clubs, on both sides of the border. The dominance of this genre over corrido-driven norteña lasted only until the late 1980s. The mid-1990s saw a surge of Mexican migration into the United States as a result of the end of tariffs on food products under NAFTA; bad Mexican farm policy, which affected an estimated twenty-five million people; and a severe economic crisis that prompted the gross devaluation of the peso, from which Mexico has not recovered (Durand, Massey, and Parrado 1999). Firmly established as the music and the voice of the Mexican immigrant population, with strong sympathies for the undocumented immigrant, norteña would increase in popularity as the decade wore on and the numbers of immigrants steadily rose.

Undocumented workers coming to the United States now had to pay a higher price for illegal transportation and fraudulent documents (Gómez-Quiñones and Maciel 1998, 44). Similarly, public opinion against undocumented workers grew harsher in the mid-1990s as the surveillance of the border, work sites, highways, and neighborhoods increased as a result of new comprehensive immigrant legislation (the Illegal Immigrant Reform Act and the Personal Responsibility and Work Opportunity Reconciliation Act of 1996). Undocumented immigrants responded by remaining in the United States, with their dependents, rather than risking the return home. They also moved away from traditional Mexican enclaves in the Southwest and settled in new communities in midwestern, northern, and southeastern states. The undocumented status of such a large number of now-permanent Mexican residents created a "new underground economy" that caused greater wage discrimination, a deterioration of working conditions, and a more impoverished community (Durand, Massey, and Parrado 1999, 528–531). Under these conditions a resurgence of narcocorridos and mojado corridos has occurred among the Mexican immigrant community.

Los Tigres' enduring success and their dominance of norteña sales on both sides of the U.S.-Mexico border (by the mid-1990s they eclipsed Ramón Ayala) is a source of some controversy. Some have criticized them for equating norteña music with narcocorridos in the minds of the public and commercial vendors. However, this group has the ability to combine fantasy with reality, mixing songs about pistol-packing outlaws and drug-smuggling bandit heroes with songs about the lives of undocumented workers and their families, as well as the political system that keeps them marginalized. In the world of Mexican immigrant popular music, cumbia norteña and banda exist primarily as modern popular dance genres, and mariachi and ranchero music endure for purposes of nostalgia and reinforcement of Mexican pride and cultural heritage; somewhere in the middle, norteña survives for its texts—its testimonials, as it were—about heroic figures past and present, real and imagined, all of whom experienced border crossing, broken families, and economic and social inequality. Ramírez-Pimienta (2004, 24–25) has written that the music of Los Tigres and other norteña artists known for recording corridos (Los Huracanes del Norte, Luis y Julián, Los Invasores del Norte, Los Tucanes de Tijuana, and others) changes very little because the public expects them to be the interpreters of their lives and their stories. The Los Tigres bandleader Hernán Hernández affirmed this notion in an August 29, 2003, interview with Claudia S. Meléndez in *Nuevo Mundo*: "Los Tigres hemos logrado esa comunicación con personas de la vida real. El protagonista de nuestras canciones es la gente, eso hace que Los Tigres del Norte estemos aquí vigentes." (Los Tigres have maintained this communication with real-life people. The protagonist in our songs is the people, and because of this, Los Tigres del Norte have continued in force.)

In the May 18, 2005, broadcast of the popular variety television program, *Don Francisco Presenta*, Los Tigres were interviewed by the show's host, Mario Kreutzberger (known as Don Francisco). The framing of the group's appearance on the program is strongly representative of how they have been promoted by their label Fonovisa and by the group members themselves: as working-class family men, as pop music icons, as Mexican immigrants, and as representatives of the undocumented immigrant. Kreutzberger began the program by talking with the group about their now-deceased father, traveling to New York with their mother to accept a Grammy award, and how they all learned to play instruments from elder brother Jorge. After renditions of early hits like "Contrabando y Traición" and "Jefe de Jefes," the group was joined by Blanca Martínez, the editor of *Furia Musical,* a norteña fanzine; she gushed about the band's deep connection with its fans and how it is one of the few popular norteña groups that saves all the handwritten song requests and dedications from fans while other groups throw them away.

Finally, the book author, news columnist, and news anchor (*Noticiero Univision*) Jorge Ramos joined the group to discuss his latest book, *Morir en el intento: La peor tragedia de inmigrantes en la historia de los Estados Unidos* (To die in the attempt: The worst immigrant tragedy in the history of the United States),[7] which documents the odyssey of seventy-three immigrants who crossed the border illegally in May 2003. They were discovered locked in a trailer truck, dehydrated and starving, with nineteen dead among them. As a tribute, Los Tigres sang a popular corrido, "José Peréz León," which tells the story of one of the dead victims whose five-year-old son also perished in the incident. "Our immigrants are not terrorists," Ramos pronounced. "They cross illegally because they have no other choice. They should not have to die this way." With that, Los Tigres ended the program with their Grammy-nominated song "De Paisano a Paisano" (From Countryman to Countryman), a testament of solidarity with

---

[7] New York: Harper Collins, 2005. Ramos is also the author of *The Other Face of America: Chronicles of the Immigrants Shaping Our Future* (New York: Harper Collins, 2003).

all Mexicans who risk their lives traveling to the United States to look for work. The song's chorus reads:

| | |
|---|---|
| De paisano a paisano | From countryman to countryman, |
| del hermano al hermano, | from brother to brother, |
| por querer trabajar | because of our desire to work |
| nos han hecho la guerra, | they have waged war on us, |
| patrullando fronteras, | by patrolling the borders, |
| no nos pueden domar. | but they cannot break us. |

To this chorus Los Tigres added the popular phrase—one that is often uttered by many norteña groups and *sonideros*—"soy mexicano, cien por ciento" (I am Mexican, 100 percent). Whether they sing about Mexicans as drug traffickers or as hard working immigrants, Los Tigres are well aware of their audience and their sentiments and plight. And though this community has been discarded by the Mexican government, criminalized and hunted in the border, and exploited in the United States, Los Tigres' songs provide unity and power through a shared imagination of a Mexican identity and immigrant nation that exists through sheer determination, hard work, and pride. As former undocumented immigrants, Los Tigres have carried on a decades-old Norteño and border-based discourse of social bandits as working-class heroes who make good. As in their songs, the group's popular music persona is constructed in the image of border heroes like Gregorio Cortez, Pancho Villa, and Emilio Varela: humble everymen who stood up against poverty, oppression, racism, and U.S. capitalist expansionism.

## Norteña Music and the Politics of Crossing Musical Borders

While the popularity of norteña has been attributed to the widespread commercialization of narcocorridos and mojado songs, the genre has met with criticism from the Mexican government and music industry. Not surprisingly, the Mexican government disapproves of narcocorridos and has asked radio stations throughout Mexico and the United States to ban them from their playlists (Wilson 1998). While many commercial stations in both countries have complied, particularly in northern Mexican states bordering the United States and in Texas and California, narcocorridos have become big business for independent Spanish-language record labels based in California, especially for Fonovisa, which started out as an independent and is now part of the Univision media conglomerate. Though the Mexican government has called for a ban on narcocorridos in the past, their resurgence in popularity has prompted more serious calls for their censorship. Because the Mexican Senate is unable to ban narcocorridos thanks to freedom-of-speech legislation, it has pressured individual states to restrict stations from playing them ("Mexico's Forbidden Songs" 2004). Between 1998 and 2003, several northern and bordering Mexican states—Baja California, Chihuahua, Sinaloa, Nuevo León, Michoacán—responded by passing legislation that "invited" stations to outlaw narcocorridos from the airwaves (Ramírez-Pimienta 2004, 22–23). In 2003, the state of Nuevo León, the birthplace of the corrido and norteña music, passed a resolution banning radio and television broadcasts of narcocorridos. This action has translated to an across-the-board avoidance of corridos by several radio stations on both sides of the border. In an interview I conducted with Hugo Morales, the station manager of Radio Bilingüe, a network of Spanish-language stations in California that syndicates its programs throughout the United States and Mexico, he said that many stations in the United States have also responded to pressure from the Mexican government for a ban on narcocorridos by simply not playing any corridos at all, regardless of the theme (personal communication). Los Tigres have declared in interviews with the press and in their shows that the government's campaign to censor narcocorridos is nothing short of editing history and muting (or even silencing) the voices of the underclass. In an interview with the Spanish press, Hernán Hernández of Los Tigres expressed this sentiment: "En México ya no se pueden hacer corridos de Pancho Villa ni de la revolución mexicana, porque ahora se viven otros tiempos, dramas, sucesos y momentos que no se pueden evitar ni esconder" (quoted in Ramírez-Pimienta 2004, 22).[8] Though no legislation regarding narcocorridos, or corridos in general, has yet surfaced in California or Texas, Morales said that many stations, particularly commercial ones, have severely limited corridos or censored them altogether. In many cases, this policy has meant limited airplay of norteña music in general, even today.

In recent years, Los Tigres and other norteña groups have turned their attention away from narcocorridos to express their opinion about Mexican politics, government corruption, U.S. immigration laws and legislation, and oppression of the undocumented worker. Ironically, more songs focusing on these themes began to appear on recordings just after the Mexican government passed a constitutional reform in 1997 that allowed first-generation Mexicans living abroad or those who have obtained U.S. citizenship to maintain their Mexican citizenship. The Mexican government's motivation is to deter assimilation of its immigrants and keep them connected to their Mexican identity and heritage so that they continue to send millions of dollars in remittances, also known as migradollars. Many Mexican sociologists have noted that the more assimilated into U.S. society and culture the immigrant becomes, the less likely he or she is to send money to extended family members or to support the construction of public facilities and services in his or her city, town, or village of origin. According to a Reuters report on March 5, 2008, remittances from Mexicans in the United

---

[8] "Now in Mexico you can't even write corridos about Pancho Villa or the Mexican Revolution because now we live in different times, where there are dramas, events, and moments that you cannot avoid or hide." The quotation from Hernández originally appeared in the article "Los Tigres del Norte defienden el contenido de sus canciones en España," published online, http://www.terra.com/ocio/articulo/html/oci34579.htm.

States totaled $24 billion in 2007. This figure represents an increase of only 1 percent over the previous year's figure, in contrast to a growth of 15 percent in 2006. Despite this decreasing growth, as a result of the current slowing of the U.S. economy, remittances still account for about 4.8 percent of Mexico's gross domestic product and have surpassed foreign direct investment flows into Mexico as well as income earned from tourism in that country.[9]

This "dual nationality" was also extended to second-generation Mexican Americans, though it did not allow them the right to vote or run for political office. In creating a more "plural and fluid" society, Mexican immigrants would become more vocal and concerned about their home country's political system (González-Gutiérrez 1999, 567). Similarly, an increase in anti-immigration sentiment among U.S. citizens has also led a new mobilization of Mexican voters who now feel more empowered to express their dissatisfactions with political affairs in Mexico as well as in the United States, giving rise to new transnational political movements (Durand, Massey, and Parrado 1999, 536). This is certainly the path Los Tigres is encouraging its listeners to take, particularly with songs like "Las Mujeres de Juárez" (The Women of Juárez), which was released on 2004's *Pacto de Sangre* (Blood Pact). The song is about the hundreds of impoverished women working in the city's U.S.-owned maquiladoras who have gone missing since 1993. It insinuates that the local police, who have been working on the case for several years without making any serious arrests, are covering up for the abductors who may in fact be some of their own. The song incited protests among the local community as well as among women's rights organizations on both sides of the border. The Mexican government called for censorship of the song, citing it as "morbid" and claiming that it not only tainted the border city's international reputation but also impeded the ongoing investigation of this case. In addition, congressional authorities in the border state of Chihuahua called upon local radios to stop playing "Las Mujeres de Juárez" and have asked the group to discontinue its promotion in Mexico ("Nueva Censura" 2004). Ironically, an American-made feature film about the missing women was released in October of 2007 and stars Jennifer Lopez as a reporter investigating the murders and the Mexican government's handling of the cases. The movie features this song and others by Los Tigres in the soundtrack.

Many norteña songs, particularly those by Los Tigres, reflect (or attempt to reflect) the concerns and opinions of people who have been disheartened by the corruption of many Mexican government officials and the economic stress this corruption imposes on their country and their lives. It all began in 1997, when Los Tigres del Norte released the double CD, *Jefe de Jefes* (Boss of Bosses), a recording that set the group on an unprecedented course as the most celebrated

---

[9]See Reuters reports in Business and Finance for May 7, 2007 (http://www.reuters.com/article/economic News/idUSN0739389720070507), and March 5, 2008 (http://www.reuters.com/article/bondsnews/idUSN0562577620080305), accessed October 29, 2008.

and prominent voice of the Mexican diaspora and, without a doubt, the most commercially and financially successful. Los Tigres' Grammy-nominated recording features songs that fervently take on a series of political, social, and moral issues, though at times they contradict themselves, particularly on the issue of drug trafficking. *Jefe de Jefes* is considered one of the most sophisticated and creative recordings of the norteña genre. More importantly, the CD represents the "plural and fluid" society of a Mexican diaspora that also embraces other non-Mexican immigrant communities and cultivates a "diasporic identity" (González-Gutiérrez 1999, 567) that is critical of both Mexican and U.S. social and political ideology. For example, "El Prisionero" is about the assassination of the presidential candidate Luis Donaldo Colosio, and "El General" tells the story of General Jesús Gutiérrez Rebollo, the Mexican contact for the Drug Enforcement Agency, who was arrested and then fired after he was accused of being on the payroll of the Ciudad Juárez drug cartel, headed by the cocaine king Amado Carrillo Fuentes (also known as the "Lord of the Skies"). "El General" not only accuses Mexican officials of leading corrupt lives but also suggests that this kind of corruption exists on the other side of the border as well. These songs, along with the title cut ("Jefe de Jefes"), "El Dolor de un Padre" (A Father's Pain), "Jesús Amado," and "También las Mujeres Pueden" (Women Can Too), warn of the dangers of drug-trafficking (regardless of age or sex), a topic that Los Tigres has turned its attention to in recent years.

Songs like "Ni Aquí ni Allá" (Neither Here nor There) speak about how political corruption, false promises, dislocation, and oppression make it difficult for the immigrant to develop an identity that is associated with either country and identify what Bhabha describes as the disruption that leads to a distinct definition (or redefinition) of national identity (1994 54–55). "Mis Dos Patrias" (My Two Countries) expresses concern about maintaining mexicanidad while living in a country that views this community as second-class and uneducated. Finally, "El Mojado Acaudalado" (The Wealthy Wetback), which is probably the CD's most popular song and its first single, is the ultimate celebration and confirmation of the Mexican immigrant's definition of mexicanidad, in which the mojado has amassed enough money to say goodbye to the United States and return to his "beloved land" where he can (finally) live a good life. While this is a reality that few immigrants can actually enjoy, a sense of loyalty to the mojado's regional and cultural heritage allows him to resist acculturation and maintain a distinct identity while still living in the United States (Martínez 1998).

Even though the Mexican government has sought to censor Los Tigres and norteña music—perhaps more in reaction to songs critical of the government than to songs about drug trafficking—*Jefe de Jefes* was the first recording in this genre to catch the attention of both Spanish- and English-language journalists who have praised this and subsequent recordings by the group. The following quote from Elijah Wald (1998) represents what many of these writers had to say about the group upon hearing the recording: "In 1997, Los Tigres released their masterpiece, a two-CD set of corridos titled *Jefe de Jefes,* which proved once and for all their artistic power, painting a musical picture of contemporary Mexican society." Until the release of *Jefe de Jefes,* Los Tigres and norteña music was rarely mentioned by writers in the mainstream North American popular music press. With *Jefe de Jefes,* Los Tigres not only reinvented themselves as the "social conscience" of the Mexican immigrant community but also extended this reach to a growing undocumented non-Mexican immigrant community, including Central Americans, Ecuadorians, and Peruvians. The album has become a classic among norteña fans and in 2005 it was certified platinum for sales of more than a million copies in the United States.

For the creation of a group that established itself in the early 1970s with a string of highly successful corridos celebrating the exploits of narcotraficantes, the message of *Jefe de Jefes* is somewhat mixed. Upon the release of this CD, Los Tigres began speaking to the North American press about their "real" feelings regarding the narcotraficante subculture they had glorified in earlier recordings: "We emphasize the fact if you are a drug dealer, if you are doing something wrong, you will end up in jail or in the hospital or dead," Hernán Hernández said in an interview with Laura Emerick, a *Chicago Sun Times* reporter. "When we made *Jefe de Jefes,* we put a lot of emphasis on that. We don't make heroes of these kinds of criminals. The people make their own heroes. We sing about what's in the news, what's reality" (Emerick 2004). On some occasions, Los Tigres have openly criticized other norteña groups who focus on the narco-corrido (even though the group created and popularized the subgenre). And though Los Tigres themselves still record and perform narcocorridos, they have been critical of those who glorify the narcotraficante lifestyle and advocate violence (e.g., Chalino Sánchez, Explosión Norteña, and Valentín Elizalde). Jorge Hernández expresses this rather conflicted view in a February 20, 2003, interview by Hiram Soto of the *San Diego Union-Tribune.* "There are several bands that have recorded songs that I can't bear to listen to because they offend me," he said. "They have turned this into a bunch of nonsense instead of using it as something cultural and a means of communicating. Our focus is corridos and not *narcocorridos.* A corrido has nothing to do with drug traffickers. We tell stories, if it happens to be about a drug trafficker, well, we tell his story."

However, the CD's title cut ("Jefe de Jefes") and some of its songs offer a different message about drug trafficking. The title cut is sung from the perspective of a drug kingpin who brags about his ability to remain untouched by the law, rival drug lords, and even journalists who seek him out to write about his exploits and glamorous lifestyle. "Jefe de Jefes" clearly challenges the authority and legitimacy of state systems (see Connell and Gibson 2003, 129), while other songs on the album warn of the consequences of a life of crime. Such songs (along with the group members' public denials) counteract rumors of the group's own underworld connections. Los Tigres tread a delicate line here. They must be clean enough to satisfy the international music industry and the media, which have begun to recognize norteña as a viable popular music form. However, as songs like "Jefe de Jefes" suggest, the group is aware of competition from a new breed of norteña groups (e.g., Los Tucanes de Tijuana, Grupo Exterminador, Explosión Norteña) who have become hugely popular by reviving the narcocorrido genre in norteña music with gangsta rap–inspired songs with lyrics containing a high degree of graphic detail and violence.

So far the U.S. public—both Mexican immigrant fans and newly acquired non-Mexican admirers—has lauded Los Tigres for their honesty, creativity, and integrity, whether the topic is drugs, immigration policy, or political corruption. And while journalists tend to focus on the group's narcocorridos, scholars, public sector presenters, and even government officials have recognized the group's importance within the Mexican immigrant community and the fact that they are willing to give money back to the community as well as the state. In 2000, Los Tigres established the Los Tigres del Norte Foundation, which provides funding to community-based nonprofit Latino organizations and offers education and outreach programs focusing on Latino arts and culture. The foundation's first gift was to the University of California, Los Angeles (UCLA) Chicano Studies Research Center in the amount of $500,000, part of which has been used to digitize over 32,000 Spanish-language recordings contained in the Strachwitz Frontera Collection (originally created by Chris Strachwitz, the founder of Arhoolie Records).[10] On the heels of the critical success of *Jefe de Jefes*, Los Tigres was the first Mexican group invited to perform at the American Music Awards in 1998. Moreover, the Chicano Studies Research Center at UCLA and the Smithsonian Institution collaborated with the group on *Corridos sin Fronteras: A New World Ballad Tradition*, a touring exhibit that opened in 2002 and that focuses on the historical development of the corrido in the New World over the past two hundred years. The exhibit features the songs, recordings, and photos of Los Tigres del Norte, though it focuses primarily on the group's financial and popular success rather than their contributions to the development of the corrido tradition. Interestingly enough, the exhibit also fails to mention the group's extensive repertoire of narcocorridos. Prominently displayed, however, is the group's first Grammy award in the newly created "Regional Mexican" category for 1987's *Gracias América, Sin Fronteras*.

Though the members of Los Tigres have been critical of growing anti-immigration sentiment in California—condemning Proposition 187 (which sought to deny health and education benefits to the undocumented immigrant) in the song "Hijos de Hernández" (Sons of Hernández)—they were honored in 2002 by the then governor Gray Davis and the California legislature in a joint

---

[10] See the Arhoolie Foundation Web site for more information about the digitizing of the Foundation's Strachwitz Frontera Collection of Mexican and Mexican American Recordings, http://www.arhoolie.com/arhoolie_foundation/projects.html. See also Los Tigres del Norte Foundation, http://lostigres delnortefoundation.org/.

resolution commending the group on their artistic career and charitable contributions to the community. In 2003, the group was also honored at a sold-out performance at the prestigious Kennedy Center in Washington, D.C. The group's success has soared on both sides of the border and is now edging toward global proportions with tours throughout Latin America and more recent stops in Japan, in Korea, and extensively in Spain.

The group's acceptance in the United States has various causes. In many cases, it is a response to the sheer numbers and youth of the Mexican immigrant community, an important group of potential consumers. In other cases, politicians anticipate this community's future influence as voters. Finally, community arts and cultural organizations recognize norteña as a way to educate North Americans at large about this population, which is visibly changing the face of many communities around the country. In some cases, these motives can outweigh the darker side of norteña. One example occurred in 2005 in New York City, which has one of the fastest-growing Mexican immigrant populations (with one of the highest percentages of undocumented residents).[11] Mayor Michael Bloomberg was given an autographed guitar from one of Los Tigres' main rivals, Los Tucanes de Tijuana (who became a top norteña group largely on the basis of their early narcocorrido output), by the group's tour sponsors, Coors Beer (González 2005). In his eagerness to connect with the fastest-growing new Latino immigrant population in the city, Bloomberg (and Coors) was probably unaware of Los Tucanes' extensive narcocorrido output or that their career was launched in the mid-1990s by such songs glorifying the narcotraficante lifestyle as "Mis Tres Animales," "Carrera Prohibida" (Prohibited Highway), "La Piedrita Colombiana" (The Little Colombian Rock), and "El Jefe X" (Boss X). "We're proud to sponsor these accomplished norteña musicians," said Melissa Coors, the brand manager for Coors Brewing Company. "Coors is committed to supporting cultural arts and higher-education initiatives in the Hispanic community" ("Coors Light *Onda Norteña Gira*"). However, Coors was more likely motivated by the group's popularity among the country's largest Latino population and its soaring CD sales and knows little (or chooses not to know at all) about the content of its songs.

Nevertheless, the Mexican government and the mainstream music industry have remained reluctant to embrace norteña, no matter how influential and internationally successful Los Tigres del Norte have been. The Mexican government is very aware of the content of songs by Los Tucanes, Los Tigres, and many other popular norteña groups. In Chicago, a resolution was passed in 2000 to create "The National Day of Los Tigres del Norte" with a portion of 26th Street in the

---

[11] New data from the U.S. Census reveal that Mexicans are New York City's fastest growing ethnic group. New York City's Mexican population ranked eleventh among major U.S. cities in 2000, at 186,872. This figure rivals the size of long-standing Mexican communities like those in San Diego, Santa Ana, and San Jose, California. See http://www.census.gov/prod/2001pubs/c2kbr01-3.pdf (accessed November 14, 2008).

Pilsner district—widely known as the main street for the Mexican community—being named after the group. The Mexican American council member who passed this resolution, Jesús García, told me in an interview that the idea came from an initiative presented to him by Mexican American community leaders. And though he invited Chicago's Mexican consular office to participate in a ceremony and a concert by the group in honor of this day and the official renaming of the street, he said the consulate did not respond to his invitation, nor did it send a representative to attend the highly publicized event (personal communication). Los Tigres' position as a popular music phenomenon, a voice of a largely undocumented immigrant community, and a powerful player in the Latin music industry has garnered for the group mixed and often conflicting responses from government officials, politicians, scholars, and journalists on both sides of the border. While North American journalists celebrate the group's eloquence in documenting the seductive world of the drug trafficker, Chicano scholars and community leaders celebrate the group's transformation from working-class immigrants to multi-millionaires, and U.S. politicians honor them as an influential voice of a large portion of the Latino population. Mexican journalists, on the other hand, have been largely critical or have avoided publicizing the group and its music; Mexican scholars tend to treat the group's music as evidence of that country's social and political decline; and the Mexican government has fought vigorously to censor their narcocorridos and, in recent years, their corridos that criticize the government and its policies. In many songs, Los Tigres are hypercritical of the Mexican political system and corrupt government officials. They also criticize the U.S. government as a willing participant in drug trafficking and for its oppressive immigration policy. However, while their songs celebrating mexicanidad are passionately patriotic and firmly maintain Spanish as their language of choice, they have put large amounts of money and support into research on and education about Mexican and Latino culture in the United States, primarily through their foundation. Mexican immigrants tend to send money back to Mexico to help their families and to support the building of roads, schools, and community centers in their villages and towns, but the members of Los Tigres have invested in keeping heritage and identity alive within Latino communities in the United States.

In spite of the group's popularity among the Mexican immigrant population, the popular music industry on both sides of the border has typically treated norteña with a degree of distance and exclusion. According to the Recording Industry Association of America, currently 60 percent of annual Spanish-language Latin music sales in the United States (over 350 million copies a year) are for "Mexican Regional" styles, which include norteña, mariachi or ranchero, and banda. Of those genres, norteña dominates in sales (Emerick 2004). Though the American Grammy Awards, presented by the National Academy of Recording Arts and Sciences (NARAS), recognized the popularity of Mexican music by creating an award for "Best Mexican/Mexican American Album" in 1983 (Pacini Hernández 2001, 63), the nod generally went to "crossover" Mexican American artists like Linda Ronstadt, Los Lobos, and Vicki Carr or to Texas-Mexican artists like Flaco Jiménez and Selena. (The only time a Grammy went to a group associated with the Mexican immigrant community was in 1988 when Los Tigres won "Best Mexican American Performance" for their album *Gracias América, Sin Fronteras.*) By honoring artists whose names are "known" to a non-Mexican and non-Latino audience, NARAS and the Grammy awards are participating in the "musical tokenism" described by Feld (2000) and Taylor (1997) in discussions of world music's mediated inclusion in the corporate mainstream music industry.

NARAS generally took a familiar, safe course in awarding its Grammy awards. This tactic is similar to that used in the first half of the 1990s, when Grammy awards in the "world music" category went to recordings made and mediated by North American or European producers and artists such as the former Grateful Dead drummer/percussionist Mickey Hart, the country-rock/folk/blues guitarist Ry Cooder (who collaborated with the *mohan vīna* player V. M. Bhatt from southern India), and the Malian singer/guitarist Ali Farka Toure (Taylor 1997, 11). In addition to creating the "Best Mexican American Performance" category, NARAS also attempted to recognize some of the ethnic and stylistic distinctions under the Latin music rubric by creating "Best Tropical" and "Best Latin Pop" categories.[12] In 1995 NARAS clearly recognized that the continued influx of new immigrants into the United States meant that there were definite distinctions between Mexican nationals (or those who identified with being Mexican) and Tejano communities, changing "Best Mexican American Performance" to "Best Mexican American/Tejano Performance" (which still lumps the music together, though the title distinguishes the communities).

Artists identifying themselves as "Mexican," however, were still left out. NARAS decided to include the label *Tejano* partly in response to the regional "explosion" of recordings produced in the early 1990s and peaking in popularity in 1994 following the death of the genre's most celebrated star, Selena Quintanilla (Ballí 2003). In fact, many Latin divisions of major labels had established offices in cities like San Antonio, Houston, and Austin, where Tejano music was being produced, and there was a great deal of energy and excitement about the "discovery" of Tejano throughout the rest of the country. One thing NARAS may not have understood is that Tejano is a U.S.-based music genre that is associated with a Texas-Mexican and Chicano community that constructed its identity as distinct, though not disconnected, from both Mexico and the United States (Limón

---

[12]The Grammy Award for Best Mexican/Mexican American Album has been awarded since 1984. The award has had several minor name changes: From 1984 to 1991 the award was known as "Best Mexican American Performance" and from 1992 to 1994 it was awarded as "Best Mexican American Album." In 1995 it returned to the title "Best Mexican American Performance," and from 1996 to 1998 it was awarded as "Best Mexican American/Tejano Music Performance." In 1999 it was presented as "Best Mexican American Music Performance," and in 2000 it was once again awarded as "Best Mexican American Performance." From 2001 it was awarded as "Best Mexican/Mexican American Album," and it continued to be presented that way until 2006, when the "Best Norteño Album" category was added.

1981; Peña 1999a, 1999b; Ballí 2003). Because Tejano music is so closely tied to Tejano identity, merging Tejano with Mexican American (which also included Mexican artists) did not sit well with most Tejano fans and artists. Similarly, many Mexican artists objected to the fact that Tejano artists (considered more "American" and accessible to the largely English-language voters) usually took the award. It took NARAS three years to respond to these criticisms, and in 1999 it created separate categories: "Best Tejano Album" for Texas-Mexican artists, and "Best Mexican American Music Performance" for Mexican and Mexican American artists (Pacini Hernández 2001). However, it was not until 2001 that NARAS recognized that it must distinguish further between Mexicans and Mexican Americans and changed the "Best Mexican American Music Performance" category to "Best Mexican/Mexican American Album." The category for both Mexican and Mexican American (not Tejano) remains under this title to this day and includes what the Latin music industry defines as "Mexican Regional" (which can also include Mexican immigrant music genres such as norteña, banda, and mariachi music primarily produced and recorded in Los Angeles and Mexico City), along with Mexican-produced pop, rock, *tropical*, and romantic ballad genres. Most winners have been artists who have some Latin crossover appeal, such as the pop singer Joan Sebastian (who won two years in a row) and the Spanish opera star Plácido Domingo (who won in 2000 for his homage to the mariachi tradition, *One Hundred Years of Mariachi*). The only norteña artist to receive this award since Los Tigres in 1988 was Ramón Ayala in 2002. However, in 2006, Los Tigres took the Grammy again, but this time in a newly created category: "Best Norteño Album." This move not only distinguished Mexican groups from Tejano groups but also finally recognized the popularity and importance of the norteña genre.

It was the much talked-about, and now historic, performance of "Livin' la Vida Loca" by Ricky Martin at the 1999 American Grammy Awards that jolted music and television executives into realizing the huge crossover potential of Latin music. The following year, the Latin Academy of Recording Arts and Sciences (LARAS) produced the first Latin Grammy Awards, honoring Spanish- and Portuguese-language recording artists, in a major televised event in Los Angeles. But the inclusion of "Mexican Regional" music in the Latin Grammy Awards has not been without controversy. There were accusations by musicians and fans that the awards were too narrowly focused on artists produced by Sony's Emilio Estefan, the husband of the Cuban American artist Gloria Estefan. A highly publicized letter written in 2000 by the salsa star and trombonist Willie Colón criticized Estefan for encouraging Latin Grammy Awards producers to boycott Cuban-based artists and those who traveled to that country to perform and for favoring artists produced by Estefan, such as Shakira and Carlos Vives.[13]

---

[13] At the time of this writing, the English translation of Colón's letter to the Latin Grammys could be accessed online at http://www.flyingserpent.net/betweenthelines/williecolon.html.

Similarly, Gilberto Moreno, the general director of Fonovisa, which produces the majority of Mexican Regional recordings sold in the United States and Mexico, publicly accused Estefan and Sony of dominating the Latin Grammy Awards and excluding Mexican Regional artists. In a Spanish-language wire report that appeared in *La Opinión* (California), Moreno claimed that the Latin Grammy Awards Presentation was "una fiesta entre Emilio Estefan y la casa discográfica Sony" (a party for Emilio Estefan and Sony Records) ("Surge polémica por discriminación de música regional mexicana" 2003).

Moreno addressed LARAS's exclusion of Mexican Regional artists as performers and as award winners at the Latin Grammy Awards: "LARAS ha ignorado a las estrellas de la música regional mexicana en favor de los artistas 'pop' y baladas de EMI y Sony."[14] Considering that more than half of Latin music sales are of Mexican Regional artists, Moreno's argument hit home. As the writer Justino Águila pointed out in an article for the *Milwaukee Journal Sentinel,* that norteña and Mexican Regional artists are extremely popular among Spanish-language audiences in the United States is little known to Latin Americans throughout the continent:

> The Latin Grammy backlash is easy to understand: More than half the Latin record sales in the United States are attributed to Regional Mexican, pushing the genre past Latin pop and tropical salsa, according to the Recording Industry Association of America. But of the 41 Latin Grammy categories, only two are specific to Regional Mexican—Best Ranchero Album and Best Regional Mexican Song. Although the genre is enjoyed by people around the world, its primary audience is in Mexico and the United States. Many Grammy voters in places such as the Caribbean and South America may not be as familiar with Regional Mexican even though it brings in millions of dollars for the industry. (Águila 2003)

It was frustration with this kind of marginalization that prompted Los Tigres del Norte to boycott the 2000 and 2001 Latin Grammy Awards, even though the group was nominated for an award in those years and won in the category of Best Norteño Performance in 2000. While it is somewhat understandable that Mexican American, Tejano, and Latino categorizations can be slippery for NARAS and the largely English-speaking audience of the American Grammy Awards, the exclusion of Mexican Regional genres at the Latin Grammy Awards would appear to be more about power and identity conflict.

When one understands the organizational structure of the Latin music industry itself and the rapid growth of Latin popular music sales since the late 1990s, it is easy to see where the conflict arises. For one thing, the Latin music industry

---

[14]"LARAS has ignored the stars of Mexican Regional music in favor of pop artists and ballads of Sony and EMI."

is primarily owned, operated, and controlled by major labels, such as Sony, Capitol EMI, WEA, PolyGram, and BMG (Pacini Hernández 2001, 61). Most of these labels created Latin music divisions that market, promote, and produce various genres (e.g., salsa, *tropical*, Tejano) in basically the same way. Pacini Hernández points out another problem with this strategy, which is the distinction between the U.S. Latino and Latin North American markets grouped into the all-inclusive "Latin Music" categorization, a distinction that the international labels have failed to recognize, thus "obscuring and ignoring the profound differences among the many styles falling under that umbrella term" (2001, 61). However, the situation with the marketing of norteña and other Mexican Regional genres like banda and ranchero is that these artists do not even fall under the "Latin Music" rubric because they are recorded, produced, marketed, and distributed by labels that are not part of the Latin divisions of major international labels.

The majority, if not all, of the top-selling Mexican norteña, banda, and ranchera—as well as some cumbia—artists are on Fonovisa (San José, California), Disa (Monterrey, Nuevo León, Mexico), Freddie (Corpus Christi, Texas) and Joey International (San Antonio, Texas). Freddie and Joey International are independently owned labels with large distribution networks (mostly in Wal-Mart, K-Mart, and Target). Fonovisa was acquired in 2002 by Univision, the Mexican media conglomerate, and that company also has a 50 percent stake in Disa Records through its Univision Music Group in Mexico.[15] Fonovisa is the largest producer of Mexican Regional music in Mexico and the United States. While independent labels like Freddie (which still holds its contract with Ramón Ayala) and Joey control about 20 percent of the Mexican Regional market in the United States and less in Mexico, the Univision Music Group controls 45 percent of the Latin music market share in the United States, making it a major player on a par with the international corporate labels. These numbers may be the very reason the Latin Grammy Awards and the international corporate labels have tried to downplay Mexican Regional's overwhelming popularity in the United States. Mexican Regional is one of the few top-selling popular music genres in which a major international label does not dominate sales, nor can it influence the tastes of the largely Mexican immigrant market that supports this music. Furthermore, Univision Music Group is a Mexican-run corporation that is part of the leading Spanish media company in the United States, controlling the Univision television and radio networks as well as the Galavisión and TeleFutura networks (Rodrigues 1993).

Another problem that the Latin music industry and Latin Grammy Awards producers seem to have with norteña (and Mexican Regional) music is that its audience is primarily made up of recent immigrants whose low incomes are unattractive to music executives, promoters, and marketers. According to the

---

[15]See the Univision Web site, http://www.univision.net/corp/en/umg.jsp.

2004 Arbitron ratings,[16] 55 percent of the Mexican Regional listening audience makes less than $25,000 a year. Arbitron's research also shows that 51 percent have not completed high school. "For music executives, these demographics are anathema to their promotions and extra products departments and discourage them from considering Mexican Regional music for crossover attempts like 'rock en español' and Latin pop," writes the journalist Gustavo Arellano (2002). Arellano claims that norteña's popularity among producers and marketers is also hampered by its rather conservative instrumentation and dance form. "There's another image problem," he explained. "Waltz and polka—introduced to Mexico by European immigrants during the late 1800s—and Mexican indigenous rhythms are the soul of the music's sound. Dancing to it means a couple holds each other in a rather old-fashioned way. It's a conservative impression that does not sit well with executives relying on marketing stereotypes of Latino culture as 'exotic' and 'sensual.'" The issue of dance is important when talking about Latin music and its appeal to a Hispanic-American and crossover audience. The fact that norteña is not associated with a popular or newly evolved dance form is part of what has kept it outside the commercially popular Latin American music industry both in the United States and throughout Latin America. Latin music styles are generally defined by a particular dance style or rhythm, such as salsa and cumbia (see, for example, Waxer 2002). In 2004, however, the Latin Grammy Awards finally made amends by creating the Best Norteño Album award, which went to Los Tigres for the superb record *Pacto De Sangre*. In 2006, the Latin Grammy Awards show traveled to New York, partly in response to criticisms of dominance by Miami- and Los Angeles–based artists and labels. Los Tigres, who performed at the event, also came away with the Best Norteño Album Award for *Historias que Contar* (Stories to Tell) and the BMI Icons award for their influence on "generations" of musicians.

In Mexico, the dancing associated with norteña music is often referred to as old-fashioned, conservative, and "rural." For this reason, norteña has received minimal airplay there (except in its heartland, Nuevo León and Tamaulipas), remaining marginalized by commercially popular styles such as the romantic ballad genre, often labeled *internacional* (performed by artists like Ana Gabriel, Luis Miguel, and Alejandro Fernández); modern ranchera (performed by artists like Vicente Fernández and Mariachi Vargas); and *rock en español*. Moreover, norteña music is almost all produced outside Mexico City, where the majority of Mexican pop, rock, and *internacional* recordings are produced. Norteña is also produced outside the "salsa matrix" that is located in New York, Miami, and

---

[16]Statistics from Arbitron's "Hispanic Radio Today" 2004 edition. The study examines radio from a national viewpoint and outlines its strength as a medium for analyzing listening behavior for six major Hispanic formats: Mexican Regional (which includes norteña, along with mariachi, banda, and *grupero*), Spanish Contemporary (i.e., *rock en español*, Latin pop, and ballads), Spanish Tropical (e.g., salsa, meringue, *bachata*, popular music, and dance from the Dominican Republic), Spanish News/Talk, Spanish Variety, and Tejano (http://www.arbitron.com/downloads/hispanicradiotoday04.pdf).

Puerto Rico (Connell and Gibson 2003, 187). In short, norteña falls outside the mainstream U.S. and Mexican recording industries.

The real problem lies with norteña's inability to assimilate into either a Mexican American (i.e., Chicano or Tejano) or Latin American definition of popular music. And while norteña is more deeply connected to its Mexican origins than other popular Mexican genres such as *rock en español* and cumbia, its association with a largely U.S.-based migrant community gives it outsider status in that country: It is "ni aquí ni allá," neither here nor there. Norteña's historical association with an autonomous, mostly rural border region and a listening audience largely made up of poor immigrants living in the United States has kept it on the fringe of the "mainstream" Latin American and Mexican music industries. As popular music recorded by independent labels located on both sides of the U.S.-Mexico border, norteña typically has low production values and widespread availability on pirated cassettes and CDs that have allowed it to remain directly connected to the attitudes and experiences of the marginalized working-class immigrant community, or subculture, that created it. While these are the very attributes that have endeared it to this audience, they are also the very things that represent the reality of the immigrant experience in the United States, which is not what the industry or the advertisers want to promote. As George Lipsitz notes, "The mechanisms of commercial culture that deprive Los Tigres del Norte of exposure to a broader audience also deprive Anglo listeners of needed knowledge about their country" (1994, 131–132).

As the scores of English-language articles that have been published about the narcocorrido phenomenon attest, there is interest in norteña, though it has been filtered through the writings of journalists who focus primarily on narcocorridos that perpetuate negative stereotypes of Mexican immigrants (and Mexicans in general) as violent and lawless. For these writers, and many readers who are otherwise unfamiliar with the lives of Mexican immigrant workers in this country, the exploits of narcotraficantes as documented in narcocorridos tend to overshadow other popular themes about illegal immigration, identity conflict, politics and corruption, nationalism, love, and death, themes that actually dominate the majority of corrido and ranchera songs recorded and performed by norteña groups throughout the Mexican diaspora. But for many non-Mexicans and audiophiles, the clandestine life of the narcotraficante who slips in and out of the no-man's-land of the border zone piques the imagination more powerfully than the life of an undocumented immigrant who struggles to maintain his dignity and identity in a society that views him only as cheap labor.

The tendency of U.S. journalists and writers to focus on narcocorridos as examples of norteña music allows for an "orientalized" interpretation of the Mexican people and their culture. It is a representation that has been promoted for years in U.S. films and popular culture, where Mexicans are portrayed as eccentric, backward, passive, sensual, and distant. And while one might argue that this interpretation of narcocorridos stems from the songs themselves and, therefore, from the Mexicans who wrote them, it reflects a particular set of assumptions. From the Mexican immigrant perspective, the narcotraficante represents mexicanidad, particularly in the way he deflects U.S. authority and rejects assimilation and acculturation. For much of the U.S. public, however, the narcotraficante symbolizes the exotic "other" whose life of crime and debauchery is merely his response to poverty, corruption, and living within a less progressive society.

## Creating New Circuits for the Corrido and Norteña Music

*Before, when norteño music was mentioned, it was only for a certain group of people and now, thank God, we've been able to transcend the music to other sectors. We've been invited to universities, there's the corrido museum in Washington [D.C.] where they have our lyrics on exhibit and other groups' lyrics as well, from years back. We've contributed instruments for display. This way we're spreading not only the music, but the lives of our people to other countries, to other social classes. So they can learn about our reality, us as Mexicans, Mexicans living in the U.S. For example, Spain, the Spanish, have more of an interesting view of the corrido. I think we've helped take it to that level, because we've taken it upon ourselves to focus on the corrido.*

—LUIS HERNÁNDEZ, LOS TIGRES DEL NORTE,
QUOTED IN AN INTERVIEW WITH NAHUM MADRID FOR *BATANGA*

In recent years, a new market has opened up for norteña in Spain, even though it arrived without being promoted or marketed by major international labels as "world music," "world beat," or "Latin pop." Typically, a popular music genre enters a foreign country via migration, as a highly marketed "international" pop music commodity, or as a breakout popular music genre from a formerly colonized diaspora. In Spain, many of the successful imported Spanish-language popular music genres are diasporic, such as salsa, Cuban son, Latin jazz, and Argentinean rock. Norteña's arrival in Spain, however, was spurred by the publication of Pérez-Reverte's novel, which created tremendous interest in the songs that inspired it.

The story of Pérez-Reverte's first encounter with "Contrabando y Traición" in a Mexico City bar popular among tourists is one that might have come from a traveler's journal. In an interview with the Spanish journalist Ángeles García in April 28, 2002, Pérez-Reverte recounts his emotional response to the song and makes a point of positioning himself inside the culture. "He ido a Sinaloa, he visitado a antiguos amigos míos que me debían favores y yo a ellos; he hablado con narcos, he estado en las cantinas oyendo música y emborrachándome con la gente," Pérez-Reverte says.[17] In this case, Pérez-Reverte's physical presence in the

---

[17] "I have been to Sinaloa; I have visited old friends of mine who have done favors for me and I for them; I have talked with narcos; I have been in bars listening to the music and getting drunk with the people."

local community and personal connection to the narcotraficante indicate that he is more than the typical "sonic traveler" or music enthusiast (Taylor 1997, 26–27). However, as a novelist, as opposed to a journalist (which he once was), musician, music researcher, or music fan, Pérez-Reverte asserts a deeper, more "lived-in" experience that allows him access to what Taylor describes as "the timeless . . . the primal, the pure, the chthonic" (1997, 26) and to which I would add "the dangerous, the clandestine, the mysterious." Perhaps this is why the corrido, or the narcocorrido in particular, was so successfully introduced in Spain in the form of literary fiction rather than by the mainstream music industry.

In his discussion of the corrido as narrative discourse, McDowell notes that the corrido "interprets, celebrates and dignifies" the history, events, beliefs, attitudes, and opinions of its audience (1981, 41). This understanding and communication of the corrido's position in the culture is something a record producer, marketing executive, disc jockey, public performance presenter, or even a scholar does not truly have. Through his book, Pérez-Reverte takes on the role of the "corridista," and in telling the story of his drug-smuggling protagonist, Teresa Mendoza, he constructs his own "informed" audience by bringing Mendoza and her narcotraficante activities from Sinaloa, Mexico to Spain, by relocating the border from U.S.-Mexico to Spain-Morocco and by transforming the corrido from an oral tradition to a long prose text.

As a musical genre, the corrido often blurs the line between reality and the imaginary. Pérez-Reverte takes great liberties in creating his own interpretations of the corrido, the narcotraficante, and the Mexican, which his book has marketed to a Spanish-speaking audience located thousands of miles away. Pérez-Reverte's book is quite a different experience from most books inspired by a popular music genre. A more typical example is Elijah Wald's hitchhiker's guide to the narcocorrido, *Narcocorrido: A Journey into the Music of Drugs, Guns, and Guerrillas* (2001). Where Wald guides his readers through sleepy Mexican villages, encounters with bored and corrupt police officers, and scores of bars, hotels, dance halls, and impromptu jam sessions as he searches for the authors of classic narcocorridos such as "La Banda del Carro Rojo," "Pacas de a Kilo," "Contrabando y Traición" and "Luis Aguirre," Pérez-Reverte writes his own narcocorrido that connects Mexico and the border to Spain and North Africa through the desperation and drive of a young woman. Wald's book fits into Taylor's (1997) definition of a world music product that claims authenticity and deep connection to the culture through the physical or bodily experience of the music that cannot be obtained through tourism. However, Wald is also a musician and journalist whose motivation is to learn more about the history of songs and the truth behind their stories, play them, and make the English-speaking public back in the United States aware of their existence. (A CD of selected narcocorridos and mojado-themed corridos is marketed with the book.) While in one sense, Pérez-Reverte is no different from Wald or musician/producers like Mickey Hart, Paul Simon, Ry Cooder, Stewart Copeland, and others acting as cultural mediators who interpret and commodify the music of non-Western artists for Western ears (Taylor 1997, 30–31), he positions himself as an intermediary for the narcocorrido in Spain: His interest lies in connecting this tradition and Mexican culture back to Spain through language, history, and a global "Hispanic" community.

As a relative of the Spanish *décima* and romance song forms, the corrido has been seriously studied by musicologists, linguists, and Spanish literary scholars. However, the narcocorrido has evolved into a commodity of popular culture and the diasporic marketplace. Pérez-Reverte says he was "seduced" by the narcocorrido and the lifestyle it documents, and, as he further reveals in the *El Pais* interview, he admires the modern-day corridista's ability to tell a story in three minutes (the typical length of a popular song recording). In order to bring the form into his own realm of understanding, Pérez-Reverte refashions the corrido into a literary novel: "Ese mundo me fascinó, pero yo no tengo la capacidad de hacer un corrido de tres minutos. No tengo ese talento. Entonces decidí hacer un corrido de 500 páginas"[18] (García 2002). Interestingly, in many of his interviews with the press, Pérez-Reverte never speaks about the Mexican immigrant community for which the narcocorrido is originally intended. His unfamiliarity with (or lack of interest in) this community allows him to create his own narcocorrido audience.

The title for each chapter of Pérez-Reverte's book is taken from an actual corrido, a means by which the author can authenticate his own corrido. By bringing the popular narcocorrido into the realm of literature, Pérez-Reverte redefines it as "high art" and allows this "decadent" popular music genre associated with poor, mostly undocumented Mexican immigrants to be admired (and accepted) as an "intellectual" work of art rather than as simply an "intelligible consumable item" (Taylor 1997, 31). Where the narcocorrido is the "noise" of a community that lives on the margin of North American society as both undocumented laborers and drug smuggling outlaws, a community whose real and imagined experiences have been transformed into the transnational popular music of the U.S.-Mexico diaspora, Pérez-Reverte's "corrido-novela" transforms this material into the narrative fiction of a modern-day "cultural explorer" from the original colonial power (Said 1994).

It is through Pérez-Reverte's narrative and interpretive lens that the narcocorrido, norteña music, and Los Tigres del Norte have been introduced to a well-educated, upper-middle-class Spanish popular music audience. The group has toured Spain three times since the release of Pérez-Reverte's book, and their music is now heard on college radio stations in Madrid, Barcelona, Bilbao, and Pamplona, cities where the group has amassed its largest fan base. Group members also participated in the "First Forum of Universal Cultures in Barcelona"

---

[18]"That world fascinated me, but I don't have the capacity to write a corrido in three minutes. I don't have this talent. So I decided to write a five hundred–page corrido."

in 2004.[19] Additionally, the Spanish label Freequency–Gran Vía Musical Records released a compilation of the group's recordings entitled *Treinta Grandes Éxitos de Los Tigres del Norte* (Thirty Great Hits of Los Tigres del Norte), which was distributed by Gran Vía Musical.

At the end of his book, Pérez-Reverte expressed his wish that, if the members of Los Tigres were to read it, they would write a three-minute corrido about it. The group duly responded shortly after Pérez-Reverte's book was released in Spain and Mexico (and later the United States) with a fourteen-song CD with the same title as the book: *La reina del sur*. Following the release of this recording, Los Tigres' record label, Fonovisa, began referring to the group in press releases as "iconic symbols" who have inspired "literature in the study of 'corrido culture.'" Although the marketing language has gone "highbrow," other than the title track, the CD's songs focus on the group's usual topics: love, the immigrant and mojado experience, and critiques of the Mexican and U.S. governments. In the wake of the recording's release in Mexico, government officials in the states of Sinaloa and Michoacán went on record denouncing narcocorridos as "having corrupted the corrido tradition" and the minds of Mexican youth who now aspire to be drug dealers (Ramírez-Pimienta 2004, 22–23). However, the title track, "La Reina del Sur," is the only narcocorrido on the CD. It recounts Pérez-Reverte's protagonist Teresa Mendoza's exploits as a Mexican narcotraficante who relocates to Spain where she immerses herself in the dangerous world of drugs and high crime. The song was written by Teodoro Bello, who has composed many narcocorridos and mojado songs for Los Tigres since the late 1990s.

The cross-cultural artistic dialogue between Los Tigres and Pérez-Reverte not only added to their popularity in Spain but also further legitimized them in the English-language press and instilled pride among the Mexican immigrant population. It is likely that the "discovery" and popularity of Los Tigres in Spain via the popularization of their narcocorrido repertoire have prompted the recent surge in criticism from the Mexican government. In spite of this resistance, Los Tigres have focused on managing the slippery, though highly profitable, enterprise of cultivating a new, better-educated audience in Spain—which views the group through Pérez-Reverte's exoticized and commodified interpretations of their musical tradition, the U.S.-Mexico border, and Mexican culture—while maintaining their position as the voice of the undocumented and underrepresented. It is the further "globalization" and intensification of the flow of technology, media, culture, and ideas (Feld 2000; Appadurai 1996) that allow Pérez-Reverte to make this music, and the corrido tradition, his own.

Los Tigres' recording of *La Reina del Sur* sold well among the Mexican immigrant community in the United States (where it debuted at number one on Billboard's "Top Latin Album" chart in November of 2002) and was, in turn, heavily

---

[19] Information from the online publication: http://www.esmas.com/espectaculos/musica/390275.html (accessed November 15, 2005).

pirated in Mexico (Univision Online 2002). The group (and norteña music by extension), finds itself in a peculiar position now that new audiences with different perceptions—often stereotyped, exoticized, or commodified—are listening to this music. Now that Los Tigres themselves have entered the "romanticized" world of Pérez-Reverte's representation of the corrido tradition and, by extension, "mexicanidad," have they become "raw material for industrialized neocolonialism" (Feld 2000, 165)? Or is it the other way around? In the end, Los Tigres have found another niche for their music and, if one can believe the following quote from this November 7, 2002, press release by their record label, Fonovisa, a sympathetic audience for the immigrant's struggle in the United States: "Los Tigres Del Norte have successfully toured throughout the land of Cervantes filling up plazas, stadiums and conquering the heart and soul of a new fan base that is gaining awareness of the perils faced by Latin American immigrants as they aspire to reach the American Dream."[20]

Whether audiences outside of the United States will truly be made aware of the Mexican immigrant experience remains to be seen. What we do know is that, though norteña music may seem old-fashioned and too text-driven for U.S.-based Latin music industry executives, too dangerous and lawless for Mexican radio, and off the musical radar for most English-speaking audiences (save a few adventurous journalists), its popularity among a very large portion of the Mexican immigrant community (and many other recent Latino immigrants) is grounded in the corrido and the transnational reach of its stories. The corrido has meaning for this community because it incorporates the celebrated defiance and mythology of the border hero, along with the constant dialogue and collaboration between communities on both sides of the border that have allowed for the creation of a dynamic popular music genre and industry.

---

[20]http://www.univision.net/corp/en/pr/Woodland_Hills_07112002-4.html (accessed March 26, 2005).

# Conclusion

A s a genre associated with an immigrant community, norteña music provides a dual sense of existence and identity within the Mexican diaspora. Among a population that has been historically marginalized, politicized, and criminalized because of its large numbers of illegal immigrants, norteña provides a new sense of Mexican identity or nationality that is based on ambivalent attachments to both the United States and Mexico and that is formed by border crossing, complex familial and community networks, and a sense of cohesion despite geographic dispersion. Norteña has continued to evolve in what David G. Gutiérrez (1999, 487) describes as the "third space," which extends from the border region—where Mexican workers have traveled, circulated, and crossed—north into the United States and south throughout Mexico. This new map of a transnational Mexican global nation also parallels norteña's own musical journey from a regional folk genre to "border music" to the music of Mexican immigrants to the voice of a transnational and transcultural working-class diaspora.

The Mexican immigrant experience in the United States is unique among those of immigrant communities in this country in that it has evolved over 150 years, much of its history playing out in the border region amid clashing political systems, intense capitalist expansion, and emerging race and class-based conflict. The history of norteña music is rooted in the revolutionary conflict of the exploited and marginalized peasant class of Mexico's northernmost territories. This dynamic took on a unique dimension as this self-sustaining community experienced a new form of discrimination once the political borderline was redrawn between the two countries and the concept of being Mexican took on new meaning. The shift from songs about working-class heroes of the revolution to those about common folk fighting for their right to work the land and to be treated as equals by the *norteamericano* (Mexican term for "white" American) would still further define the genre's narrative ballad form: the corrido.

Today, norteña, like the people for whom it is named, has become the voice of a nation of travelers who still fervently wave the Mexican flag even though they may never return to their home country again. Norteño history, Norteño culture, and Norteño autonomy set in motion the creation and development of a distinct popular music style that was radically different from the mestizo string-based son ensembles of the culturally distinct regions of Mexico and from the modern mariachi ensemble now recognized as the national music of Mexico. Norteña evolved on its own and was supported by an independent recording industry that developed first on the Texas side—in the lower Rio Grande Valley—and later in the sprawling industrialized city of Monterrey. It was music made by and for traveling migrant laborers, first those who came from rural Mexican villages throughout the northeastern states to Monterrey and later those who ventured north of the border.

The domination of clarinets, flutes, and eventually the accordion in this region, which represented an interest in the music of other immigrant communities (Germans and Czechs in particular) coming into the area in the nineteenth and early twentieth centuries, set this region apart from the rest of Mexico. Though the corrido was not unique to northern Mexico, it was cultivated in novel ways by a predominantly illiterate local population as a means of communication, reporting, storytelling, and entertainment. As these people sought to negotiate their rapidly changing social and economic status and the encroachment of a foreign culture and society that viewed them as inferior, they expressed their sentiments in the corrido, which allowed for the articulation of a collective understanding and imagination in a rapidly changing and modernizing world that was encroaching from both sides. Where the corrido was decidedly "Mexican" and distinctly "Norteño," the accordion and bajo sexto musical core that would become the song form's primary vehicle represented the merging of the Mexican and "the other"—the *norteamericano*—and reflected an emerging "border experience." The accordion, in particular, traveled with workers on both sides of the border, where it came to symbolize accomplishment and modernity for those who returned to Mexico and pride in one's working-class identity and roots among migrants in Texas.

In the 1960s, the presence of a Mexican American middle class throughout the Southwest, the new migratory movements across the United States, the increased militarization of the border zone, and the ongoing economic crisis in Mexico gave undocumented migrants new incentives to remain abroad (Durand,

Massey, and Parrado 1999, 535). During this time, accordion and bajo sexto ensembles in Texas moved away from the corrido, and a new dance hall sound—increasingly identified as conjunto—focused more on dancing and instrumental virtuosity rather than on songs about migration for work. Conjunto would give birth to orquesta tejana and later música tejana, the sound of a now politically and socially visible Texas-Mexican or Mexican American population distinguishing itself as "Chicano," "Tejano," "Hispanic," or "Latino." Audiences for Texas-Mexican conjunto and *música tejana* are region-specific, concentrated primarily in the Southwest. By contrast, norteña's association with the borderlands, the corrido, and the Mexico-identified migrant profoundly affected the expansion of its reach and the cultivation of a transnational diaspora that still maintained ties with modern-day Mexico.

The emergence of Texas-Mexican conjunto and its modern incarnations presents a fascinating opportunity to study the construction of a separate regional society and identity based on selective local acculturation and assimilation. However, norteña's ability to embody a new sense of personal, regional, and transnational history and identity allows for a dynamic exploration by both scholars and music enthusiasts of a newly mobilized population in response to the undocumented status of a large portion of its members. Despite limited socioeconomic advancement, many immigrants draw strength from extensive networks that span the diaspora, together creating an "imagined community," one that is based on strong attachments to Mexican heritage and culture but not to the Mexican geopolitical state.

Norteña's constant references to border history, mythology, and social banditry reflect the reality of living as an "illegal alien," a life that makes assimilation and acculturation extremely difficult. Similarly, the loss of legitimate legal status once one crosses the border is connected to the loss of identity and power, particularly among this population. Norteña music, however, with its songs that celebrate the courage, defiance, pride, and strong will of both the undocumented traveler and the modern-day social bandit, the drug smuggler, has transformed itself from a regionally specific, border-based genre into a transnational phenomenon associated with the real and imagined experiences of this traveling immigrant community. The solidarity and collective identity contained in this music and the reconstruction of mexicanidad through historically based Norteño cultural references represents a dramatization of the experience of traveling between two countries with complex and always changing political and social relations.

The corrido's two most popular protagonists, the mojado and the narcotraficante, embody both the real and imagined manifestations of Mexican migrant travel and life in an increasingly hostile and unwelcoming North American society. While Mexican immigrants remain marginalized in both Mexico and the United States because of low educational attainment, the impossibility of socioeconomic advancement, and the anti-immigration sentiment of the U.S. population, they also operate in a sphere beyond the control of either government.

A new era of migration inaugurated by the Immigration Reform and Control Act in late 1986 only encouraged the long-term stay of Mexicans in the United States at the same time that it prevented the many undocumented from assimilating into the population at large or into the Chicano and Tejano communities. These conditions have produced a Mexican diaspora that is profoundly affecting and transforming U.S. society. Moreover, these conditions have only been exacerbated; the increase of border patrol agents and the closing off of strategic entry points beginning in 1996 further criminalized the act of border crossing and illegal migration. It was at this point that norteña's most popular and politically vocal group, Los Tigres del Norte, transformed the genre and the corrido by recording songs that criticized U.S. and Mexican immigration policies and high-level corruption within both governments. Most importantly, Los Tigres and a number of norteña groups have rediscovered the power of the corrido as a tool for mobilizing their now massive community of largely undocumented Mexican fans into working to defend their rights in the United States while also encouraging political change in Mexico.

# Glossary

**bajo sexto.** A combination bass/rhythm guitar with twelve (six double-course) strings. It is found in the Texas-Mexican border region and is believed to be originally from the state of Durango in Mexico. The instrument is common in Texas-Mexican conjunto and Mexican norteña music styles, and most of those played by Texas-Mexican conjunto and norteña musicians are handcrafted by builders in San Antonio, Texas, and Monterrey, Nuevo León, Mexico. Some instruments are factory-produced in other cities in Mexico, but most musicians consider them to be of very low quality.

**banda.** Large brass ensemble with roots in nineteenth-century Spanish and European military orchestras. Regional ensembles are found throughout Mexico, particularly in the states of Sinaloa, Oaxaca, and Guerrero. Contemporary bandas, featuring keyboards and electric instruments, became popular in Mexico and among immigrant populations in Los Angeles in the early 1990s. Banda's popularity spread to other cities in the United States, particularly in the West and the Midwest and gave rise to a popular dance called *quebradita*.

**bolero.** A slow-tempo dance rhythm that originated in Spain in the eighteenth century. It is in triple time with a triplet on the second beat of each bar. The Cuban bolero is danced and sung in moderate tempo and duple meter. It is the Cuban version that migrated almost immediately after its inception to Mexico (initially to the Yucatán) and, later, throughout Latin America. The bolero was popularized in Mexico in the early nineteenth century by trios featuring acoustic guitars and rich vocal harmonies. Song texts deal with classic romantic and love story material. (Also, canción romántica.)

**bracero.** This term refers to an individual who does manual labor. From 1942 to 1964, the U.S. government administered the Bracero Program, which legally brought hundreds of thousands of Mexican laborers into the country to work on building railroads and in the agriculture industry.

**canción-corrido.** Modern song form of the norteña genre that merges the strophic, narrative corrido and elements of the popular canción ranchera (i.e., it includes a refrain).

**canción ranchera.** Mexican country/folk songs with a refrain and generally played in waltz or polka dance tempos. Canción ranchera lyrics draw on rural traditional folklore or "ranch life" and are typically written in the AABAB song form. The songs are often played in waltz-time, a slow 6/8, or 2/4 polka meter (the latter more common in the border region). The canción ranchera emerged in the 1940s and was conceived as a symbol of a new national consciousness in reaction to the aristocratic tastes of the era. See ranchera.

**cancíon romántica.** Romantic song form dating back to the nineteenth century. See bolero.

**carpas.** Traveling tent shows.

**charro.** A Mexican cowboy, who often dressed in an opulently decorated riding costume symbolizing his connection to rural aristocracy, and who helped define the macho singing cowboy (particularly in its prototype, Jorge Negrete) in the national consciousness during the 1940s.

**Chicano.** A term derived from *mexicano,* which is also pronounced *mechicano. Chicano* is used to describe a Mexican American living in the United States. The literary and political movements of the late 1960s and 1970s among Mexican Americans established *Chicano* as a term of ethnic pride, and it is properly written today as a proper noun with a capital *C.* See *El Movimiento.*

**comedia ranchera.** A popular Mexican film genre that reached its height of popularity during the 1930s and 1940s. Comedy, music, and dancing were typical of these films, as were nostalgia themes of an idyllic pastoral life that has been corrupted by modernity and urban migration.

**conjunto.** A music ensemble featuring accordion, bajo sexto, bass, and drums and distinguished by its use of Mexican song forms (e.g., canción ranchera, canción romántica, cumbia) and European rhythms (e.g., polka, waltz, mazurka). Conjunto evolved in the Texas-Mexican border region among working-class Mexican Americans shortly after the turn of the twentieth century and remains a popular dance music form or ensemble in South Texas and parts of the Hispanic Southwest.

*copla.* Couplet. Spanish-derived narrative genre with four, octosyllabic verses in which the last words of the second and fourth lines rhyme.

**corrido.** Popular Mexican narrative ballad descended from the Spanish romance and featuring the verse form of the *copla.*

**cumbia.** Contemporary dance rhythm rooted in the northern Colombian folk tradition that has grown in popularity among Latin American countries, especially in Mexico and Central America. The tempo is moderate and the harmony is fairly simple.

*décima.* A Spanish poetic form consisting of one or more stanzas, each with ten octosyllabic lines. Traditionally, Spanish *décimas* were composed in the style known as *espinela,* after the Spanish poet, novelist, and musician Vicente Espinel (1544–1624), who in 1591 published ten-line verses of poetry with an abbaaccddc rhyme scheme. Though the tradition has all but died out in Spain except for parts of the Canary Islands, it has survived in countries throughout Latin America (e.g., Mexico, Puerto Rico, Cuba, Chile, and Argentina), where it is often performed in a competitive context (Chase 1941, 271–272).

**diatonic accordion.** Initially popular because of their great simplicity, sound output, light weight, and low cost, these accordions are bisonoric, meaning each button produces two notes: one when the bellows is compressed, another while it is expanded. The note pattern of the keyboard is usually identical to that of the harmonica. Since the mid-1950s, the accordion of choice for modern norteña and Texas-Mexican conjunto musicians has been the three-row button accordion with the third row either a semitone higher than the original (now middle) row or a fourth above the second row.

**dueto.** Vocal or instrumental duet.

*El Movimiento.* The Chicano political movement during the late 1960s and 1970s that mobilized Mexican Americans in the United States to promote ethnic pride and to fight for better social, political, and economic status. Some have criticized *El Movimiento* for its inability to connect with the working class. The Chicano Movement took inspiration from an indigenous Mexican and American past. Community leaders, scholars, activists, artists, educators, and students ushered in the movement, which took hold in the Southwest. Leaders such as Reís López Tijerina, Corky González, César Chávez, and Dolores Huerta gave the movement national voices and called attention to the issues facing Chicanos. Part of the Chicano initiative was to set various educational goals: reduction of school dropout rates, improvement of educational attainment, development of bilingual and bicultural programs, and expansion of higher education fellowships and support services. Other goals included the development of Chicano-centered curricula, the creation of courses and programs in Chicano studies, and an increase in the number of Chicano teachers and administrators. Thousands of students also mobilized and formed student organizations geared towards education reform, activism, and peer support (Gonzales 1999, 191–222).

*el otro lado.* Literally, "the other side." Mexicans often use this slang term to refer to the United States, which is on the other side of the Rio Grande River. However, when used by an immigrant living in the United States, the phrase might also refer to Mexico.

*gente.* The people or common folk.

**gringo.** A non-Latino, North American individual. Depending on the context, the term can have derogatory connotations.

*grito.* Celebratory shout or yell, often heard in Texas dance halls where conjunto music is played.

*güero.* A person who is blonde or of light complexion.

**huapango.** Mexican folk dance rhythm with rapidly alternating rhythmic pattern (hemiola). It is associated with regional folk genres such as the son *jarocho* and son *huasteco.* Typically both major and minor keys are used.

*internacional.* Mainstream Mexican popular music that features highly produced programmed music and romantic songs. It is patterned after American pop.

*jarana.* A small, deep-bodied rhythm guitar, usually with eight strings: three double courses and two single.

*la mica.* "Green card." An official document verifying permanent U.S. residency.

*la migra.* Slang term for Immigration and Naturalization Service (now part of the Department of Homeland Security) agents, or the border patrol.

*malinchista.* Generally translated as "traitor." However, the term has often been used by Mexican immigrants when referring to Chicanos or U.S.-born Mexican Americans who deny their Mexican roots or look down upon those who are from Mexico. The term is taken from "La Malinche," the name given to the Aztec woman who reportedly traveled with Cortés as he conquered Mexico.

**maquiladora.** Assembly or manufacturing operation that is partly or entirely owned by U.S., Canadian, Japanese, or other foreign interests and typically located in Mexican cities and towns bordering the United States. Maquiladoras are attractive to foreign manufacturers because they can avoid health, safety, and environmental restrictions and can pay low wages to impoverished workers.

**mariachi.** A traditionally string-based folk ensemble originally from the state of Jalisco, Mexico (trumpets were added in the late 1930s). A mariachi consists of at least two violins, two trumpets, one Spanish guitar, a *vihuela* (high-pitched, five-string guitar), and a *guitarrón* (large, deep-bodied, six-string bass guitar), though it can expand to up to thirty musicians. After the Mexican Revolution, the mariachi came to represent a "united" Mexico and was popularized in numerous Mexican films and by well-known ranchera singers such as Javier Solís and Vicente Fernández. Popular as strolling musicians in restaurants and clubs, birthday celebrations, weddings, and numerous life-cycle events, mariachis are made up of professional and semi-professional musicians and have become known throughout the United States.

**mazurka.** A Polish dance from the Masuria region of northeastern Poland. It is similar to the polka and is a moderate dance in triple measure (3/8 or 3/4) with a strong accent on the second measure.

**merengue.** Dance music originating in the Dominican Republic. The rhythm is distinguished by fast, composite patterns.

**Mexican American War.** Also called the U.S.-Mexico War, it was fought between the United States and Mexico from 1846 to 1848. In the United States it is also known as the Mexican War, and in Mexico it is also known as the U.S. Intervention, the U.S. Invasion of Mexico, the United States War against Mexico, and the War of Northern Aggression. The war grew out of unresolved conflicts between Mexico and Texas after the latter won its independence from Mexico in 1836. The Republic of Texas was annexed by the United States in 1845, even though the southern and western borders were still in dispute. The Mexican government regarded this as a declaration of war. The Treaty of Hidalgo, signed on February 2, 1848, ended the war. It confirmed U.S. claims to Texas and set its boundary at the Rio Grande. Mexico also agreed to cede to the United States California and New Mexico (which included present-day California, Nevada, and Utah, and parts of Arizona, New Mexico, Colorado, and Wyoming) in exchange for $15 million. The treaty was ratified by the U.S. Senate on March 10, 1848 (Gonzales 1999, 64–72).

**mexicanidad.** Mexicanness. Historically a nationalist and patriotic identity that embraces Mexico's indigenous cultures. The period of reconstruction in Mexico (1920 to 1930) witnessed the early political consolidation of the Revolution as well as the search for a means of expressing a new sense of nationality, or mexicanidad. This ethnonational self-identity recaptured indigenous culture along with a modern and idealist Mexico that embraced progress and technology. However, among recent Mexican immigrants, mexicanidad is celebrated as the essence of being Mexican within an expanding transnational Mexican diaspora.

**mojado.** Loose translation of the phrase *espaldas mojadas,* which is itself a translation of the derogatory term *wetback.* Though the term is associated with illegal migration and border crossing, it also indicates low economic status. For most assimilated and upwardly mobile Chicanos and Mexican Americans, *mojado* is a highly undesirable term; however, many Mexican immigrants use it liberally to denote an individual who has sacrificed much for a better life for him/herself and family. (Also, wetback.)

*música duranguense.* A popular music genre that grew out of a blending of banda and norteña among Chicago's Mexican immigrant population during the mid-1990s. The music and its artists have become a sensation among immigrant youth in communities throughout the United States. and, more recently, in Mexico. Today, it is quite popular in communities on both sides of the border and top groups such as Montéz de Durango and K-Paz de la Sierra now rival top banda and norteña groups in popularity.

*música tejana.* Spanish-language popular music genre aimed primarily at upwardly mobile, young Texas-Mexican middle class. It incorporates popular pan-Latino rhythms like cumbia and salsa along with rancheras from conjunto and American popular music styles like country, pop, and rhythm and blues. (Also, tejano, *grupo tejano, la onda chicana.*)

**norteña.** A music style similar in instrumentation to Texas-Mexican conjunto but more focused on corridos (both traditional and new) and the cumbia rhythm than conjunto music. The lyrics tend to focus on experiences in Mexico and immigrant communities throughout the United States. *Norteña* initially referred to music of northern Mexico and South Texas (once a province of Mexico). Before the 1930s, norteña and conjunto were stylistically interchangeable, but as Texas-Mexicans began to develop an identity of their own, apart from Mexico, conjunto evolved to accommodate their experiences. Norteña, however, remains popular in northern Mexico and among Mexican immigrant laborers in the United States. (Also, música norteña.)

**Norteño.** Typically, *Norteño(a)* refers to an individual who was born in one of Mexico's northernmost states such as Tamaulipas; Nuevo León; Coahuila; Chihuahua; Baja California; Sonora; and sometimes Durango, Sinaloa, and Zacatecas. Today the term is often used to describe an individual of Mexican descent living in the United States.

*onda grupera.* Also cumbia norteña or Mexican Regional *tropical.* The term *onda grupera* initially referred to any music group that utilized synthesizers or keyboards. Today the term refers to groups who primarily perform cumbias. Cumbia norteña groups became popular in Monterrey, Nuevo León, Mexico, in the late 1970s and sometimes featured accordion or saxophone or both. They also dressed in the Norteño charro (horseman) outfits typically worn by música norteña groups.

**orquesta tejana.** Popular Mexican American music form that evolved in the 1940s and 1950s in response to an expanding Texas-Mexican middle class. The music merged American popular styles such as swing, jazz, and rock and roll; Mexican song forms like rancheras and corridos; Latino rhythms such as cumbia and salsa; and elements of conjunto. This style is the predecessor to contemporary *música tejana*.

*patrón.* Employer or boss.

*pelado.* Literally the "skinned one" or the shirtless one, typically a bumbling, though at times sharp-witted, character in Mexican vaudeville and traveling tent shows (carpas). The *pelado* is further defined in modern Mexican cinema as "a person who is totally marginalized from mainstream society and who, in turn, is spiritually and psychologically empty due to this marginalization" (Martínez 1998, 33). This character is most popularly portrayed as a poor slum-dweller and a product of rural to urban migration in Mexico during the late 1920s through the 1940s. The comic actor Cantinflas immortalized the *pelado* on-screen during this period.

*peón.* Laborer or peon.

*pocho.* This can be a pejorative term referring to an "Americanized" person of Mexican descent. Like *mojado* and *gringo,* however, this term has been reinterpreted by many as a source of pride and ethnic identity.

*quinceañera.* An important coming-of-age celebration, or coming-out party, that occurs on a young girl's fifteenth birthday.

**ranchera.** The song form that emerged in the late nineteenth century and became popular during the Mexican Revolution. Many consider it Mexico's first popular music genre. Sung to different rhythms—from polka to waltz to bolero—its lyrics traditionally celebrate rural life, Revolutionary heroes, and the struggles of love and life in a changing and modernizing world. Though both norteña and tejano groups perform rancheras (Mexican "country" songs sung in the polka rhythm), the ranchera genre refers more specifically to popular Mexican singers who dress in the mariachi charro (Spanish-inspired equestrian) suits and sing classic ranchera songs and popular ballads. Some of the best known ranchera stars include Vicente Fernández, Javier Solís, and Pepe Aguilar. (Also, canción ranchera.)

**redova.** Also *redowa.* Traditionally known as *vals bajito* in northern Mexico and along the Texas-Mexican border, this dance rhythm of European origin was typically played in the lower register of the accordion and is in 9/8, with a fast waltz-like feel. The redova's melody is strongly accented on the first and third beat. The redova is always played instrumentally and is known among Texas-Mexican accordionists as a "show piece." Due to the number of notes one could play in a measure, the redova is more complex than the other rhythms (except the Mexican huapango) and is reserved for seasoned players. Today, very few young Texas-Mexican and Mexican accordionists play redovas; most younger players are completely unfamiliar with them (García Flores 1991, 10).

*rinche.* According to Paredes, the word *rinche* comes from the border Mexicans' distortion of the word "ranger." He also states that *rinche* can apply to any other American "armed and mounted and looking for Mexicans to kill." The Texas Rangers were known to have exaggerated the number of Mexicans they apprehended or killed at the border (1958, 24).

**rock en español.** An umbrella term for Spanish-language rock. This loosely defined Latin take on rock emerged in Mexico in the mid-1960s, and soon after in Argentina, and came of age in the Ibero-American world in the 1980s.

**romance.** The Spanish romance is a classic poetic song form dating back to the 1500s. Like the corrido, it features octosyllabic lines alternating in pairs with rhymed assonance in the even lines. For further discussion (and debates) about the romance's relationship to the corrido, see Duvalier 1937 and Paredes 1954.

**son (trio or ensemble).** Mestizo folk music tradition that is defined by regional styles throughout Mexico. Most styles, such as son *jarocho,* son *jalisciense,* son *huasteco,* and son *arribeño* are distinct string ensemble traditions.

*sonidero.* A deejay who mixes cumbia and sometimes other popular Spanish-language music genres at dances in urban cities in Mexico and, more recently, in the United States. He selects new and cutting-edge cumbias and reads dedications over the mix. The dedications are then duplicated and mailed to individuals on both sides of the border. The *sonidero* scene originated in the slums of Mexico City and Monterrey in the late 1970s and has spread to villages, particularly in southern states like Puebla and Guerrero. In North America, the *sonidero* phenomenon emerged in the early 1990s in cities like New York, Chicago, Las Vegas, and Atlanta. (See Ragland 2003.) The term is also used to describe the Mexican cumbia groups who have become popular as a result of this deejay-driven phenomena. It refers to both the deejay-driven dances and the cumbia groups that the deejays meticulously select to play. They tend not to be groups heard on mainstream Latin American or Latino radio.

**son jarocho.** Rural folk music tradition originating in the Jarocho region of Mexico, which includes parts of Veracruz, San Luis Potosí, and Tamaulipas. The ensemble generally includes a large thirty-two– to thirty-six–string wooden harp, *jarana* (guitar-like instrument with five courses of strings, three double and two single), *requinto jarocho* (three-quarter size guitar with four strings, similar to a Spanish requinto, but tuned higher), a frame drum, and occasionally other percussion instruments. The huapango rhythm, which is associated with *jarocho* and *huasteco* styles, is a fast 6/8 syncopated against 3/4 (*sesquiáltera*).

*technobanda.* Modern-day spin-off of banda, which was based on the village brass band tradition that still exists in western Mexican states such as Sinaloa, Nayarit, and Jalisco. *Technobanda* adds keyboards and synthesizers. Along with *sonidero* and *música duranguense,* it is a popular working-class Mexican immigrant music genre that has emerged in the diaspora within the past twenty years. Helena Simonett associates the mid-1990s explosion of this music and dance genre, which is popular among Mexican youth in Los Angeles, with anti-immigrant rhetoric by the then-governor Pete Wilson and supporters of Proposition 187 (see Simonett 2001a).

**Tejano.** A Mexican American born in Texas.

**tejano.** Uncapitalized, this term is used to refer to the popular South Texas music style (also known as *música tejana*) and as an umbrella term for music played by Texas-born Mexican Americans (i.e., tejano conjunto, orquesta tejana, etc.).

**tololoche.** The Mexican name for a handmade contrabass typically used in Texas-Mexican conjunto and Mexican norteña music groups prior to the late 1950s. This instrument can still be found in norteña ensembles in Mexican border towns. It has since been replaced by the electric bass.

*tropical.* A popular Latin American music form featuring romantic songs with cumbia rhythms. In the United States, this music is especially popular among Mexican immigrant laborers.

*varsovienne.* A dance that originated in France during the 1850s. It is a genteel variation of the mazurka, incorporating elements of the waltz. Its name is taken from the French translation for "women of Warsaw." Its tempo is rather slow, and its music is characterized by strong accents on the first beats of the second and fourth complete bars. (See Brown.)

**wetback.** Derogatory term for undocumented (Mexican) immigrant. *Wetback* was first used in 1944 by border patrol officials when the number of illegal Mexicans traveling into the United States increased by a significantly large percentage. (Also, *mojado.*)

*yerba mala.* Marijuana.

*zonas de tolerancia.* Similar to "red-light districts." In the early part of the twentieth century, these *zonas* emerged in working-class *colonias* (neighborhoods) on the edge of Monterrey. The dance salons and bars in these districts generally provided music, dancing, floor shows, room accommodations, and food service. These *zonas* still exist today, though the cantinas and clubs are generally for men only and prostitution is more rampant. Local norteña groups can still be found performing in these locations (Molina Montelongo and Quezada Molina 1995a, 97–98).

# References

Águila, Justino. 2003. "Mexican Superstar Still Feels like Afterthought in World of Latin Grammys." *Milwaukee Journal Sentinel*, September 3.

Alanís Támez, Juan. 1994. *Los Montañeses del Álamo 1938–1994*. Santiago, Nuevo León, Mexico: El Cercado.

Alemán, Jesse. 1998. "Chicano Novelistic Discourse: Dialogizing the Corrido Critical Paradigm." *MELUS* 23 (1): 49–64.

Allensworth, Elaine. 1997. "Earnings Mobility of First and '1.5' Generation Mexican-Origin Women and Men: A Comparison with U.S.-Born Mexican Americans and Non-Hispanic Whites." *International Migration Review* 31:386–410.

Alonzo, Ana María. 1995. *Thread of Blood: Colonialism, Revolution, and Gender on Mexico's Northern Frontier*. Tucson: University of Arizona Press.

Anderson, Stuart. 2004. "When a More Open Border Is Better." *Washington Post*, January 26.

Anzaldúa, Gloria. 1987. *Borderlands/La Frontera: The New Mestiza*. San Francisco: Spinsters/Aunt Lute.

Appadurai, Arjun. 1990. "Disjuncture and Difference in the Global Cultural Economy." *Theory, Culture, and Society* 7 (2–3): 295–310.

———. 1991. "Global Ethnoscapes: Notes and Queries for a Transnational Anthropology." In *Recapturing Anthropology: Working in the Present*, edited by Richard G. Fox, 191–210. Santa Fe, N.M.: School of American Research Press.

———. 1996. *Modernity at Large: Cultural Dimensions of Modernity*. Minneapolis: University of Minnesota Press.

———. 2003. "Sovereignty without Territoriality: Notes for a Post-national Geography." In *The Anthropology of Space and Place: Locating Culture*, edited by Setha Low and Denise Lawrence-Zuñiga, 337–349. Oxford: Blackwell.

Argüelles Franco, Manuel Ángel. 1995. "Banda de música de Cadereyta Jiménez." In *Tradiciones y costumbres de Nuevo León*, edited by Rogelio Velázquez de León and Francisco Javier Alvarado Segovia, 151–157. Monterrey, Nuevo León: Departamento de Investigaciones Históricas, Secretaría de Desarrollo Social del Gobierno del Estado de Nuevo León.

Arizpe, Lourdes. 2004. "Migración y cultura. Las redes simbólicas del futuro." In *Los retos culturales de México*, edited by Lourdes Arizpe, 19–42. Mexico City: Centro Regional de Investigaciones Multidisciplinarias, Universidad Autónoma de México.

Arrelano, Gustavo. 2002. "Latin Grammys Hide the Big, Uncool Truth." *Pacific News Service*, September 21, http://news.pacificnews.org/news/view_article.html?article_id=1a5c27b1266cbf0238738691302fdb3f (accessed November 15, 2003).

Arreola, Daniel, and James R. Curtis. 1993. *The Mexican Border Cities: Landscape, Autonomy, and Place Personality.* Tucson: University of Arizona Press.

Astorga, Luis 1996a. *Mitología del narcotraficante en México.* Mexico City: Plaza y Valdés.

———. 1996b. *El siglo de las drogas.* Mexico City: Espasa Calpe.

Ayala Duarte, Alfonso. 1995. "El Jazz en Monterrey: Los fabulosos años 20's." In *Tradiciones y costumbres de Nuevo León*, compiled by Celso Garza Guajardo, 27–33. Monterrey, Nuevo León: Grafo Print Editores.

Ballí, Cecilia. 2003. "It's Not about Music No More: Inter-Ethnic Conflict and Compromise in the Regional Mexican Music Industry." *Tonantzin* 28 (n.p.).

———. 2004. "King of the Accordion." *Texas Monthly,* April, 140–187.

Basch, Linda, Nina Glick Schiller and Cristina Szanton Blanc. 1994. *Nations Unbound: Transnational Projects, Postcolonial Predicaments, and Deterritorialized Nation-States.* New York: Routledge.

Berestein, Leslie. 2006. "Border Deaths on Record Pace." *San Diego Tribune,* July 22, http://www.signonsandiego.com/news/mexico/tijuana/20060722-9999-1n22crossers.html (accessed October 21, 2008).

Berrones, Guillermo. 1995. *Ingratos ojos míos: Miguel Luna y la historia de El Palomo y El Gorrión.* Monterrey, Nuevo León: OFICIO Ediciones, Universidad Autónoma de Nuevo León.

Bhabha, Homi K. 1994. *The Location of Culture.* London: Routledge.

Bourdieu, Pierre. 1993. *The Field of Cultural Production.* Edited and introduced by Randal Johnson. New York: University of Columbia Press.

Brown, Maurice J. E. "Varsovienne." *Grove Music Online,* edited by Laura Macy, http://www.grovemusic.com (accessed October 25, 2004).

Calavita, Kitty. 1992. *Inside the State: the Bracero Program, Immigration, and the I.N.S.* New York: Routledge.

Canclini, Néstor García. 2000. "From National Capital to Global Capital: Urban Change in Mexico City." *Public Culture* 12 (1): 207–213.

Carillo, Iván. "Tigres del Norte retan a la censura: Tigres del Norte de gira con La Reina del Sur." *Univisión Online,* http://www.univision.com/content/ (accessed September 25, 2003).

Carrizosa, Toño. 1997. *La onda grupera: Historia del movimiento grupero.* Mexico City: Edamex.

Chandler, Billy J. 1978. *The Bandit King: Lampiao of Brazil.* College Station: Texas A&M Press.

Chapa, Jorge. 1990. "Trends in Educational and Occupational Attainment of Mexican Americans." *Journal of Hispanic Policy* 4:3–18.

Chase, Gilbert. 1941. *The Music of Spain.* New York: Dover.

Chávez, Leo. 1992. *Shadowed Lives: Undocumented Immigrants in American Society.* New York: Harcourt Brace College Publishers.

Chipman, Donald E. 1992. *Spanish Texas, 1519–1821.* Austin: University of Texas Press.

Clearley, Anna. 2007. "Songs about Mexican Drug Cartels Proving Dangerous for Performers." *San Diego Union Tribune,* January 2, http://www.signonsandiego.com/news/mexico/tijuana/20070102-9999-1n2nortena.html (accessed March 12, 2007).

Clifford, James. 1992. "Traveling Cultures." In *Cultural Studies,* edited by Lawrence Grossberg, Cary Nelson, and Paula Treichler, 96–116. New York: Routledge.

———. 1997. *Routes: Travel and Translation in the Late Twentieth Century.* Cambridge, Mass.: Harvard University Press.

Cobo, Leila. 2004. "Los Tigres del Norte: Music with a Social Conscience." *Hispanic Magazine,* July/August.

Connell, John, and Chris Gibson. 2003. *Sound Tracks: Popular Music, Identity and Place.* London: Routledge.

"Coors Light *Onda Norteña Gira* (Norteño New Wave Tour) 2005." Online press release, *P.R. Newswire—United Business Media,* June 9, http://www.prnewswire.com/ (accessed June 10, 2005).

Cuéllar, José B. 2001. "El Saxofón in Tejano and Norteño Music." In *Puro Conjunto: An Album in Words and Pictures. Writings, Posters and Photos from the Tejano Conjunto Festival en San Antonio, 1982–1998,* edited by Juan Tejeda and Alvelardo Valdez, 135–156. Austin: CMAS Books, University of Texas Press.

de la Cruz López, Raymundo. 1978. *Corridos y Voces del Pueblo.* Torreón, Coahuila: Ediciones Mayrán.

de la Vega Alfaro, Eduardo. 1995. "Origins, Development and Crisis of the Sound Cinema (1929–64)." In *Mexican Cinema,* edited by Paulo Antonio Paranaguá, 79–93. London: British Film Institute.

Durand, Jorge, Douglas S. Massey, and Emilio A. Parrado. 1999. "The New Era of Mexican Migration to the United States." *Journal of American History* 86 (2): 518–536.

Duvalier, Armando. 1937. "Romance y corrido." *Crisol: Revista de Crítica* (June): 35–43, (September): 8–16, and (November): 35–41.

Edberg, Mark Cameron. 2004. *El Narcotraficante: Narcocorridos and the Construction of a Cultural Persona on the U.S.-Mexico Border.* Austin: University of Texas Press.

Emerick, Laura. 2004 "Blood ties to homeland, a 'Pacto de Sangre.'" Interview of Hernán Hernández of Los Tigres del Norte. *Chicago Sun-Times,* April 4.

Epstein, Edward Jay. 1977. *Agency of Fear: Opiates and Political Power in America.* New York: Putnam and Sons.

Erlmann, Veit. 1993. "The Politics and Aesthetics of Transnational Musics." *World of Music* 35 (2): 3–15.

Espinel, Vicente. 1980. *Diversa rimas (Acta Salamanticensia).* Salamanca, Spain: Universidad de Salamanca.

Etzioni, Amitai. 1993. *The Spirit of Community.* New York: Crown Publishers.

Feld, Steven. 2000. "A Sweet Lullaby for World Music." *Public Culture* 12 (1): 145–171.

Fleshman, Karen. 2002. "Abrazando Mexicanos: The United States Should Recognize Mexican Workers' Contributions to Its Economy by Allowing Them to Work Legally." *New York Law School Journal of Human Rights* 18 (2): 237–269.

Flores, Juan. 1993. *Divided Borders: Essays on Puerto Rican Identity.* Houston: Arte Público Press.

Fowler, Gene, and Bill Crawford. 2002. *Border Radio: Quacks, Yodelers, Pitchmen, Psychics, and Other Amazing Broadcasters of the American Airwaves.* Austin: University of Texas Press.

Fraisse, Paul. 1982. "Rhythm and Tempo." In *The Psychology of Music,* edited by Diana Deutsch, 149–180. New York: Academic Press.

Frith, Simon. 1981. *Sound Effects: Youth, Leisure, and the Politics of Rock 'n' Roll.* New York: Pantheon.

Galán, Héctor. 1996. *Chicano! History of the Mexican American Civil Rights Movement.* Video. NLCC Educational Media.

Galarza, Ernesto. 1978. *Merchants of Labor: The Mexican Bracero Story.* Charlotte, N.C.: McNally and Loftin Publishers.

Gamio, Manuel. 1969. *Mexican Immigration to the United States.* New York: Arno and *New York Times.*

García, Ángeles. 2002. "He escrito un corrido mexicano de 500 páginas." Interview of the Spanish writer Arturo Pérez-Reverte. *El País* (Madrid, Spain), April 28.

García, Mario T. 1996. "La Frontera: The Border as Symbol and Reality in Mexican-American Thought." In *Between Two Worlds: Mexican Immigrants in the United States,* edited by David G. Gutiérrez, 89–118. Wilmington, Del.: Scholarly Resources.

García Flores, Raúl. 1991. "Treasury of Northeastern Mexican Music." Liner notes to the CD *Treasury of Northeastern Mexican Music Volume I: Nuevo León,* various artists. Monterrey, Nuevo León: Consejo Nacional para la Cultura/Las Artes y Instituto Nacional de Antropología e Historia.

García Hernández, Arturo G. 1999. "Piporro, un gran improvisador de la tradición: Monsiváis." *La Jornada* (Mexico City), March 25.

———. 2005. "Prejuicios e ignorancia detrás del llamado a censurar antología de corridos." *La Jornada* (Mexico City), April 7.

García y Griego, Manuel. 1996. "The Importation of Mexican Contract Laborers to the United States, 1942–1964." In *Between Two Worlds: Mexican Immigrants in the United States,* edited by David G. Gutiérrez, 45–85. Wilmington, Del.: Scholarly Resources.

Garza Guajardo, Celso. 1993. *Me decían Tanguma . . . y bailaba "El Cerro de la Silla."* Zuazua, Nuevo León: Centro de Información de Historia Regional Hacienda de San Pedro.

Gilroy, Paul. 1993. *The Black Atlantic: Modernity and Double Consciousness.* Cambridge, Mass.: Harvard University Press.

Glick Schiller, Nina, Linda Basch, and Cristina Blanc-Szanton, eds. 1992. *Towards a Transnational Perspective on Migration: Race, Class, Ethnicity, and Nationalism Reconsidered.* New York: Academy of Sciences.

Gómez Flores, Carlos Jesús. 1997. *A tambora batiente.* Monterrey, Nuevo León: Dirección General de Culturas Populares/Unidad Regional Norte.

Gómez-Peña, Guillermo. 1996. *The New World Border: Prophecies, Poems, and Loqueras for the End of the Century.* San Francisco: City Lights.

Gómez-Quiñones, Juan, and David R. Maciel. 1998. "What Goes Around Comes Around: Political Practice and Cultural Response to the Internationalization of Mexican Labor." In *Culture across Borders: Mexican Immigration and Popular Culture,* edited by David R. Maciel and María Herrera-Sobek, 27–65. Tucson: University of Arizona Press.

Gonzales, Manuel G. 1999. *Mexicanos: A History of Mexicans in the United States.* Bloomington: Indiana University Press.

González, Damaso. 2005. "El alcalde Michael Bloomberg: ¡México vive en Gracie Mansion!" *El Diario* (New York), May 6, http://www.eldiariony.com/noticias/detail_archive.aspx?

section=17&desc=&id=1141940&Day=6&Month=5&Year=2005 (accessed May 15, 2005).

González Gutiérrez, Carlos. 1999. "Fostering Identities: Mexico's Relations with Its Diaspora." *Journal of American History* 86 (2): 545–567.

González Ramírez, Eulalio. 1999. *Autobiogr . . . ajúa y anecdo . . . taconario.* Mexico City: Editorial Diana.

Graham, Otis L. 1995. "Tracing Liberal Woes to '65 Immigration Act." *Christian Science Monitor,* December 28. Center for Immigration Studies Web site, http://www.cis.org/articles/1995/olg12-28-95.html (accessed March 3, 2003).

Guilbault, Jocelyne. 1993a. *Zouk: World Music in the West Indies.* Chicago: University of Chicago Press.

———. 1993b. "On Redefining the 'Local' through World Music." *World of Music* 35 (2): 33–47.

Gupta, Akhil, and James Ferguson. 1997. "Culture, Power, Place: Ethnography at the End of an Era." In *Culture, Power, Place: Explorations in Critical Anthropology,* edited by Akhil Gupta and James Ferguson, 1–46. Durham, N.C.: Duke University Press.

Gutiérrez, David G. 1995. *Walls and Mirrors: Mexican Americans, Mexican Immigrants, and the Politics of Ethnicity.* Berkeley and Los Angeles: University of California Press.

———. 1999. "Migration, Emergent Ethnicity, and the 'Third Space': The Shifting Politics of Nationalism in Greater Mexico." *Journal of American History* 86 (2): 481–517.

Gutiérrez, Ramón A. 1987. "Unraveling America's Hispanic Past: Internal Stratification and Class Boundaries." *Aztlán* 17 (1): 79–100.

Hagan, Carla J., Dan Dickey, and Felix Peña. 1979. "La Compuzimos Pizcando: Texas Migrant Ballads." Manuscript, Migrant Border Ballads Project Records, Benson Latin American Collection, University of Texas Libraries, the University of Texas, Austin.

Hagan, Jacqueline, and Nestor Rodríguez. 2002. "Resurrecting Exclusion: The Effects of 1996 U.S. Reform on Communities and Families in Texas, El Salvador, and Mexico." In *Latinos: Remaking America,* edited by Marcelo M. Suárez-Orozco and Mariela M. Páez, 190–201. Berkeley and Los Angeles: University of California Press.

Hall, Stuart. 1981. "Notes on Deconstructing 'the Popular.'" In *People's History and Socialist Theory,* edited by Raphael Samuel, 227–240. London: Routledge.

———. 1994. "Cultural Identity and Diaspora." In *Colonial Discourse and Post-Colonial Theory: A Reader,* edited by Patrick Williams and Laura Chrisman, 392–401. London: Harvester Wheatsheaf.

———. 1997a. "Old and New Identities, Old and New Ethnicities." In *Culture, Globalization, and the World System: Contemporary Conditions for the Representation of Identity,* edited by Anthony D. King, 41–68. Binghamton: State University of New York.

———, ed. 1997b. *Representation: Cultural Representation and Signifying Practices.* Thousand Oaks, Calif.: Sage.

Hebdige, Dick. 1979. *Subculture: The Meaning of Style.* London: Methuen.

Hernández, Guillermo E. 1999. "What Is the Corrido?" *Studies in Latin American Popular Culture* 18:69–92.

Herrera-Sobek, María. 1979. *The Bracero Program: Elitelore versus Folklore.* Los Angeles: UCLA Latin American Center Publications.

———. 1982. "The Acculturation Process of the Chicana in the Corrido." *De Colores: Journal of Chicano Expression and Thought* 6:7–16.

———. 1990. *The Mexican Corrido: A Feminist Analysis.* Bloomington: Indiana University Press.

———. 1993. *Northward Bound: The Mexican Immigrant Experience in Ballad and Song.* Bloomington: University of Indiana Press.

———. 1998. "The Corrido as Hypertext: Undocumented Mexican Immigrant Films and the Mexican/Chicano Ballad." In *Culture across Borders: Mexican Immigration and Popular Culture,* edited by David R. Maciel and María Herrera-Sobek, 227–258. Tucson: University of Arizona Press.

Hobsbawm, Eric J. 1981. *Bandits.* New York: Pantheon.

———. 1983. "Introduction: Inventing Tradition." In *The Invention of Tradition,* edited by Eric Hobsbawm and Terrence Ranger, 1–14. Cambridge: Cambridge University Press.

Kanellos, Nicolás. 1984. *Hispanic Theatre in the United States.* Houston: Arte Público Press.

Kaplan, Caren. 1996. *Questions of Travel: Postmodern Discourses of Displacement.* Durham, N.C.: Duke University Press.

Keil, Charles, and Steven Feld. 1994. *Music Grooves: Essays and Dialogues.* Chicago: University of Chicago Press.

Lauer, A. Robert. 2002. "Spanish Metrification." Online article, January 25, http://faculty-staff.ou.edu/L/A-Robert.R.Lauer-1/METRIFICATION.html (accessed January 12, 2004).

Lefebvre, Henri. 1991. *The Production of Space.* Oxford: Blackwell.

Levy, Andre. 2000. "Diasporas through Anthropological Lenses: Contexts of Postmodernity." *Diaspora* 9 (1):137–158.

Limón, José E. 1981. "The Folk Performance of Chicano and the Cultural Limits of Political Ideology." In *"And Other Neighborly Names": Social Process and Cultural Image in Texas Folklore,* edited by Richard Bauman and Roger D. Abrahams, 197–225. Austin: University of Texas Press.

———. 1983. "Folklore, Social Conflict, and the United States–Mexico Border." In *Handbook of American Folklore,* edited by Richard M. Dorson, 191–225. Bloomington: Indiana University Press.

———. 1992. *Mexican Ballads, Chicano Poems: History and Influence in Mexican-American Social Poetry.* Berkeley and Los Angeles: University of California Press.

———. 1998. *American Encounters: Greater Mexico, the United States, and the Erotics of Culture.* Boston: Beacon Press.

Lipsitz, George. 1994. *Dangerous Crossroads: Popular Music, Postmodernism, and the Poetics of Place.* New York: Verso.

Lomnitz, Claudio. 1994. "Decadence in Times of Globalization." *Cultural Anthropology* 9:257–267.

———. 1996. "Fissures in Contemporary Mexican Nationalism." *Public Culture* 9 (1): 55–68.

Lowe, Lisa. 1996. *Immigrant Acts: On Asian American Cultural Politics.* Durham, N.C.: Duke University Press.

Lytle, Kelly. 2003. "Constructing the Criminal Alien: A Historical Framework for Analyzing Border Vigilantes at the Turn of the 21st Century." University of San Diego, Center for Comparative Immigration Studies, Vigilante Panel. Working Paper no. 83, October 7, 2003, http://www.ccis-ucsd.org/PUBLICATIONS/wrkg83.pdf (accessed January 4, 2005).

Maciel, David R., and María Rosa García-Acevedo. 1998. "The Celluloid Immigrant: Narrative Films of Mexican Immigration." In *Culture across Borders: Mexican Immigration and Popular Culture,* edited by David R. Maciel and María Herrera-Sobek, 149–202. Tucson: University of Arizona Press.

Madrid, Alejandro L. 2003. "Navigating Ideologies in 'In-Between' Cultures: Signifying Practices in Nor-tec Music." *Latin American Music Review* 24:270–286.

Mailman, Stanley. 1995. "California's Proposition 187 and Its Lessons." *New York Law Journal,* January 3, http://www.ssbb.com/article1.html (accessed July 13, 2004).

Malkin, Elizabeth. 2008. "Mexicans Barely Increased Remittances in '07." *New York Times,* February 26.

Manuel, Peter. 1993. *Cassette Culture: Music and a People's Medium in North India.* Chicago: University of Chicago Press.

———. 1995. "Music as Symbol, Music as Simulacrum: Postmodern, Pre-modern, and Modern Aesthetics in Subcultural Popular Musics." *Popular Music* 14 (2): 227–239.

Marcus, George E. 1995. "Ethnography in/of the World System: The Emergence of Multi-sited Ethnography." *Annual Review of Anthropology* 24:95–117.

Martínez, Glenn A. 1998. "Mojados, Malinches, and the Dismantling of the United States/ Mexico Border in Contemporary Mexican Cinema." *Latin American Issues* 14:31–50.

Martínez, Jesús. 1995. "Tigers in a Gold Cage: Binationalism and Politics in the Songs of Mexican Immigrants in Silicon Valley." In *Ballads and Boundaries: Narrative Singing in an Intercultural Context,* ed. James Porter, 325–338. Los Angeles: Department of Ethnomusicology and Systematic Musicology, University of California.

Martínez, Rubén. 1993. *The Other Side: Fault Lines, Guerrilla Saints, and the True Heart of Rock and Roll.* London: Vintage.

Massey, Douglas, Jorge Durand, and Nolan J. Malone. 2002. *Beyond Smoke and Mirrors: Mexican Immigration in an Era of Economic Integration.* New York: Russell Sage Foundation.

Mato, Daniel. 1998. "On the Making of Transnational Identities in the Age of Globalization: The U.S. Latina/o–Latin American Case." *Cultural Studies* 12:598–620.

McDowell, John Holmes. 1972. "The Mexican Corrido: Formula and Theme in a Ballad Tradition." *Journal of American Folklore* 85:205–220.

———. 1981. "The Corrido of Greater Mexico as Discourse, Music, Event." In *"And Other Neighborly Names": Social Process and Cultural Image in Texas Folklore,* edited by Richard D. Bauman and Roger D. Abrahams, 44–75. Austin: University of Texas Press.

McKinley, James, Jr. 2008. "Mexico's New President Sends Thousands of Federal Officers to Fight Drug Cartels." *New York Times,* January 19.

McLynn, Frank. 2001. *Villa and Zapata: A Biography of the Mexican Revolution.* London: Pimlico.

Medina de la Serna, Rafael. 1995. "Sorrows and Glories of Comedy." In *Mexican Cinema,* edited by Paulo Antonio Paranaguá, 163–170. London: British Film Institute.

Meier, Matt, and Feliciano Ribera. 1993. *Mexican Americans, American Mexicans: From Conquistadors to Chicanos.* New York: Hill and Wang.

Meléndez, Claudia S. 2003. "Retratos del pueblo: Los Tigres del Norte." Interview of Hernán Hernández of Los Tigres del Norte. *Nuevo Mundo* (San Jose, California), August 29.

Mendoza, Vicente T. 1939. *El romance español y el corrido mexicano.* Mexico City: Ediciones de la Universidad Nacional Autónoma de México.

———. 1954. *El corrido mexicano; antología.* Mexico City: Ediciones de la Universidad Nacional Autónoma de México.

———. 1964. *Lírica narrativa de México: El corrido.* Mexico City: Universidad Nacional Autónoma de México, Instituto de Investigaciones Estéticas.

"Mexico's Forbidden Songs." 2004. Reported by Chris Summers and Dominic Bailey, *BBC News Online,* October 3, http://news.bbc.co.uk/2/hi/americas/3552370.stm (accessed January 4, 2005).

Middleton, Richard. 1990. *Studying Popular Music.* Philadelphia: Open University Press.

Molina Montelongo, Filiberto, and Guadalupe Quezada Molina. 1995a. "Nuevo León y su música de acordeón 1941–1961." In *Tradiciones y costumbres de Nuevo León,* edited by Rogelio Velázquez de León and Francisco Javier Alvarado Segovia, 97–104. Monterrey, Nuevo León: Departamento de Investigaciones Históricas, Secretaría de Desarrollo Social del Gobierno del Estado de Nuevo León.

———. 1995b. "Nuevo León y su música tambora y clarinete." In *Tradiciones y costumbres de Nuevo León,* edited by Rogelio Velázquez de León and Francisco Javier Alvarado Segovia, 93–95. Monterrey, Nuevo León : Departamento de Investigaciones Históricas, Secretaría de Desarrollo Social del Gobierno del Estado de Nuevo León.

Monsiváis, Carlos. 1995. "Mythologies." In *Mexican Cinema,* edited by Paulo Antonio Paranaguá, 117–127. London: British Film Institute.

Moreno, Julio. 2003. *Yankee Don't Go Home! Mexican Nationalism, American Business Culture, and the Shaping of Modern Mexico, 1920–1950.* Chapel Hill: University of North Carolina Press.

Moreno Rivas, Yolanda. 1979. *Historia de la música popular mexicana.* Mexico City: Alianza Editorial Mexicana, Consejo Nacional para la Cultura y las Artes.

Nicolopulos, James. 1997. "The Heroic Corrido: A Premature Obituary?" *Aztlán: Journal of Chicano Studies* 22:115–138.

"Norteño Music Icons Los Tigres del Norte Debut #1 on the Billboard Top Latin Album Chart with their New Album 'La Reina del Sur.'" 2002. Univision online, July 11. [Fonovisa press release to promote the release of the CD *La Reina del Sur* by Los Tigres del Norte], http://www.univision.net/corp/en/pr/Woodland_Hills_07112002-4.html (accessed December 12, 2004).

"Nueva censura a Los Tigres del Norte." 2004. EFE online [the Spanish-language associated press] April 24, http://www.esmas.com/espectaculos/musica/359483.htm (accessed November 4, 2004).

Oliver, Paul. 1984. *Songsters and Saints: Vocal Traditions on Race Records.* Cambridge: Cambridge University Press.

Olvera, Juan José. 1992. "Continuidad y cambio en la música colombiana en Monterrey." Monterrey, Nuevo León: Actas del IV Congreso Latinoamericano de la Asociación Internacional para el Estudio de la Música Popular.

Ortiz Guerrero, Armando Hugo. 1992. *Vida y muerte en la frontera.* Monterrey, Nuevo León: Hensa Editores.

Osante, Patricia. 1997. *Orígenes del Nuevo Santander, 1748–1772.* Mexico City: Universidad Nacional Autónoma de México, Ciudad Victoria: Universidad Autónoma de Tamaulipas.

Pacini Hernández, Deborah. 1993. "The Picó Phenomenon in Cartagena, Colombia." *América Negra* 6:69–95.

———. 2001. "Race, Ethnicity and the Production of Latin/o Popular Music." In *Global Repertoires: Popular Music within and beyond the Transnational Music Industry,* edited by Andreas Gebesmair and Alfred Smudits, 57–72. Aldershot, UK: Ashgate Publishing.

Paranaguá, Paulo Antonio. 1995. "Ten Reasons to Love or Hate Mexican Cinema." In *Mexican Cinema,* edited by Paulo Antonio Paranaguá, 1–14. London: British Film Institute.

Paredes, Américo. 1958. *"With His Pistol in His Hand": A Border Ballad and Its Hero.* Urbana: University of Illinois Press.

———. 1963. "The Ancestry of Mexico's Corridos: A Matter of Definitions." *Journal of American Folklore* 76:231–235.

———. 1976. *A Texas-Mexican Cancionero: Folksongs of the Lower Border.* Austin: University of Texas Press.

———. 1978. "The Problem of Identity in a Changing Culture: Popular Expressions of Culture Conflict along the Lower Rio Grande Border." In *Views across the Border: The United States and Mexico,* edited by Stanley Ross, 68–94. Albuquerque: University of New Mexico Press.

———. 1993. *Folklore and Culture on the Texas Mexican Border.* Austin: University of Texas Press.

Passel, Jeffrey S. 2005. "Estimates of the Size and Characteristics of the Undocumented Population." *Pew Hispanic Center Online,* March 21, http://pewhispanic.org/reports/report.php?ReportID=44 (accessed April 14, 2005).

Patoski, Joe Nick. 1996. *Selena: Como la Flor.* New York: Little, Brown.

Paz, Octavio. 1985. *The Labyrinth of Solitude and Other Writings.* New York: New Grove Press.

Peña, Manuel H. 1981. "The Emergence of Texas-Mexican Conjunto Music, 1935–1960: An Interpretive History." Ph.D. dissertation, University of Texas, Austin.

———. 1985. *The Texas-Mexican Conjunto: Music of a Working-Class People.* Austin: University of Texas Press.

———. 1999a. *Música Tejana: The Cultural Economy of Artistic Transformation.* College Station: Texas A&M Press.

———. 1999b. *The Mexican American Orquesta: Music, Culture, and the Dialectic of Conflict.* Austin: University of Texas Press.

Pérez-Reverte, Arturo. 2002. *La Reina del Sur.* Miami: Santillana USA Publishing.

Quiñones, Sam. 1997–1998. "San Jose's Los Tigres del Norte Have Remade Mexican Pop Music Twice Over." *Silicon Valley Metro,* December 31–January 7, http.//www.metroactive.com/papers/metro/12.31.97/los-tigres-9753.html (accessed March 4, 2004).

———. 1998. "Narco Pop's Bloody Polkas; On Both Sides of the Border, Drug Lord Ballads Shoot to the Top." *Washington Post,* March 1.

———. 2001. *True Tales from Another Mexico: The Lynch Mob, the Popsicle Kings, Chalino, and the Bronx.* Albuquerque: University of New Mexico Press.

Ragland, Cathy. 1994. "La Voz del Pueblo Tejano: The Construction of Tejano Identity and Conjunto Music in South Texas." Master's thesis, University of Washington, Seattle.

———. 2000. "Raíces musicales . . . raíces de la raza: Maintaining Tradition in Conjunto Style." *Tonantzin* 25 (n.p.).

———. 2001a. "With His Accordion in His Hand: The Impact of the Accordion during the Formative Years of Modern Texas-Mexican *Conjunto* Music (1930s–1950s)." *Free Reed Journal* 2:25–33.

———. 2001b. "La Voz del Pueblo Tejano: The Construction of Identity and Conjunto Music in South Texas." In *Puro Conjunto: An Album in Words and Pictures. Writings, Posters and Photos from the Tejano Conjunto Festival en San Antonio, 1982–1998,* edited by Juan Tejeda and Alvelardo Valdez, 211–227. Austin: CMAS Books, University of Texas Press.

———. 2003. "Mexican Deejays and the Transnational Space of Youth Dances in New York and New Jersey." *Ethnomusicology* 47 (3): 338–354.

———. 2004. "Shifting Borders, New Identities: Toward a Mapping of Working-Class Popular Music in the Mexican Diaspora" (paper presented at the forty-ninth annual meeting of the Society for Ethnomusicology, Tucson, Arizona, November 3–7).

Ramírez Berg, Charles. 1992. *Cinema of Solitude: A Critical Study of Mexican Film, 1967–1983.* Austin: University of Texas Press.

Ramírez-Pimienta, Juan Carlos. 1998. "Corrido de narcotráfico en los años ochenta y noventa: Un juicio moral suspendido." *Bilingual Review* 23 (2): 145–156.

———. 2004. "Del corrido de narcotráfico al narcocorrido: Orígenes y desarrollo del canto a los traficantes." *Studies in Latin American Popular Culture* 23:22–41.

Ramos, Mario Arturo. 2002. *Cien corridos: Alma de la canción mexicana.* Mexico City: Editorial Océano.

Ramos Aguirre, Francisco. 1994. *Historia del corrido en la frontera tamaulipeca (1844–1994).* Ciudad Victoria, Tamaulipas: Fondo Nacional para la Cultura y las Artes.

Reisler, Mark. 1976a. *By the Sweat of Their Brow: Mexican Immigrant Labor in the United States, 1900–1940.* Westport, Conn.: Greenwood Press.

———. 1976b. "Always the Laborer, Never the Citizen: Anglo Perceptions of the Mexican Immigrant during the 1920s." *Pacific Historical Review* 2:231–254.

Reséndez, Andrés. 1999. "National Identity on a Shifting Border: Texas and New Mexico in the Age of Transition, 1821–1846." *Journal of American History* 86 (2): 668–688.

Reyna, José R., and María Herrera-Sobek. 1998. "Jokelore, Cultural Differences, and Linguistic Dexterity: The Construction of the Immigrant in Chicano Humor." In *Culture across Borders: Mexican Immigration and Popular Culture,* edited by David R. Maciel and María Herrera-Sobek, 203–226. Tucson: University of Arizona Press.

Rodrigues, América. 1993. *Made in the USA: The Constructions of Univision News.* Ph.D. dissertation, University of California, San Diego.

Rodríguez, Néstor. 1996. "The Battle for the Border: Notes on Autonomous Migration, Transnational Communities, and the State." *Social Justice* 23 (3): 21–37.

Rodríguez, Néstor, and Rogelio Núñez. 1986. "An Exploration of Factors That Contribute to Differentiation between Chicanos and Indocumentados." In *Mexican Immigrants and Mexican Americans: An Evolving Relation,* edited by Harley L. Browning and Rodolfo De La Garza, 138–156. Austin: CMAS Publications, University of Texas.

Rouse, Roger. 1991. "Mexican Migration and the Social Space of Postmodernism." *Diaspora* 1 (1): 8–23.

Rumbaut, Rubén. 1997. "Assimilation and its Discontents: Between Rhetoric and Reality." *International Migration Review* 31:923–960.

Said, Edward W. 1994. *Culture and Imperialism.* New York: Vintage Books.

Saldívar, José David. 1997. *Border Matters: Remapping American Cultural Studies.* Berkeley and Los Angeles: University of California Press.

Samora, Julián. 1971. *Los Mojados: The Wetback Story.* Notre Dame, Ind.: University of Notre Dame Press.

Sánchez, George J. 1993. *Becoming Mexican American: Ethnicity, Culture, and Identity in Chicano Los Angeles, 1900–1945.* New York: Oxford University Press.

Simmons, Merle. 1963. "The Ancestry of Mexico's Corridos." *Journal of American Folklore* 76:1–15.

Simonett, Helena. 1996. "Waving Hats and Stomping Boots: A Transborder Music and Dance Phenomenon in Los Angeles' Mexican American Communities." *Pacific Review of Ethnomusicology* 8 (1): 41–50.

———. 2000. "Popular Music and the Politics of Identity: The Empowering Sound of Technobanda." *Popular Music and Society* 24 (2): 1–23.

———. 2001a. *Banda: Mexican Musical Life across Borders.* Middletown, Conn.: Wesleyan University Press.

———. 2001b. "Narcocorridos: An Emerging Micromusic of Nuevo L.A." *Ethnomusicology* 45 (2): 315–337.

Singer, Autrey, and Douglas Massey. 1998. "The Social Process of Undocumented Border Crossing among Mexican Migrants." *International Migration Review* 32:561–592.

Slobin, Mark. 1993. *Subcultural Sounds: Micromusics of the West.* Hanover, N.H.: Wesleyan University Press.

Smith, Robert C. 2000. "How Durable and New Is Transnational Life? Historical Retrieval through Local Comparison." *Diaspora* 9 (2): 203–234.

———. 2003. "Migrant Membership as an Instituted Process: Transnationalism, the State, and the Extra-Territorial Conduct of Mexican Politics." *International Migration Review* 37:297–343.

Soja, Edward W. 1996. *Thirdspace: Journeys to Los Angeles and Other Real-and-Imagined Places.* Malden, Mass.: Blackwell.

Sosa Plata, Gabriel. 2002. "80 años de radio mexicana: Primeras transmisiones en México." *Historias de Radio Mexicana,* http://radiomexicana.tripod.com.mx/historiasradio/id10.html (accessed June 12, 2004).

Soto, Hiram. 2003. "The Return of the People's Band." Interview of Jorge Hernández of Los Tigres del Norte. *San Diego Union-Tribune,* February 20.

Stevenson, Robert. 1952. *Music in Mexico: A Historical Survey.* New York: Thomas Y. Crowell.

Suárez-Orozco, Marcelo. 1998. *Crossings: Mexican Immigration in Interdisciplinary Perspective.* Cambridge, Mass.: Schenkman.

"Surge polémica por discriminación de música regional mexicana." EFE online [the Spanish-Language Associated Press], http://www.terra.com/ocio/articulo/html/oci8275.htm (accessed September 13, 2003).

Taylor, Timothy. 1997. *Global Pop: World Music, World Markets.* New York: Routledge.

Tejeda, Armando G. 2002. "Ya no hay revolución . . . lo que hay es mucho tráfico de droga, afirman Los Tigres del Norte." *La Jornada* (Mexico City), September 11.

Thompson, Ginger. 2003. "Mexican Immigrants Boost Economy Back Home." *New York Times,* October 28.

Valenzuela Arce, José Manuel. 2002. *Jefe de jefes: Corridos y narcocultura en México.* Mexico City: Plaza y Janés Editores.

Wade, Peter. 2000. *Music, Race, and Nation: Música Tropical in Colombia.* Chicago: University of Chicago Press.

Wald, Elijah. 1998. "The Ballad of a Mexican Musical Tradition: Corridos Are Still Celebrating Outlaws, Even in the Age of the War on Drugs." *Boston Globe,* January 18.

———. 2001. *Narcocorrido: A Journey into the Music of Drugs, Guns, and Guerrillas.* New York: Rayo.

Waxer, Lise (ed.). 2002. *Situating Salsa: Global Markets and Local Meaning in Latin Popular Music.* New York: Routledge.

Wilson, William. 1998. "Ballads That Tell Borderline Truths." *Washington Post,* June 23.

Winant, Stephen Louis. 2002. "Out of the Rhythm Section: The Role of the Bajo Sexto in Tejano Conjunto." Master's thesis, University of Washington, Seattle.

Zamarripa, Armando. "Zamarripa's of the Hacienda San Martin." *Buber's Basque Page,* http://www.buber.net/Basque/Diaspora/Immigrant/zamarripa.html (accessed March 6, 2003).

Zitner, Aaron. 2001. "Immigrant Tally Doubles in Census." *Los Angeles Times,* March 10.

# Selected Discography

Alegres de Terán, Los. 1996. *Los Alegres de Terán: Tomás Ortiz y Eugenio Abrego* (CD), EMI Music Mexico 077779600922 (reissue).

———. 2004a. *Los Alegres de Terán: Grabaciones Originales 1952–1954* (CD), Arhoolie Records 9048.

———. 2004b. *Quince de Colección* (CD), EMI Latin 73188.

*Borderlands: From Conjunto to Chicken Scratch, Music of the Rio Grande Valley of South Texas and Southern Arizona* (CD). 1993. Various artists, Smithsonian/Folkways SF CD40418.

Bronco y Los Bukis. 2004. *Crónica de Dos Grandes* (CD), Fonovisa 808835-12790-5.

Capos de México, Los. 1998. *Corridos Mafiosos* (CD), Fonovisa TFL/2529.

Conjunto Bernal. 1987. *Veinte Exitos* (cass./CD), Scorpio Productions SRP-409.

———. 2007. *Mi Único Camino* (CD), Ideal/Arhoolie Records (reissue) 344.

*¡Conjunto! Texas-Mexican Border Music, Volume I* (CD). 1988. Various artists, Rounder 6023.

Donneños, Los. 1989. *Mario y Ramiro* (cass.), Joey International (reissue) 6003.

———. 1990. *Corridos y Tragedias* (cass.), Freddie Records FRE-ECO-224.

Dos Gilbertos, Los. 1993. *Bajo Sexto y Acordeón* (cass./CD), Capitol/EMI Latin 42803 4 1.

Emilio Navaira and the Rio Band. 1991. *Shoot It!* (CD), Capitol/EMI-Latin H2H42455.

Explosión Norteña. 1998. *Catorce Detonantes Corridos* (CD), 724349645820.

———. 2006. *Entre Corridos y Norteñas* (CD), Vene Music Emm, 827865013422.

Fernández, Vicente. 1993. *A Pesar de Todo* (cass./CD), Sony Internacional, B000002DNE (reissue).

González, Lalo "El Piporro." 1995. *Lo Mejor de El Piporro* (CD), Musart 2552.

Grupo Tayer. 1997. *Viejo Canto Norestense* (CD), Agave Music SDL22111.

Huracanes del Norte, Los. 1996. *Corridos Pesados* (CD), Musivisa 053308-60432-6.

———. 1997. *Treinta Norteñas Perronas* (3 CDs with DVD), Fonovisa 053308-07192-0.

———. 2000. *Corridos pa'l Pueblo* (CD), Discos DLV/Fonovisa (reissue) 053308-60812-6.

Invasores y Los Gavilanes, Los. 1984. *Agarrón Norteño* (cass./CD), Freddie Records FR-1289.

Jiménez, Flaco. 1979. *Ay Te Dejo en San Antonio* (CD), Arhoolie Records 318.

———. 1989. *Arriba el Norte* (CD), Rounder 6032.

Jiménez, Santiago. 1994. *Don Santiago Jiménez: His First and Last Recordings,* 1937 and 1979 (CD), Arhoolie Records 414.

La Rosa, Tony de. 1991. *Así Se Baila en Tejas* (CD), Rounder 6046.

———. 1995. *Atotonilco* (CD), Arhoolie Records (reissue) 362.

Longoria, Valerio. 1990. *Caballo Viejo* (cass./CD), Arhoolie Records 336.

Martínez, Narciso. 1993. *The Father of Tex-Mex Conjunto* (CD), Ideal/Arhoolie Records (reissue) 361.

*Más Grande Homenaje a Los Tigres del Norte, El* (CD). 2001. Various artists, Fonovisa 053308-61372-4.

Maya y Cantú. 1999. *El Primero Conjunto Norteño Famoso* (CD), Folklyric/Arhoolie Records (reissue), 9013.

*Mexican American Border Music, Vols. 6 and 7: Corridos y Tragedias de la Frontera* (2 CDs). 1994. Various artists, Arhoolie/Folklyric CD 7019/7020.

Mingo Saldívar y Los Tremendos Cuatro Espadas. 1992. *I Love My Freedom, I Love My Texas* (CD), Rounder Records 6047.

Montañeses del Álamo, Los. 2002. *Los Montañeses del Álamo: First Recordings, 1940–1950* (CD), Folklyric/Arhoolie Records (reissue) 7021.

*Música de Puro Nortè* (CD). 1989. Various artists, Freddie Records FRC-1460.

Ramón Ayala y Los Bravos del Norte. 1990. *Rinconcito en el Cielo* (CD), Freddie Records FR-1312.

———. 1991. *Corridos del '91* (CD), Freddie Records FMC-1572.

———. 1995. *Corridos Auténticos* (CD), Freddie Records 1715.

———. 2002. *El Número 100* (CD), Freddie Records JMCD 1845.

Relámpagos del Norte, Los. 1995. *Rey de Reyes* (CD), Fonovisa (reissue) 0883 50115 2.

*Roots of the Narcocorrido, The* (CD). 2001. Various artists, Down Home Music 7053.

*San Antonio's Conjuntos in the 1950s* (CD). 1994. Various artists, Arhoolie Records 376.

Sánchez, Chalino. 1989. *Al Estilo Norteño* (CD), Brentwood/BCI Music 287927.

———. 1991. *Corridos Villistas* (CD), Brentwood 89032.

———. 2001. *Trece Mejores Éxitos* (CD), Brentwood/BCI (reissue) 87089, 2001.

Selena. 1992. *Entre a Mi Mundo* (CD), Capital/EMI Latin, H2 42635.

*Tejano Roots: The Women* (CD). 1991. Various artists, Arhoolie Records 343.

Terribles del Norte, Los. 1990. *Los Grandes Corridos* (CD), Freddie Records FRC-1534.

———. 2003. *Los Meros Jefes* (CD), Freddie Records JMCD 1858.

*Texas Mexican Border Music—Vol. III* (CD). 1995. Various artists, Folklyric/Arhoolie Records 7016.

Tigres del Norte, Los. 1991. *Ídolos del Pueblo* (CD), Fonovisa 053308-88002-7.

———. 1997. *Jefe de Jefes* (2 CDs), Fonovisa 80711.

———. 2000. *Contrabando, Traición y Robo* (CD), Los Tigres del Norte, Fonovisa (reissue) 053308-50282-0.

———. 2002a. *Corridos Prohibidos* (CD), Fonovisa FP-8815 (reissue) 053308-88152-9.

———. 2002b. *De Paisano a Paisano* (CD), Fonovisa 053308-60922-2.

———. 2002c. *El Otro México* (CD) Fonovisa (reissue) 053308-50432-9.

———. 2002d. *Jaula de Oro* (CD), Fonovisa 808835-03922-2.

———. 2002e. *Reina del Sur* (CD), Fonovisa 707395-06662-7.

———. 2003. *Herencia Musical: Veinte Corridos Inolvidables* (2 CDs and DVD with 7 videos), Fonovisa 0883 50880 0.

———. 2004. *Pacto de Sangre* (CD), Fonovisa 808835124522.

———. 2006. *Historias que Contar* (CD), Fonovisa, B000ERU39M.

*Treasury of Northeastern Mexican Music, Volume I: Nuevo León* (CD). 1991. Various artists, Instituto Nacional de Antropología e Historia, Mexico 29.

Tucanes de Tijuana, Los. 2000. *Corridos de Primera Plana* (CD), Universal Music Latino, 440013021-2.

———. 2002. *Catorce Tucanazos Bien Pesados* (CD), Universal Music Latino (reissue) 017 672.

*Veinte Tex-Mex Corridos Famosos* (cass./CD). 1992. Various artists, Hacienda SC-171.

Villa, Beto. 1992. *Father of Orquesta Tejana* (CD), Ideal/Arhoolie Records (reissue) 364.

# Interviews

All interviews were conducted by me unless otherwise noted in the citation. Interview transcriptions and translations in the text of this book are also mine unless otherwise noted.

**Alanís Támez, Juan.** Historian of the early group Los Montañeses del Álamo. Monterrey, Nuevo León, Mexico, August 11, 1998 (conducted in Spanish).

**Almeida, Santiago.** The original bajo sexto player who accompanied the accordionist Narciso Martínez on his first recordings, thus establishing the instrumental core of norteña and tejano conjunto music. Sunnyside, Washington, July 5, 1993 (conducted in Spanish).

**Ayala, Ramón.** Accordionist and leader of the important norteña group Ramón Ayala y Los Bravos del Norte. McAllen, Texas, October 7, 1998 (conducted in Spanish).

**Barco, Juan.** Noted tejano songwriter, singer, and bajo sexto player. Seattle, Washington, June 13, 1996.

**Berrones, Guillermo.** Music historian and author of *Ingratos ojos míos: Miguel Luna y la historia de El Palomo y El Gorrión.* Monterrey, Nuevo León, Mexico, July 11, 1998, and June 4, 2003 (conducted in Spanish).

**Cano, Joel.** Top norteña promoter in Mexico and the United States. Monterrey, Nuevo León, Mexico, July 9, 1998 (conducted in Spanish).

**Cavazos, Ramiro.** Bajo sexto player and founding member of the seminal border group Los Donneños. McAllen, Texas, October 6, 1998, and August 6, 2003 (conducted in Spanish).

**Flores, Oscar.** Top promoter of Tejano music in northern Mexico. Monterrey, Nuevo León, Mexico, August, 20, 1998 (conducted in Spanish).

**García, Gilberto, Sr., and Bobby Salinas.** Conjunto accordionist/bandleader and bajo sexto player for Los Dos Gilbertos. Edinburg, Texas, August 11, 1991.

**García, Jesús.** Pilsner (in Chicago) district council member. Chicago, April 13, 2003.

**García, Rogelio.** Longtime, important radio deejay. Monterrey, Nuevo León, Mexico, August 13, 1998, and August 7, 2003 (conducted in Spanish).

**García Flores, Raúl.** Anthropologist, musicologist, and researcher of music of northeastern Mexico. Monterrey, Nuevo León, Mexico, July 19, 1998 (conducted in Spanish).

**Garza, Julián.** Coleader of the norteña group Luis y Julián. Monterrey, Nuevo León, Mexico, July 6, 1998, and August 4, 2003 (conducted in Spanish).

**Garza Guajardo, Celso.** Researcher and historian in the Department of Historical and Cultural Research at the Universidad Autónoma de Nuevo León. Monterrey, Nuevo León, Mexico, June 5, 1998 (conducted in Spanish).

**Gómez Flores, Carlos.** Music historian and author of *A tambora batiente*. Monterrey, Nuevo León, Mexico, July 6, 1998 (conducted in Spanish).

**González Ramírez, Eulalio.** Pioneering norteña songwriter, singer, and actor. Mexico City, Mexico, May 12, 1999 (conducted in Spanish).

**Hernández, Jorge.** Interview by Elijah Wald, 1999, online transcript, http://www.elijah wald.com/jhernan.html (accessed December 19, 2004).

**Hernández, José.** Bajo sexto maker. Monterrey, Nuevo Léon, Mexico, June 10, 2003 (conducted in Spanish).

**Hernández, Luis.** Bajo sexto player for Los Tigres del Norte. Interview by Nahum Madrid, "Norteño Exposure: Los Tigres Del Norte's Music Speaks to the Man on the Street," *Batanga*, http://www.batanga.com/en/articles/LosTigresDelNorte043005.asp (accessed May 12, 2005).

**Javier, Pablo and Santiago.** Accordionist and bajo sexto player for Suspenso del Norte. New York City, April 12, 2002, and August 9, 2003 (conducted in Spanish).

**Javier, Roberto.** Accordionist and father of Pablo and Santiago. Santa Inés, Puebla, Mexico, June 14, 2003 (conducted in Spanish).

**La Rosa, Tony de.** Conjunto accordionist/bandleader. Riviera, Texas, July 20, 1991.

**Longoria, Valerio.** Conjunto accordionist and bandleader. San Antonio, Texas, April 16, 1991 (conducted by Pat Jasper for Texas Folklife Resources).

**Luna, Miguel.** Accordionist and founding member of El Palomo y el Gorrión. Monterrey, Nuevo León, Mexico, July 8, 1998 (conducted in Spanish).

**Marroquín, Carmen.** Half of the singing sister duo Carmen y Laura, who were among the first artists to record on Ideal Records. Interview with Héctor Galán for Galán Productions, transcript no. 135, Houston, Texas, May 7, 1996(?). Translation and transcription by interviewer.

**Martínez, Freddie, Jr.** Freddie Records Promotions Director. Corpus Christi, Texas, October 18, 1991.

**Martínez, Narciso.** Conjunto accordionist. La Paloma, Texas, November 9, 1991 (conducted by Michael Stone and Cathy Ragland).

**Morales, Hugo.** Director of Radio Bilingüe (which has stations across the Southwest and is syndicated in Mexico). Fresno, California, March 24, 2004.

**Ortiz Guerrero, Armando Hugo.** Music historian and author of *Vida y muerte en la frontera*. Monterrey, Nuevo León, Mexico, July 9 and August 19, 1998 (conducted in Spanish).

**Salazar, Carlos.** Founding member of the top norteña group Carlos y José. Terán, Nuevo León, Mexico, August 12, 1998 (conducted in Spanish).

**Saldívar, Mingo.** Conjunto accordionist/bandleader. San Antonio, Texas, October 21, 1994, and May 28, 2003.

**Silva, Juan.** Accordionist and musician formerly with Los Rancheritos del Topo Chico and El Piporro. Monterrey, Nuevo León, Mexico, July 8, 1998 (conducted in Spanish).

**Villagomez, Poncho.** Leader of the early norteña group Los Coyotes del Río Bravo and owner of Del Bravo Records. Monterrey, Nuevo León, Mexico, August 21, 1998 (conducted in Spanish).

# Index

*Note:* Page numbers in italics indicate figures.

**Cathy Ragland** is Assistant Professor of Music and the Arts at Empire State College/SUNY. She is a former music critic for the *San Antonio Express-News, Seattle Times,* and *Austin American-Statesman,* where she wrote about Texas-Mexican music and música norteña, among other popular genres. She also cofounded the Mariachi Academy of New York, a community-based music program for youth in East Harlem.